MANAGING THE EFFECTIVE SCHOOL

MANAGING THE EFFECTIVE SCHOOL

Edited by
Margaret Preedy

at The Open University

Published in association with
The Open University

P·C·P
Paul Chapman
Publishing Ltd

Paul Chapman Publishing Ltd
144 Liverpool Road
London
N1 1LA

British Library Cataloguing in Publication Data
Managing the Effective School
I. Preedy, Margaret
371.2

ISBN 1 85396 210 4

Index compiled by Indexing Specialists,
Hove, East Sussex BN3 2DJ
Typeset by Inforum, Rowlands Castle, Hants
Printed and bound by Athenaeum Press, Newcastle-upon-Tyne

B C D E F G H 9 8 7 6 5 4 3

CONTENTS

PREFACE

This reader comprises a collection of papers published in connection with the Open University courses E326, *Managing Schools: Challenge and Response*, and E630, *Managing for School Effectiveness*.

This reader is one part of an Open University integrated teaching system and the selection is therefore related to other material available to students. The editors have attempted nevertheless to make it of value to all those concerned with school management. Opinions expressed in it are not necessarily those of the course team or of the University.

It is not necessary to become an undergraduate of The Open University in order to take the course of which this reader is part. Further information about the courses and about the Advanced Diploma in Educational Management, of which E326 can form a component, may be obtained by writing to: Central Enquiry Service, PO Box 200, The Open University, Milton Keynes MK7 6YZ.

Acknowledgements

Very grateful acknowledgements are made to Sindy York for secretarial support, and to Ron Glatter, for his helpful comments on an earlier draft of the introduction.

The chapters in this collection come from the following sources, to whose publishers grateful acknowledgement is made.

1. Mortimore, P., Sammons, P., Stoll, L., Lewis, D. and Ecob, R. (1988) *School Matters: The Junior Years*, Open Books, Wells, ch. 12, pp. 248–62.
2. Gray, J. (1990) The quality of schooling: frameworks for judgement, *British Journal of Educational Studies*, Vol. 38, no. 3, pp. 204–23.
3. Morgan, G. (1986) Strengths and limitations of the culture metaphor, in *Images of Organisation*, Sage, Newbury Park, California, pp. 134–40.
4. Torrington, D. and Weightman, J. (1989) The culture and ethos of the school, in *The Reality of School Management*, Blackwell, Oxford, ch. 2. Reproduced by permission of Simon & Schuster Education, Hemel Hempstead, UK.
5. Shipman, M. (1990) The management of learning: using the information, in *In Search of Learning*, Blackwell, Oxford, ch. 9. Reproduced by permission of Simon & Schuster Education, Hemel Hempstead, UK.
6. Weston, P. and Barrett, E. with Jamison, J. (1993) Review and reflection: the quest for coherence, in *The Quest for Coherence: Managing The Whole Curriculum 5–16*, National Foundation for Educational Research, Slough.
7. Campbell, R. J., Evans, L., Neill, S. R. St J. and Packwood, A.(1991) The National Curriculum and the management of infant teachers' time. Revised version of paper entitled 'The use and management of infant teachers' time: some policy issues', presented to Policy Analysis Unit seminar, University of Warwick, 15 November. Reproduced by permission of the authors.
8. Gilbert, C. (1990) Local management of schools: an introductory summary, in C. Gilbert (ed.) *Local Management of Schools: A Guide for Governors and Teachers*, Kogan Page, London, pp. 13–34.
9. Levačić, R. (1992) Coupling financial and curriculum decision-making in schools. Copyright © The Open University.
10. Downes, P. A. (1991) Costing the curriculum, *Managing Schools Today*, Vol. 1, no. 3. Reproduced by permission of *Managing Schools Today*, published by The Questions Publishing Company Ltd., 6–7 Hockley Hill, Birmingham B18 5AA.
11. Kennedy, J. (1991) Interfacing finance, *Managing Schools Today*, Vol. 7, no. 2, pp. 20–1. Reproduced by permission of *Managing Schools Today*, published by The Questions Publishing Company Ltd., 6–7 Hockley Hill, Birmingham B18 5AA.
12. Lancaster, D. (1989) Aspects of management information systems, in B. Fidler and G. Bowles (eds.) *Effective Local Management of Schools*, Longman, Harlow, pp. 174–83.
13. Beare, H., Caldwell, B. and Millikan, R. (1989) *Creating an Excellent School*, Routledge, London, ch. 5, pp. 99–123.
14. Singleton, C. (1989) Women deputy headteachers in educational management. Extract from MSc thesis (CNAA), 'Women in educational management', chs 4 and 5. Reproduced by permission of the author.
15. Poster, C. and Poster, D. (1991) Headteacher appraisal, in *Teacher Appraisal*, Routledge, London, ch. 10.
16. Macbeth, A. (ed.) (1989) A minimum programme and a signed understanding, in *Involving Parents: Effective Parent–Teacher Relations*, Heinemann Publishers, Oxford, ch. 2.
17. Deem, R. (1992) Educational reform and school governing bodies in England 1986–92. Commissioned article, copyright © The Open University.
18. Dennison, W. F. (1990) Performance indicators and consumer choice, *International Journal of Educational Management*, Vol. 4, no. 1, pp. 8–11.
19. Hargreaves, D. H. and Hopkins, D. (eds.) (1991) School effectiveness, school improvement and development planning, in *The Empowered School*, Cassell, London, ch. 14, pp. 109–24.

INTRODUCTION

This collection of articles explores school effectiveness in the context of various key aspects of the school – culture or ethos, curriculum, resources, staff and leadership, and relations with the external environment. In drawing together these articles we have been concerned to reflect various theoretical perspectives and recent research studies. The purpose of the volume is to promote analysis and critical reflection about the concept of school effectiveness, its management implications and applicability to the main areas of the school's work. The intention is thus not prescriptive ('how to do it') but exploratory – seeking a deeper understanding of a range of approaches and issues and their relevance to various areas of school management. It is hoped that the volume will be of use to teachers and others with an interest in school effectiveness and management, and to those engaged in INSET activities and courses related to these themes.

But what is school effectiveness, and what part does management play in developing it? The articles here provide a number of valuable pointers, drawing on recent empirical research. Nonetheless, these are large and complex questions to which there *are* no definitive answers that provide a clear step-by-step recipe for producing 'the effective school'. Indeed, if there were, school management would comprise little more than following the recipe and monitoring its results.

The articles in this volume highlight a number of issues arising from the concept of school effectiveness. First, as suggested above, effectiveness is a complex matter with no universally applicable prescriptions. It is often defined in terms of goal achievement – a school, or any other organization, is effective in so far as it fulfils its goals or objectives. This raises the problem of organizational goals – how far do schools and their staffs have agreed and realistic goals which they attempt to achieve in practice? Many commentators have pointed out that schools tend to have multiple and often ambiguous goals, expressed in broad terms, which are therefore difficult to operationalize and realize (see, for example, Hoyle, 1986). Different departments or subunits may well have competing priorities, leading to conflict rather than the common pursuit of shared goals (see Ball, 1987).

Second, there is the question of *which* goals relate to *which* areas of the school's work. We can identify three main ways in which effectiveness in terms of goal achievement is conceptualized: (1) in terms of outcomes, e.g. pupil examination results and social and personal development; (2) with respect to process factors, such as culture or ethos, and levels of staff and student satisfaction with the way the school operates; (3) in terms of the school's success in acquiring inputs, e.g. pupils or financial and staff resources. Item (1) is a widely used and obvious approach – assessing school effectiveness in terms of pupil outcomes is clearly important for parents and pupils as well as teachers. However, looking at pupil outcomes alone does not tell us anything about the effects of the school, the 'value added', unless outcomes are assessed in relation to intake characteristics. Thus, for example, school A might seem much more effective than school B if we look at examination results alone, but may well turn out to be less effective when pupil attainment levels on entry to the school are taken into account. Empirical studies have shown that process factors (item (2) above) are also very important, though difficult to assess and measure in precise terms (see, for example, Rutter *et al.*, 1979; Mortimore *et al.*, 1988; Reynolds, 1991). Thus effective schools, as well as having good examination results, are also characterized by a positive ethos, shared values and good relationships among staff and pupils. Item (3) above, effectiveness in gaining inputs, is clearly important given local management of schools (LMS), more open enrolment and parental choice, which create a context where schools are in competition for pupils. However, it does not resolve the question of the effectiveness of the system overall.

Third, there is the issue that judgements about effectiveness are based on values and criteria that differ between the various groups and individuals with an interest in the school. Thus parents, teachers, pupils and school governors do not necessarily agree about what the major constituents of an effective school are. Priorities within and between groups of stakeholders associated with any particular school are likely to show marked disparities.

Fourth, evidence from a number of effectiveness studies has suggested that the impact of schools may be different for different groups (see, for example, Nuttall *et al.*, 1989; Reynolds, 1991). Thus schools seem to be differentially effective for particular subgroups of pupils. Similarly, different departments in the same school may be significantly more or less effective.

Finally, approaches to effectiveness change in response to changing circumstances and needs. Given that notions of effectiveness are dependent on particular contexts, goals and values, and that these are constantly evolving, then effectiveness, too, cannot be static, but must be continually reassessed for each school in its own particular circumstances. Bearing in mind these issues we now turn to look briefly at the contents of this collection.

Part 1 addresses two broad themes: (a) the range of factors associated with school effectiveness; (b) the importance of school climate or ethos, which research studies have shown is a key variable in effective schools. Chapter 1 by Mortimore *et al.* reports the findings of a large-scale longitudinal study. The research looked at pupils' intake characteristics, their educational outcomes, and at the effects of various measures of the classroom and school environment in influencing these outcomes. The study identified significant variations in outcome, taking into account the differences in pupil intakes. In this extract from the research, Mortimore *et al.* identify the twelve key management policy factors contributing to the differences between the more and less effective schools. The factors identified are similar to those reported in studies of secondary schools, both in the UK and USA, and thus are likely to be broadly generalizable across both sectors.

Chapter 2 by Gray explores the debate on the range of factors that need to be taken into account in judging school effectiveness or quality. He argues for just three simple measures: one relating to outcomes – academic progress – and two for process factors – pupil satisfaction and pupil–teacher relationships. The article makes the important point that much of effective teaching and learning cannot be captured or assessed by checklists of performance indicators. Schools and teachers should attempt to identify and celebrate their own 'moments of excellence'.

The two final chapters in Part 1 examine the significance of culture or ethos. Morgan's chapter, drawn from the general management literature, looks at the pros and cons of attempting to influence organizational cultures. While managers can affect the evolution of culture by attempting to foster desired values, they cannot control or shape it as has sometimes been suggested. Thus an understanding of school culture is important but provides no simple measures for enhancing effectiveness.

Drawing on a research study of twenty-four secondary schools, Torrington and Weightman (Chapter 4) explore the nature of school culture, and argue that effective management of schools is built round a shared sense of unity based 'on a few central ideals about which there is a high degree of consensus'.

Studies of school effectiveness have consistently emphasized the central importance of a clear focus on teaching and learning. Part 2 of this volume looks at various aspects of these issues and their management implications. Chapter 5 is an extract from Shipman's (1990) book in which he argues the need for school managers to regard *learning* as their main priority, rather than procedural and organizational matters. Here he suggests that the effective use of information is a key aspect of the management of learning. Legislative requirements to collect a wide range of pupil data provide an important opportunity for teachers to analyse and act upon the information provided by such data about the impact of the school's policies and practices on pupil learning.

Students' performance and experiences of schools are likely to be adversely affected unless the curriculum is planned as a cohesive whole across the school and, indeed, between schools. Chapter 6 (Weston and Barrett, with Jamison), drawing on a large-scale NFER research project, examines the extent to which schools are achieving curriculum coherence and managing the curriculum as a whole within schools and between primary and secondary sectors.

An important issue in the management of teaching and learning, which has previously received little attention in the literature, is the interface between teachers' perspectives on their roles and use of time, and management expectations about these factors. The chapter by Campbell *et al.* (Chapter 7) explores the nature of teachers' work, how they interpret their roles and how their time is deployed both within and beyond the classroom. The authors then identify a number of management policy implications arising from their research.

Part 3 of the collection turns to look at the management of financial and other resources in the context of local management of schools (LMS). Gilbert (Chapter 8) describes the main features of LMS, and argues that it provides the opportunity for staff to develop a shared and coherent approach to planning and thus to enhance the effectiveness of teaching and learning. Given the competitive market forces ideology underlying LMS, she suggests that it is all the more important for staff to attempt to develop strategies for *co-operation*, rather than competition *between* schools.

Effective resource management requires schools to develop decision-making processes and techniques which enable budget decisions to reflect educational aims and priorities. Levačić (Chapter 9) examines the ways in which schools can achieve this by coupling financial and curriculum decision-making. Specific budget planning techniques for linking financial and educational planning are put forward by Downes (Chapter 10) and Kennedy (Chapter 11). A key theme running through all these pieces is the importance of appropriate information for management decision-making. In Chapter 12 Lancaster explores the notion of information as a strategic resource, raising issues similar to those addressed by Shipman in Chapter 5. Lancaster goes on to discuss how effective management information systems can help schools in the major management functions of planning, monitoring and communicating.

The theme of Part 4 is the management of staff and leadership in schools, a key component in effectiveness. Beare, Caldwell and Millikan, in Chapter 13, summarize the main findings of recent leadership studies which stress the importance of a range of leadership factors: in particular, developing a shared vision, power sharing (leadership density) and institutionalizing the vision so that it informs and shapes the day-to-day activities of the school.

Chapter 13 notes that regardless of the gender of the leader, both male and female stereotype qualities are important in outstanding/excellent leadership. Singleton, Chapter 14, takes up this issue in a study of the management styles of women deputy heads. She explores the barriers to women in educational management posed by traditional masculine stereotypes of leadership. The chapter argues that so-called 'feminine' qualities and skills have an important and increasingly recognized part to play in leadership: 'if management is to be effective it requires a balance of "feminine" and "masculine" skills'.

The importance of effective leadership in schools highlights the need for clear criteria and frameworks for headteacher appraisal. Poster and Poster

(Chapter 15) explore the issues raised by the appraisal of heads and propose criteria and approaches, arguing that the appraisal of all staff, particularly heads, should be linked with the School Development Plan.

Part 5 of this volume looks at the management of the school's relationship with the environment, an issue which is of even greater importance in the light of the legislative changes of the late 1980s and early 1990s. Macbeth (Chapter 16) examines links with parents, arguing that they should be treated as partners as well as clients of the school. He suggests the importance of recognizing parents' rights *and* responsibilities with respect to their childrens' schooling, by means of a clear programme for parent–teacher liaison and a signed agreement outlining parents' obligations. Chapter 17 by Deem examines the role of school governors in the 1990s, in the light of recent legislative changes, and the implications for school management. She explores the ambiguities in school governors' responsibilities and the emergence of more proactive business-oriented governors who are prepared to challenge the traditional 'rubber stamping' role of governing bodies.

In Chapter 18 Dennison looks at the important question of marketing schools. Despite resistance by many teachers to this concept, he argues that given LMS, more open enrolment and heightened consumer awareness among parents, schools have little choice but to develop effective marketing strategies, which take into account the expectations of parents as consumers of the services that schools provide. The chapter proposes a number of factors which, it is suggested, schools need to consider in attempting to meet consumer expectations and professional requirements.

The final chapter provides an overview of recent school effectiveness and improvement literature. Hargreaves and Hopkins (Chapter 19) summarize the findings of a number of major studies and examine their implications for school development planning.

Margaret Preedy
The Open University, 1992

REFERENCES

Ball, S. (1987) *The Micro-Politics of the School*, Methuen, London.
Hoyle, E. (1986) *The Politics of School Management*, Hodder & Stoughton, London.
Mortimore, P., Sammons, P., Stoll, L., Lewis, D. and Ecob, R. (1988) *School Matters*, Open Books, Wells.
Nuttall, D., Goldstein, H., Prosser, R. and Rabash, H. (1989) Differential school effectiveness, *International Journal of Educational Research*, Vol. 13, no. 10, pp. 769–76.
Reynolds, D. (1991 Linking school effectiveness knowledge and school improvement practice. Paper presented to ICSEI, Cardiff, January.
Rutter, M., Maughan, B., Mortimore, P. and Ouston, J. (1979) *Fifteen Thousand Hours*, Open Books, Wells.
Shipman, M. (1990) *In Search of Learning*, Blackwell, Oxford.

PART 1:

Effectiveness and School Culture

1

KEY FACTORS FOR EFFECTIVE JUNIOR SCHOOLING

Peter Mortimore, Pamela Sammons, Louise Stoll, David Lewis and Russell Ecob

This material has been abridged

[A] major question addressed by the Junior School Project concerned the factors which contributed to school effectiveness. We found that much of the variation between schools in their effects on pupils' progress and development was explained by differences in policies and practices, and by certain given characteristics. By investigating the interconnections between the many factors linked with school effects on pupils' progress and development, we have been able to identify some of the mechanisms by which effective junior schooling is promoted. In particular, we have shown that the given features of schools and classes are closely related to many aspects of policy and practice. Moreover, effective school policies are associated with the adoption of more effective teaching strategies within the classroom.

The relationships [. . .] have enabled us to draw together [. . .] twelve key factors. However, it must be emphasized that these factors are not purely statistical constructs. They have not been obtained solely by means of quantitative analyses. Rather, they are derived from a combination of careful examination and discussion of the statistical findings, and the use of educational and research judgement. They represent the interpretation of the research results by an inter-disciplinary team of researchers and teachers.

KEY FACTORS FOR EFFECTIVE JUNIOR SCHOOLING

[. . .] Many [. . .] factors had an impact on a range of different outcomes. Similarly, features of the school and the classroom frequently were related to each other and, through a detailed investigation of these links, we have developed a framework of key factors that we believe contribute to effective junior schooling. This framework, however, is not intended to be a blueprint for success. Inevitably there were aspects of school life which we could not examine during the course of the Project. Furthermore, schools, like all institutions, are perpetually changing. Our survey was carried out between 1980 and 1984, and it was not possible to take full account of all the changes (particularly in approaches to the curriculum) that were evolving in schools and classrooms during that period. Nonetheless, a large number of factors were related consistently to effective junior schooling. Those factors which come under the control of the head, the staff or the class teacher we have grouped together under twelve headings. Before examining these factors over which schools and teachers can exercise control, we shall [examine] briefly the less flexible characteristics of schools [. . .] – the school and class givens. It is clear that certain of these given features make it easier to create an effective school.

Key given factors

Schools that cover the entire primary age range, where pupils do not have to transfer at age seven, appear to be at an advantage, as do voluntary-aided schools. Even though voluntary schools tend to have more socio-economically advantaged intakes than county schools, we still found that voluntary schools tended to be more effective. Smaller schools, with a junior roll of around 160 or fewer, also appear to benefit their pupils. Research by Galton at Leicester University has also suggested that smaller schools tend to be more effective. Class size is also relevant: smaller classes (with fewer than 24 pupils) had a positive impact upon pupil progress and development, especially in the early years, whereas in classes with 27 or more pupils the effects were less positive.

Not surprisingly, a good physical environment, as reflected in the school's amenities, decorative order and immediate surroundings, was a positive advantage. Extended periods of disruption, due to building work and redecoration, can have a negative impact on pupils' progress. This was in line with [the] findings [of Rutter *et al.*] (1979) concerning the care of school buildings. The stability of the school's teaching force is also an important factor. Changes of head and deputy headteacher, though inevitable, have an unsettling effect upon the pupils. Every effort, therefore, should be made to reduce the potentially negative impact of such changes. Similarly, where there is an unavoidable change of class teacher during the school year, careful planning will be needed to ensure an easy transition, and to minimize disruption to the pupils. Where pupils experience continuity with one class teacher through the whole year, progress is more likely to occur. It is, however, not only continuity of staff that is important. Although major or frequent changes tend to have negative effects, schools were less effective where the headteacher had been in post for a long time. In the more effective schools, heads had usually been in post for between three and seven years.

It is clear, therefore, that some schools are more advantaged in terms of their size, status, environment and stability of teaching staff. Nonetheless, although these favourable given characteristics contribute to effectiveness, they do not, by themselves, ensure it. They provide a supporting framework within which the head and teachers can work to promote pupil progress and development. However, it is the factors within the control of the head and teachers that are crucial. These are the factors that can be changed and improved.

The twelve key factors described below are not arranged in any order of importance. However, we have grouped them into factors that concern school policy (1 to 4), those that relate to classroom policy (5 to 9), and, finally, aspects of relevance to school and class policy (10 to 12).

The twelve key factors

(1) Purposeful leadership of the staff by the headteacher;
(2) The involvement of the deputy head;
(3) The involvement of teachers;
(4) Consistency amongst teachers;
(5) Structured sessions;
(6) Intellectually challenging teaching;
(7) The work-centred environment;
(8) Limited focus within sessions;
(9) Maximum communication between teachers and pupils;
(10) Record keeping;
(11) Parental involvement;
(12) Positive climate.

1. Purposeful leadership of the staff by the headteacher

Purposeful leadership occurred where the headteacher understood the needs of the school and was involved actively in the school's work, without exerting total control over the rest of the staff. In effective schools, headteachers were involved in curriculum discussions and influenced the content of guidelines drawn up within the school, without taking complete control. They also influenced the teaching strategies of teachers, but only selectively, where they judged it necessary. This leadership was demonstrated by an emphasis on the monitoring of pupils' progress, through teachers keeping individual records. Approaches varied – some schools kept written records; others passed on folders of pupils' work to their next teacher; some did both – but a systematic policy of record keeping was important. With regard to in-service training, those heads exhibiting purposeful leadership did not allow teachers total freedom to attend any course: attendance was encouraged for a good reason. Nonetheless, most teachers in these schools had attended in-service courses.

Thus, effective headteachers were sufficiently involved in, and knowledgeable about, what went on in the classrooms and about the progress of individual pupils. They were more able to feel confident about their teaching staff and did not need to intervene constantly. At the same time, however, they were not afraid to assert their leadership where appropriate.

2. The involvement of the deputy head

Our findings indicate that the deputy head can have a major role to play in promoting the effectiveness of junior schools. Where the deputy was frequently absent, or absent for a prolonged period (due to illness, attendance on long courses, or other commitments), this was detrimental to pupils' progress and development. Moreover, a change of deputy head tended to have negative effects. The responsibilities undertaken by deputy heads also seemed to be significant. Where the head generally involved the deputy in policy decisions, it was beneficial to the pupils. This was particularly true in terms of allocating teachers to classes. Thus, it appears that a certain amount of delegation by the headteacher, and the sharing of responsibilities, promoted effectiveness.

3. The involvement of teachers

In successful schools, the teachers were involved in curriculum planning and played a major role in developing their own curriculum guidelines. As with the deputy head, teacher involvement in decisions concerning which classes they were to teach, was important. Similarly, we found that consultation with teachers about decisions on spending was associated with greater effectiveness. It appears that schools in which teachers were consulted on issues affecting school policy, as well as those affecting them directly, were more likely to be successful. We found a link between schools where the deputy was involved in policy decisions and schools where teachers were involved. Thus, effective primary schools did not operate a small management team – everyone had their say.

4. Consistency amongst teachers

We have already shown that continuity of staffing had positive effects. Not only, however, do pupils benefit from teacher continuity, but it also appears that consistency in teacher approach is important. For example, in schools where all teachers followed guidelines in the same way (whether closely or selectively), the impact on progress was positive. Where there was variation between teachers in their usage of guidelines, this had a negative effect.

5. Structured sessions

The Project findings indicate that pupils benefitted when their school day was given some structure. In effective classes, pupils' work was organized in broad outline by the teacher, who ensured that there was always plenty of work to do. We also found that the progress of pupils benefitted when they were not given unlimited responsibility for planning their own daily programme of work, or for choosing work activities, but were guided into areas of study or exploration and taught the skills necessary for independently managing that work. In general, therefore, teachers who organized a framework within which pupils could work, and yet encouraged them to exercise a degree of independence, and allowed some freedom and choice within this structure, were more successful. Children developed and made progress particularly in classrooms where most pupils were able to work in the absence of constant support from their teachers. Clearly, when pupils can work autonomously in this way the teacher is freed to spend time in areas she or he considers a high priority.

6. Intellectually challenging teaching

Not surprisingly, the quality of teaching was very important in promoting pupil progress and development. Our findings show clearly that, in those classes where pupils were stimulated and challenged, progress was greatest. The content of teacher–pupil classroom talk was vitally important. Progress was encouraged where teachers used more higher-order questions and statements, when they encouraged pupils to use their creative imagination and powers of problem solving. Additionally, in classrooms which were bright and interesting, where the context created by the teacher was stimulating, and where teachers communicated their own interest and enthusiasm to the children, greater pupil progress occurred. In contrast, teachers who frequently directed pupils' work without discussing it, or explaining its purpose, were less effective.

A further important feature was the expectation in the more effective classrooms that pupils could manage independently the tasks they were engaged upon. In such classes teachers only rarely intervened with instructions and directives, yet everyone in the class knew what to do and could work without close supervision.

7. Work-centred environment

In schools where teachers spent more of their time discussing the content of work with pupils, and less time on routine matters and the maintenance of work activity, the effect was positive. Time devoted to giving pupils feedback about their work also appeared to be very beneficial.

The work-centred environment was characterized by a high level of pupil industry in the classroom. Pupils appeared to enjoy their work and were eager to commence new tasks. The noise level was low, although this is not to say that there was silence in the classroom. In fact, none of the classes we visited was completely silent. Furthermore, pupil movement around the classroom was not excessive, and was generally work related. These results receive support from the views of pupils. Even in the third year over 40 per cent of pupils reported that they had difficulty in concentrating on their work most of the time. Where levels of noise and movement were high, concentration seems to be more difficult to maintain. Work-centred classrooms, therefore, had a business-like and purposeful air, with pupils obviously enjoying the work they were doing. Furthermore, where classrooms were work centred, lessons were found to be more challenging.

8. *Limited focus within sessions*

It appears that pupils made greater progress when teachers tended to organize lessons around one particular curriculum area. At times, work could be undertaken in two areas and also produce positive effects, but, where the tendency was for the teacher regularly to organize classroom work such that three or more curriculum areas were running concurrently, then pupils' progress was marred. This finding is related to a number of other factors. For example, pupil industry was lower in classrooms where mixed activities occurred, noise and pupil movement were greater, and teachers spent less time discussing work and more time on routine issues and behaviour control. Thus, such classrooms were less likely to be work centred. More importantly, in mixed-activity sessions the opportunities for communication between teachers and pupils were reduced (see key factor 9 below).

A focus upon one curriculum area does not imply that all the pupils should do exactly the same work. On the contrary, effects were most positive when the teacher geared the level of work to pupils' needs, but not where all pupils worked individually on exactly the same piece of work. It seems likely that, in mixed-curriculum sessions, the demands made upon the teachers' time, attention and energy can become too great for them to ensure effective learning with all groups. Furthermore, it becomes more difficult in such sessions for the teacher to call the class together should the opportunity arise to share an interesting point that may emerge from the work of a particular group or pupil. We recognize that there are many occasions when teachers may wish to diversify the work in the classroom, and beyond, into more than one curriculum area. Sometimes such diversification is unavoidable, perhaps through the constraints of timetabling or because of the nature of the work in progress, but, for the reasons cited above, we would urge the utmost caution over the adoption of a mixed-curriculum methodology as a basis for teaching and learning.

9. *Maximum communication between teachers and pupils*

We found evidence that pupils gained from having lots of communication with the teacher. Thus, those teachers who spent higher proportions of their time not interacting with the children were less successful in promoting progress and development. The time teachers spent on communications with the whole class was also important. Most teachers devoted most of their attention to speaking with individuals. Each child, therefore, could only expect to receive a fairly small number of individual contacts with their teacher. In fact, [. . .] for each pupil the average number of such contacts over a day was only eleven. Given that some children demand, and receive, more attention than the average from their teachers, this means that others have very few individual contacts per day. By speaking to the whole class, teachers increased the overall number of contacts with children, as pupils become part of the teacher's audience more often in such circumstances. Most importantly higher-order communications occurred more frequently when the teacher talked to the whole class.

We are not, however, advocating traditional class teaching. Our findings did not show any such approach to be beneficial for pupils and, in fact, we found no evidence of readily identifiable teaching styles at all. We feel that teaching is far too complex an activity for it to be categorized in this way. On the contrary, our results indicate the value of a flexible approach, that can blend individual, class and group interaction as appropriate. Furthermore, where children worked in a single curriculum area within sessions (even if they were engaged on individual or group tasks) it was easier for teachers to raise an intellectually challenging point with all pupils. Such exchanges tended to occur when teachers were introducing a topic to the class, before pupils were sent off to work individually or in groups. Class discussions were also a popular forum for gathering all pupils together, as was storytelling. These activities offered teachers a particular opportunity to challenge and stimulate their pupils.

10. Record keeping

We have already commented upon the value of record keeping in relation to the purposeful leadership of the headteacher. In addition, it was also an important aspect of teachers' planning and assessment. Where teachers reported that they kept written records of pupils' work progress, in addition to the authority's primary yearly record summary, the effect on the pupils was positive. The keeping of records concerning pupils' personal and social development was also found to be generally beneficial. Furthermore, in many effective schools, teachers kept samples of pupils' work in folders to be passed on to their next teacher.

11. Parental involvement

Our findings show parental involvement in the life of the school to be a positive influence upon pupils' progress and development. This included help in classrooms and on educational visits, and attendance at meetings to discuss children's progress. The headteacher's accessibility to parents was also important, schools operating an informal, open-door policy being more effective. Parental involvement in pupils' educational development within the home was also clearly beneficial. Parents who read to their children, heard them read, and provided them with access to books at home, had a positive effect upon their children's learning. Curiously, however, formal parent–teacher associations were not found to be related to effective schooling. Although the reasons for this are not clear it could be that some parents find the formal structure of such bodies to be intimidating and are thus deterred from involvement, rather than encouraged. We also found that some parents feel that PTAs tend to be run by small cliques of parents. We would not wish to advocate, of course, that schools disband their PTAs, but if a school has an association and is not involving parents in other ways it would perhaps be worth considering how parent–school relationships could be opened up.

12. *Positive climate*

The Junior School Project provides confirmation that an effective school has a positive ethos. Overall, we found the atmosphere to be more pleasant in the effective schools, for a variety of reasons. Both around the school and within the classroom, less emphasis on punishment and critical control, and a greater emphasis on praise and reward was beneficial. Where teachers actively encouraged self-control on the part of pupils, rather than emphasizing the negative aspects of their behaviour, progress and development were enhanced. What appeared to be important was firm but fair classroom management. The class teachers' attitude to pupils was also important. Positive effects resulted where teachers obviously enjoyed teaching their classes, valued the fun factor, and communicated their enthusiasm to the children. Their interest in the children as individuals, and not just as learners, also fostered progress. Those who devoted more time to non-school chat or small talk increased pupils' progress and development. Outside the classroom, evidence of a positive climate included: the organization of lunchtime and after-school clubs for pupils; involvement of pupils in the presentation of assemblies; teachers eating their lunch at the same tables as the children; organization of trips and visits; and the use of the local environment as a learning resource.

It is important to note that the climate in effective schools was not only positive for the pupils. The teachers' working conditions also contributed to the creation of a positive climate. Where teachers had non-teaching periods, the impact on pupil progress and development was positive. Thus, the climate created by the teachers for the pupils, and by the head for the teachers, was an important aspect of school effectiveness. This further appeared to be reflected in effective schools by happy, well-behaved pupils who were friendly towards each other and outsiders, and by the absence of graffiti around the school.

LINKS WITH OTHER STUDIES

Many of these key factors have been identified in the results of other studies or reports and we will describe some of the links between our study and the findings of other research here. However, it must be stressed that the selection of studies is not intended to be exhaustive. [. . .]

Positive leadership

A number of other studies have pointed to the importance of the headteacher's leadership in promoting school effectiveness. For example, [. . .] work by Armor *et al.* (1976) examined schools which had been especially successful in promoting the reading achievement of minority children. They concluded that schools where the principal achieved a balance between a strong leadership role for themselves and maximum autonomy for teachers were more effective. [. . .] The California State Department of Education (1980) compared schools where pupils' reading scores were improving with those where reading scores were decreasing. This study also confirmed the value of positive leadership, and noted that such leadership was more effective when it included the sharing of responsibility for decision-making and planning. Our results support this conclusion. Tomlinson (1980) and Levine and Stark (1981) have also drawn attention to the importance of the principal's leadership in effective schools. In the British context, Rutter *et al.* (1979), in a major study of secondary schools in inner London, noted the importance of the headteacher's leadership in the promotion of school effectiveness. More recently, the Thomas Report (1985), which examined ways of improving primary schools in the Inner London Education Authority, commented on the necessity for clear and sensitive leadership by the headteacher.

The involvement of the deputy head

This finding is in accordance with the suggestions of Plowden (1967) and Coulson and Cox (1975) that deputies should be more involved in decision-making. [. . .] It was often the duty of the deputy head to take charge of the day-to-day organization of schools and to ensure that everything ran smoothly. Furthermore, many deputy heads had a particular pastoral role in the school, relating both to pupils and other teachers. Finally, they placed great emphasis on their role as a link between the head and the rest of the staff, a role of which many headteachers were also aware.

Far less attention has been paid to the role of the deputy head in previous studies of school effects. There is evidence, however, that the sharing of responsibility for decision-making and planning is an important aspect of effective leadership by the head (see the study by the California State Department of Education, 1980). Our findings indicate clearly the value of involving the deputy head in such decision-making and planning. [. . .]

The involvement of teachers

Staff involvement is, therefore, related to the first factor, the headteacher's purposeful leadership. An authoritarian style of leadership will not encourage staff participation and involvement in decision-making. The study by the California State Department of Education (1980) pointed to the importance of sharing the responsibility for decision-making and planning with other staff. Glenn (1981) conducted case-studies of four urban elementary schools. Amongst other factors, she suggested that school effectiveness was enhanced where there was joint planning by the staff. [. . .] Moreover, the conclusions of the Thomas Report (1985) noted the value of staff involvement in decision-making in primary schools. The authors state 'it is a matter of high priority that each school should have a sense of wholeness. That can be achieved . . .

after the adjustments that inevitably follow staff discussions arranged to consider proposals' (p. 66).

Consistency amongst teachers

Glenn's study (1981) also pointed to the benefits of consistency amongst teaching staff, particularly in the use of through-the-grades reading and mathematics programmes. Edmonds (1979a, 1979b) emphasized the importance of school-wide policies and agreement among teachers in their aims. [. . .] In the secondary sector, Rutter *et al.* (1979) found that consistency amongst teachers promoted effectiveness, and noted that staff consensus on the value and aims of the school as a whole was related to greater success in promoting pupils' educational outcomes.

Structured sessions

Structure was also shown to be important by Traub, Weiss and Fisher (1976) who found that higher pupil performance in basic skills occurred where there was an emphasis on a more structured approach to learning in which students did not have complete freedom to decide their programme of activities. [. . .] Solomon and Kendall (1976) found that excessive pupil choice and responsibility for planning their own work were disadvantageous for pupil achievement and self-esteem. These authors argued it was not a choice between teacher control and pupil control, rather a question of teacher control versus lack of control of learning activities.

Intellectually challenging teaching

Many studies [. . .] have indicated that high expectations of pupils are beneficial (see [. . .] Rutter *et al.*, 1979; California State Department of Education, 1980; Glenn, 1981; and reviews by Brophy, 1983, and Pilling and Kellmer Pringle, 1978). Evidence of the value of intellectually challenging teaching is also provided in the study of junior pupils conducted by Galton and Simon (1980). In addition, Levine and Stark (1981) have noted that effective elementary schools emphasized the development of higher-order cognitive skills such as reading comprehension, and problem solving in mathematics.

Work-centred environment

Weber's (1971) study also emphasized the importance of an atmosphere of order, purposefulness, and pleasure in learning. Work by Rosenshine and Berliner (1978) has indicated that, where academic engaged time was higher, pupil progress in basic skills was promoted. [. . .]

Work in junior schools in Britain has also shown that the amount of teacher time spent communicating with pupils about their work was related positively to pupil progress. Galton and Simon (1980) noted 'all three groups of successful teachers had more task interactions than the typical teacher in the sample' (p. 196). In addition, Tomlinson (1980) stressed the importance of the efficient use of classroom time. Fisher *et al.* (1980), in a study which examined the characteristics of good schools, found that academic learning time was increased, while Glenn's (1981) work has noted the importance of efficient, coordinated scheduling and planning of activities.

Our findings also support those of Armor *et al.* (1976), which demonstrated that an orderly atmosphere in schools was associated with greater effectiveness. Rutter *et al.* (1979) also indicated that strategies of classroom management which kept students actively engaged in learning activities had a beneficial effect on pupils' educational outcomes.

Limited focus within sessions

We have found no references in published studies of school effectiveness to the identification of a limited focus as defined in our research being an important aspect of effectiveness. This is likely to reflect the absence in past studies of data about the way teachers mix different curriculum activities.

Maximum communication

Work by Galton and Simon (1980) similarly found that the amount of teacher–pupil contact was important. They noted for all three groups of successful teachers [that] 'the most striking and perhaps the most important feature was that the teachers all achieved above-average levels of interactions with their pupils' (p. 186). Our results demonstrate that one of the ways teachers were able to increase the level of communication with pupils was by the use of a balance of class and individual contacts. Galton and Simon (1980) also found that one of their groups of more successful teachers were the 'class enquirers', who combined whole-class teaching with individual work. As with our Project, these authors also found a positive link between the use of higher-order questions and statements and maximum communication.

The Thomas Report also noted that teacher communication with the whole class could be valuable. Thus, the authors commented:

> Here and there our visits to classrooms coincided with an intensive piece of work by a teacher using exposition and discussion with a group of children or the whole class. Almost always this teaching brought a sense of eagerness and involvement to the work that was less often apparent when children were working on their own.
>
> (Thomas Report, 1985, p. 32)

They also noted that arrangements for individual work on any large scale frequently break down 'because teachers find it impossible to give sufficient individual attention to children and have to engage children too much in work that is simply time-filling'. [. . .]

Record keeping

A number of previous studies of effectiveness have also noted the importance of school-wide systems for the monitoring and evaluation of pupil progress. Thus, Weber's (1971) work noted the value of careful evaluation of student progress. Edmonds (1979a, 1979b, 1981) found that the frequent monitoring of pupil progress was related positively to effectiveness. [. . .] Dean (1980) also reported that 'record-keeping is an essential ingredient in making education continuous' (p. 14).

Parental involvement

Studies conducted in the USA have also suggested that parental involvement is an influential aspect of school effectiveness. Thus, Armor *et al.* (1976) noted the value of high levels of parent–teacher and parent–headteacher contact. In Britain, work by Hewison and Tizard (1980) has demonstrated a link between parental involvement and reading attainment for junior pupils. [. . .] Hargreaves (1984) and Thomas (1985) have also noted the value of increasing parental involvement in secondary and in primary schools. [. . .]

Positive climate

Other studies have reached similar conclusions concerning a positive climate. [. . .] Trisman, Waller and Wilder (1976) found that more effective schools tended to have a good school atmosphere including student–teacher rapport. Work by Moos (1978) noted the importance of a positive classroom climate. Brookover *et al.* (1979) found the quality of the school's social climate was related positively to the promotion of pupil achievement. Edmonds (1979a, 1979b) and Edmonds and Frederiksen (1979) have also reported that a school climate conducive to learning was necessary to promote achievement. In Britain, the work of Rutter *et al.* (1979) [. . .] indicated that the school ethos was influential in determining effectiveness. It also noted the importance of praise and of the emphasis on rewards rather than punishments.

SUMMARY

It is clear, therefore, that there are many links between the factors identified as important in the Junior School Project, and those found to contribute to school effectiveness in previous research. Nonetheless, some factors have received less attention in past studies: in particular, the key role of the deputy head, and the value of a limited focus in the classroom. Although a few studies have noted the value of maximizing communication between teachers and pupils, in general this aspect has received only limited attention in most analyses of school effectiveness.

The twelve key factors point to effective schools as being friendly, supportive environments, led by heads who are not afraid to assert their views and yet are able to share management and decision-making with the staff. Class teachers within effective schools provide a structured learning situation for their pupils but give them freedom within this framework. By being flexible in their use of whole class, group and individual contacts, they maximize communications with each pupil. Furthermore, through limiting their focus within sessions, their attention is less fragmented. Hence, the opportunities for developing a work-centred environment and for presenting challenging work to pupils are increased.

Whilst the twelve key factors we have outlined may not constitute a recipe for effective junior schooling, they can provide a framework within which the various partners in the life of the school – headteacher and staff, parents and pupils, and governors – can operate. Each of these partners has some role to play in fostering the overall success of the school, and when each makes a positive contribution, the result can be an increase in the school's effectiveness. [. . .]

REFERENCES

Armor, D., Conry-Oseguera, P., Cox, M., King, N., McConnell, L., Pascal, A., Pauly, E. and Zellman, G. (1976) Analysis of the School Preferred Reading Program in selected Los Angeles Minority Schools. (Report No. R–2007–CAUSD), Santa Monica FA. The Rand Corporation.

Brookover, W.B., Beady, C., Flood, P. and Schweitzer, J. (1979) *School Systems and Student Achievement: Schools Make a Difference*, Praeger, New York.

Brophy, J. (1983) Research on the self fulfilling prophecy and teacher expectations, *Journal of Educational Psychology*, Vol. 75, no. 5, pp. 631–61.

California State Department of Education (1980) Report on the special studies of selected ECE schools with increasing and decreasing reading scores. Office of Program Evaluation and Research, Sacramento, California.

Coulson, A. and Cox, M. (1975) What do deputies do? *Education 3–13*, Vol. 3, no. 2, pp. 100–103.

Dean, J. (1980) Continuity, in C. Richards (ed.) *Primary Education: Issues for the Eighties*, A & C Black, London.

Edmonds, R.R. (1979a) Effective schools for the urban poor, *Educational Leadership*, Vol. 37, no. 1, pp. 15–27.

Edmonds, R.R. (1979b) Some schools work and more can, *Social Policy*, Vol. 12, no. 2, pp. 56–60.

Edmonds, R.R. (1981) Making public schools effective, *Social Policy*, Vol. 12, pp. 56–60.

Edmonds, R.R. and Frederiksen, J.R. (1979) Search for effective schools: the identification and analysis of city schools that are instructionally effective for poor children. (ERIC Document Reproduction Service No. ED 170 396).

Fisher, C.W., Berliner, D.C., Filby, N.N., Marliave, R., Cahen, L.S. and Dishaw, M.M. (1980) Teaching behaviours, academic learning time, and student achievement: an overview, in C. Denham and A. Lieberman (eds.) *Time to Learn*, Department of Education, Washington D.C.

Galton, M. and Simon, B. (1980) *Progress and Performance in the Primary Classroom*, Routledge & Kegan Paul, London.

Glenn, B.C. (1981) *What Works? An Examination of Effective Schools for Poor Black Children*, Center for Law and Education, Harvard University, Cambridge, Mass.

Hargreaves, D. (1984) *Improving Secondary Schools*, ILEA, London.

Hewison, J. and Tizard, J. (1980) Parental involvement and reading attainment, *British Journal of Educational Psychology*, Vol. 50, part 3, pp. 209–15.

Levine, D.U. and Stark, J. (1981) Extended summary and conclusions: institutional and organizational arrangements and processes for improving academic achievement at inner city elementary schools. Center for the Study of Metropolitan Problems in Education, University of Missouri-Kansas City, Kansas City.

Moos, R.H. (1978) A typology of junior high and high school classrooms, *American Educational Research Journal*, Vol. 15, pp. 53–66.

Pilling, D. and Kellmer Pringle, M. (1978) *Controversial Issues in Child Development*, National Children's Bureau, Paul Elek, London.

Plowden Report (1967) *Children and their Primary Schools*, HMSO, London.

Rosenshine, B. and Berliner, D.C. (1978) Academic engaged time, *British Journal of Teacher Education*, Vol. 4, part 1, pp. 3–16.

Rutter, M., Maughan, B., Mortimore, P. and Ouston, J. (1979) *Fifteen Thousand Hours*, Open Books, London.

Solomon, D. and Kendall, A.J. (1976) Final report: individual characteristics and children's performance in varied educational settings. Spencer Foundation Project, Chicago.

Thomas, N. (1985) *Improving Primary Schools*: Report of the Committee on Primary Education (The Thomas Report). ILEA, London.

Tomlinson, T.M. (1980) Student ability, student background and student achievement: another look at life in effective schools. Paper presented at the Educational Testing Service Conference on Effective Schools. New York, May 1980.

Traub, R., Weiss, J. and Fisher, C. (1976) Openness in schools: an evaluation, *Research in Education: Series 5*, OISE, Toronto.

Trisman, D.A., Waller, M.I. and Wilder, C.A. (1976) A descriptive and analytic study of compensatory reading programs: final report. Educational Testing Service, Princeton, N.J.

Weber, G. (1971) *Inner-City Children can be Taught to Read: Four Successful Schools*, Council for Basic Education, Washington, D.C.

2

THE QUALITY OF SCHOOLING:
Frameworks for Judgement

John Gray

INTRODUCTION

[. . .] With the passage of the 1988 Education Reform Act a concern with 'quality' in the education service has become something of an obsession. [. . . It] is a potentially elusive concept. It undoubtedly has something of the 'best buy' features so assiduously researched and celebrated in *Which* magazine in relation to washing machines, TV sets and electric food mixers. Few people, however, would be happy with definitions that were restricted to these kinds of 'qualities'. They are undoubtedly looking for more. Articulating what that 'more' is will be a major challenge for the next few years but will come, I hope, to form the cornerstone of how schools find themselves judged over the next decade.

Different groups have different criteria for judging a school's quality. Rhodes Boyson is reported to have three 'instant tests'. The first is the amount of litter in the playground. The second is the amount and quality of graffiti in the loos. And the third is the angle at which children hold their heads, forty-five degrees being the optimum. Below that, they are clearly fast asleep; beyond it, in open revolution!

SOME QUANTITATIVE INDICATORS OF QUALITY

In the attempt to understand quality many people turn to such traditional indicators of educational outcomes as exam results and staying-on rates. Using the Youth Cohort Study of England and Wales [. . .] I have picked out some relevant statistics (Gray *et al.*). Two of these are also available from official sources but the other two (the proportions of pupils truanting and pupils' attitudes) are not [Table 2.1].

Table 2.1   Some traditional indicators of the quality of secondary schools

Pupil outcome measure*	1987 (%)	1986 (%)	1985 (%)
Obtaining one or more 'higher grade' *exam passes* in year eleven	52	51	51
Staying on after year eleven	42	41	40
Truanting during year eleven			
'seriously'	7	7	7
'seriously or selectively'	17	17	17
Saying: *'School was a waste of time'*	11	12	11

Note: * These various measures were obtained from the Youth Cohort Study of England and Wales.

The picture over the three years 1985, 1986 and 1987 is a pretty stable one. Whichever of the four measures are employed things don't seem to have changed very much. [. . .] When the full pictures from GCSE results in later years come on stream we may find the 'improvement' so considerable that a new series of statistics to serve as benchmarks is required. Whatever the 'quality' in absolute terms of the education on offer in the secondary system, its quality (as judged by small and steady improvements over time) does not appear to have altered much in recent years.

THE VIEW FROM HM INSPECTORS

National responsibility for monitoring the quality of what goes on in schools is vested in members of HM Inspectorate. [. . .]

HMI follow events more closely than statisticians ever could. They visit institutions which are directly affected by events, both intended and un-intended. Not surprisingly, their account is of a system which has had a bump-ier ride. Policy initiatives actually affect what is happening.

[. . .] They reported that in 1988–9:

> Across schools and colleges around 70–80 per cent of the work seen was judged to be satisfactory or better: roughly one-third of it at all levels was adjudged good or very good. That is *not* a profile of a service in great difficulty about its general standards of work. But . . . there are serious problems of low and under-achievement; of poor teaching; and of inade-quate provision. It is particularly troubling that in schools some 30 per cent . . . of what HMI saw was judged poor or very poor. Those figures, if replicated throughout the system, represent a large number of pupils . . . getting a raw deal.
>
> (DES, 1990a).

These conclusions are undoubtedly disturbing and merit urgent attention. But what do the reports tell us about how quality has been changing over time? To establish this I looked back at the annual reports from previous years.

Anyone embarking on such a venture needs to be aware that comparing HMI judgements over time is not an easy matter. There are several reasons for this. The most obvious of these is that, in attempting to capture the complete strengths and weaknesses of the educational system as a whole within a few pages of a report, much of the detailed basis for the judgements is inevitably omitted.

But the difficulties are further compounded by the fact that HMI have, in fact, been using *three* summary judgements when they visit a school rather than just one. The report on the 1986 academic session provides the clearest discussion of this point (DES, 1987):

- the *first* measure is an assessment of 'the overall quality of work in schools visited';
- the *second* is an assessment of 'the quality of provision for each class (or lesson) seen';
- the *third* is an assessment of 'pupils' response for each class (or lesson) seen'.

Interestingly, HMI nowhere comment on secondary schools' exam results in their annual report. The focus is truly on the processes of teaching and learning!

The 1986 report suggests that for:

- 'overall quality' a figure of around 80 per cent satisfactory or better is to be expected;
- for 'quality of provision' around 70 per cent; and
- for 'pupils' response' around 80 per cent – to their credit the pupils are apparently achieving in spite of the odds and the provision!

It is the evidence for the first of these three measures that I have attempted to assemble in Table 2.2. This was not always easy. The report on 1987/88, for example, refers to 'most of the work seen by HMI' rather than a specific percentage, and the figure '4 lessons out of 5', the only quantified statement about secondary schools offered, relates in fact to their report on GCSE and is accompanied by the statement that this was 'a higher proportion than is usually reported in our inspection findings' (DES, 1989a).

By way of complete contrast the previous year's results (that is 1986/87) were quoted to a satisfyingly precise single decimal place. [. . .] Probably the only useful conclusion to be drawn is that, over the years, HMI have consistently found that somewhere between 70 per cent and 80 per cent of the schools they have visited have been of 'satisfactory or better' quality.

Table 2.2   HMI's judgements of school quality

Year	Proportion judged to be 'satisfactory or better'*
1988/1989	'70% to 80% of work seen'
1987/1988	'Four lessons out of five'
1986/1987	'83% of work seen'
1985/1986	'81% of work seen'
1982 to 1986	'Nearly three-quarters of schools'

Note: * 'Satisfactory' is the mid-point on a five-point scale running 'from excellent to poor'.
Sources: Sources were as follows. 1988/89: DES report published in 1990; 1987/88: DES, 1989; 1985/86 and 1986/87: DES, 1987; 1982–6: DES, 1988. All cited above.

In practice, as I shall argue later, broad judgements of this kind are the only useful ones to be made. What is important, when judging the quality of schools, is to note those occasions on which there are *marked* variations from the expected norms. Small fluctuations, one way or the other, are neither here nor there. At the national level at least, things do not appear to have changed very much in recent years whether one is looking at the quantitative indicators or the qualitative ones.

A 'POOR' SCHOOL BY ANY YARDSTICK

This is not to deny that there are marked variations in the quality of different schools, a point forcibly brought home by HMI's report on a Hackney secondary school published in [1990]. 'Only 20 per cent of the lessons seen reached satisfactory standards of teaching and learning. . . . As many as 50 per cent were of the poorest quality, lacking a clear sense of purpose, pace, progression or direction' (DES, 1990b).

The gap between the national picture and the local one presented here is so stark that the apparent precision offered by the statistics is unnecessary. The school's 'overall standards' would surely be recognized as 'exceptionally low' by anyone. The environment in the upper school was 'squalid', the graffiti 'very offensive' and the toilets 'insanitary'. 'Many lessons failed to start on time' and 'pupils' attendance and punctuality gave serious cause for concern'. 'Teacher–pupil relationships . . . varied from the kindly, supportive, interested and positive to the distant, aggressive and, on occasions, the verbally abusive. Many teachers did not have the classroom management skills to maintain discipline.' 'Overall the school [was] not managed effectively and in some respects it was badly managed.'

Even by the standards of the measured language of evaluation employed by HMI it is clear that something had gone very wrong indeed. The 1983 HMI report on the Liverpool Institute for Boys was the last occasion on which I read about a similarly neglected institution. On this latter occasion, after almost 18 years of increasing neglect, the LEA eventually closed it down.

THE NATIONAL POSITION

How many secondary schools might be like these two nationally? The honest answer is that it is hard to say. The Hackney and Liverpool schools are doubtless at one extreme. [. . .]

Part of the answer to our question lies in how you choose to draw the line between the 'good' and the 'not so good'. To those who would maintain that the 'figures speak for themselves' I would merely observe that I have yet to find a single figure that could speak, let alone for itself.

Over the years I have noted a number of different strategies for drawing the line. HMI's preference, using a five-point scale running from 'excellent' to 'poor', is to draw the line below the third category; hence 80 per cent of lessons are 'satisfactory' (the mid-point) or 'better' (good or excellent). By way of contrast most LEAs, in my experience, like to draw the line halfway down the list; this enables them to offer the insight that half the schools in the authority are above the LEA average and half below it.

My own preference is to draw two lines on the assumption that the majority of schools are performing at or around the average. I am looking, therefore, for ways in which schools may be said to differ from this average as well as for reasons; either they are a good deal above it or, alternatively, a good deal below. Most of the time there is nothing exceptional about their performance. They achieve what you would expect.

THE POLITICS OF SCHOOL EVALUATION

Setting the line is not just a matter of statistics or personal preference. As those who have tried to introduce improved strategies for schools' evaluation have found, more is at stake. In any system for evaluating schools there will be winners and losers. In selecting the overall approaches and the particular criteria this needs to be borne in mind. However, we could scarcely have a system more unfair than that which exists at present. By insisting that schools and LEAs publish their 'raw' exam or test results we run the distinct risk of rewarding schools for the 'quality' of the intakes they can attract rather than what they actually do with pupils.

[. . .] There are basically two ways in which the quality of a school's performance can be judged. The easiest way is to compare this year's performance with last year's and the year before that and so on. On the assumption that the intake has remained much the same over the years, how do the results compare?

The second approach is to compare like with like. How much progress have the pupils in this school made compared with pupils at similar starting points in other schools?

Ideally, one would use both approaches at the same time. In practice, most school effectiveness studies have concentrated on comparing like with like.

HOW MUCH DIFFERENCE DO SCHOOLS MAKE?

The debate about whether schools 'make a difference' has raged since the 1960s. Like most such debates there has been ample scope for misunderstanding. The simple and unequivocal answer to the question whether they make a difference is a positive one – of course they do. The crucial questions are how much? and why?

Back in the early 1970s Christopher Jencks argued that at least half the differences in pupils' performances in their late teens were due to differences in their social backgrounds and prior attainments; the remaining unexplained half he attributed to 'other factors' (Jencks *et al.*, 1972). Whilst these 'other

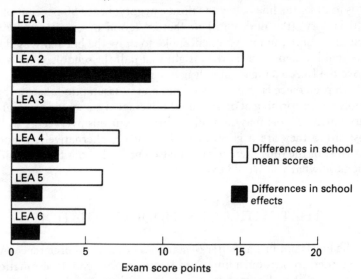

Figure 2.1   The size of school effects (inter-quartile ranges)

factors' undoubtedly included the schools young people attended, he maintained that no-one could actually identify which were the more effective schools, prior to the event, or what precisely made them more effective. As far as predicting outcomes was concerned, schools, to all intents and purposes, made only rather small differences to life chances.

Jencks's overall analysis of the *relative* importance of home and school continues to be the most comprehensive available and his conclusion that, relatively speaking, what pupils bring to school with them is considerably more important than what schools can do to or with them has scarcely been quarrelled with since then.

Our own recent work confirms the sorts of estimates that have been made up till now (Gray, Jesson and Sime, 1990). Working with data from six different LEAs, and using the most sophisticated statistical techniques currently available (multi-level modelling), we found that when differences in schools' intakes are taken into account the differences between schools' results are roughly halved. We have seen this happen so frequently with the data sets we have analysed that we have come to refer to this phenomenon as the 'rule of half'.

Figure 2.1 nonetheless shows that there were differences in the results of pupils attending schools of differing 'effectiveness'. The unshaded blocks show the difference in the actual exam performances of pupils attending different schools. These are the kinds of figures and differences the press reports.

The lengths of the heavily shaded blocks show the number of exam points difference between schools that just fell into the top quarter of 'effectiveness' in an authority and schools which just fell into the bottom quarter. In some LEAs, it can be seen, these differences were quite small (2 to 4 points); in one or two cases they were rather larger than this.

FACTORS WHICH SEEM TO MAKE A DIFFERENCE

What causes the differences? [. . .] Whichever account one reads of research on school effectiveness a prominent place is given to the centrality of the institution's values. In a nutshell, the more effective or successful schools seem to know what they are about and where they are going. They have, as Lightfoot puts it in her account of six 'good' American high schools, visible and explicit ideologies (Lightfoot, 1984). The particularly interesting (and with hindsight not unexpected) feature, however, is that staff and pupils alike can provide a reasonably good account of what the school is all about as well; the schools' aims and objectives are not merely the creation of, and confined to, their heads and senior teachers.

Teaching and learning are, of course, at the heart of any school's activities. What particularly distinguishes the more effective ones, Oakes argues in her wide-ranging review of the literature, is their 'press for achievement' (Oakes, 1987). Teachers expect their pupils to achieve and pupils, in turn, find themselves stretched and challenged in the classroom. Again there appears to be some mutuality of perceptions between pupils and teachers.

A third area in which the more effective schools make their contribution is in terms of relationships (Goodlad, 1984). Certainly, there is an absence of conflict between pupils and teachers; frequently there is some kind of mutual respect or 'rapport'. But crucially, at least in Lightfoot's study, there are plentiful opportunities for pupils to make good or, as she puts it, 'vital' relationships with one or more adults.

These sorts of things do not, of course, just happen; they are managed. Each of the various studies underlines, to a greater or lesser extent, the role of the school's leadership. Indeed I am still looking for a *research* study which demonstrates convincingly that the headteacher was not at the centre of things and yet the school, for which they were responsible, still functioned effectively.

More recently studies have gone beyond the headteacher to emphasize the role of senior management, the strategies that they implement and the ways in which they seek to support their more junior colleagues. A constant search for ways of evaluating and improving their institution's current performance also seems to be characteristic of the leaders of successful schools.

All four of these areas are ones to which Jencks paid scant attention. He would doubtless argue that the later research had given insufficient attention to the question of causal directions and there could be some truth in this charge. Taken collectively, however (and bearing in mind the qualitative accounts of how teachers and pupils actually behaved in the more successful schools), the balance of probabilities is that these things happened directly *because* of the efforts made by heads and their staffs. The most convincing demonstration would probably be to see how these factors were developed in a school over a period of time; but to date few researchers have been in a position to follow a school's development over this longer sort of period.

There is one area in which Jencks's conclusions have had to be modified a little, namely in relation to resourcing schools. This is the one area in which those responsible for a school, but nonetheless outside it, can influence matters directly. For much of the 1970s it was fashionable amongst researchers and policy-makers to assert that resources couldn't buy success. Class sizes, for example, didn't make a difference; indeed researchers frequently reported that children did better in larger ones!

With hindsight nearly all the studies cited in support of these conclusions have been shown to be seriously flawed from the point of view of research design. One or two more recent studies (and notably the ILEA's Junior School Project in this country) have shown that smaller classes do make some difference, although the effects have not been startling (Mortimore *et al.*, 1988). Within any one LEA pupil–teacher ratios are not usually allowed to vary by that much.

Adequate levels of resourcing, then, seem to be a necessary but not sufficient condition for a school to be effective; quite wide mixes of resources seem to be associated (and I emphasize the word associated) with success. Several caveats are, however, necessary.

The first is that in twenty years of reading research on the characteristics of effective schools I have only once come across a case of an 'excellent' school where the physical environment left something to be desired; interestingly, in that particular case, working on the environment of the school had been one of the new principal's first priorities, as indeed it appears to be with most new headteachers.

Second, in seven years of reading HMI's published reports on secondary schools I can only remember two or three occasions where their overall rating was highly favourable and the roof (or something similar) was in need of repair; and someone was always in the process of doing something about it.

Third, I have never read an account of a 'good' school which had serious staffing difficulties.

One further point needs to be made about the current research on school effectiveness. In general terms, it provides a relatively good introductory guide to the factors that make a difference. As a rule, schools which do the kinds of things the research suggests make a difference, tend to get better results (however these are measured or assessed). The problem is that these are tendencies, not certainties. In betting terms the research would be right around seven out of ten times, especially if it could be supported by professional assessments.

Around three out of ten times, however, schools seem to achieve 'good' results without scoring particularly highly on all the 'key factors' identified by researchers' blueprints. The collective wisdom of researchers and experienced practitioners is quite simply not good enough to hold individual institutions to account. To do so would be to run the risk of hampering, perhaps even damaging them.

The focus has tended to turn, as a result, from assertions about what schools must do to what schools must achieve. In particular, rather a lot of time has been spent debating the frameworks within which schools' performance will be judged.

PERFORMANCE INDICATORS: SOME LESSONS FROM NORTH AMERICA

As we begin in this country to consider the introduction of performance indicators we can learn something from experiences in North America. During 1987 Secretary Bennett of the US Department of Education introduced his infamous 'Wallchart'. This summarized, for the benefit of state superintendents, key features of pupils' performance in each of the states on certain nationally administered attainment tests as well as providing information about their respective levels of resourcing. In addition it included columns specifying the improvements or gains in pupils' performance that would be needed 'to meet President Reagan's 1990 challenge'. Controversially, these targets seem to be the same for states as diverse as Massachusetts and Mississippi.

During the 1980s the USA [. . .] began to take the whole business of monitoring test performance fairly seriously as one major strategy for raising standards. Individual states have increasingly been administering nationally normed standardized achievement tests (of one kind or another) and reporting the results to their communities. However, little in the British experience, apart from the dodges of car manufacturers' mpg claims, could have prepared us for what has come to be known as the Cannell controversy [see Shephard (1989) for a fuller discussion].

Cannell looked at the reports all 50 states had provided on their test results (Cannell, 1987). According to him, all 50 claimed to be above the national average and around 70 per cent of all students across the nation were told they were achieving at 'above average' levels. Cannell found this hard to believe. Surely there was some mistake?

In the subsequent debates some qualifications in relation to Cannell's conclusions were put forward. But, surprisingly, it emerged that he was essentially right. In a situation where each state had some freedom to determine which particular tests they would use as yardsticks it was perfectly possible for all or most to report 'above average' levels of performance.

There were several reasons for this but they mostly involved forms of 'teaching to the test'. In many states the testing environment was a 'high-stakes' one; pupils, teachers and their schools simply couldn't afford to do badly because life chances were at stake. In others the schools' curricula were either aligned to the test or, rather more frequently, the tests were aligned to the schools' curricula. Pupils were prepared more frequently for testing situations. There were also some doubts about what were euphemistically referred to as test security and familiarity. Clearly some part of the gains states were reporting was illusory. But then, in a situation where there was no national body taking responsibility for maintaining some kind

of overall perspective, there was scope for quite a few unintended consequences.

SOME EARLY INITIATIVES IN RELATION TO PERFORMANCE INDICATORS

The initial push for the introduction of performance indicators in Great Britain
came from the Audit Commission during the early 1980s. Auditors are usually
accountants by training and inclination. Naturally, therefore, they asked to see
the accounts. The education service provided them with some fairly promptly.
It was only several months later that it became clear that the education service's 'accounts' lacked the structure that a modern, performance-driven accountant might be seeking.

The accountant's dream that every educational activity and outcome could
be allocated to a cost heading and given a precise cost was some way off
becoming reality. To an accountant such imprecision is disconcerting. Before
much progress could be made the education service needed to determine where
it was headed and to establish some performance indicators by which it could
be judged. [. . .] Judgements about performance require a context within
which they can be located. Equally importantly, given the firmly embedded
nature of some existing approaches to school evaluation, they require some
overall co-ordination, if publicly credible judgements that have the power to
challenge existing assumptions and prejudices are to be produced. Orchestrat-
ing such 'agreements' is not merely a technical activity but involves influencing
the social organization of 'educational knowledge' as well.

DEVELOPING SOME PRINCIPLES

[In 1989 and 1990] I and my colleagues worked on these issues with members
of about one in five of the English LEAs. A number of problems have emerged
in our discussions about how their LEAs are responding to the new demands of
the 1988 Education Reform Act. [. . .]

First, few LEAs have sophisticated procedures in place already for judging
the performance of their schools; indeed, as a recent HMI report confirmed, a
majority of LEAs have not yet got round to establishing suitable procedures for
interpreting schools' examination results (DES, 1989b). Lacking such approaches, they and their schools have recently found themselves falling victim
to individuals or pressure groups who have been prepared to employ whatever
crude yardsticks were to hand.

Second, they have only recently begun to develop procedures for systematically sharing information about schools' performances, let alone judging them.
Few LEAs to date can rely on a consensus amongst their officers and advisers
about what it is important to concentrate on. Should they, for example, look at
outcomes as well as processes? And, in either case, which particular ones?

Table 2.3   Some general principles for the construction of performance indicators

Performance indicators should:
(1) be about schools' performance
(2) be central to the processes of teaching and learning
(3) cover significant parts of schools' activities (but not all)
(4) reflect competing educational priorities
(5) be capable of being assessed
(6) allow meaningful comparisons: over time and between schools
(7) allow schools to be seen to have changed their levels of performance by dint of their own efforts
(8) be few in number

Third, even where the beginnings of some consensus have begun to emerge, there is considerable uncertainty about what precise evidence to collect. There is mounting pressure in many LEAs to use whatever happens to be on the shelf because time is short. But there is also widespread unease that what may currently be readily available or easily measurable is not necessarily central to the educational enterprise. Data collected for one purpose may not lend themselves to others.

Fourth, and most importantly of all, we have found it important to establish some general principles for the construction of performance indicators. Table 2.3 represents the latest attempt of my colleague David Jesson and myself to introduce some coherence to the debate by developing some general principles (Gray and Jesson, 1990).

The most important consideration relating to the construction of performance indicators is that they should *directly measure or assess schools' performance*. Many of the proposals we have encountered to date seem only indirectly related to actual performance.

They should be *central to the processes of teaching and learning* which we take to be schools' prime objectives.

They should *cover significant parts of schools' activities* but not necessarily (and certainly not to begin with) all or even most of them.

They should be chosen to *reflect the existence of competing educational priorities*; a school which did well in terms of one of them would not *necessarily* be expected (or found) to do well in terms of the others.

They should be *capable of being assessed*; we distinguish assessment here from measurement, which implies a greater degree of precision than we intend.

They should *allow meaningful comparisons* to be made over time and between schools.

They should be couched in terms that would *allow schools, by dint of their own efforts* and the ways in which they chose to organize themselves, *to be seen to have changed their levels of performance*; that is to have improved or, alternatively, to have deteriorated relative to previous performance and other schools.

Finally, they should be *few in number*; three or four might be enough to begin with. After some experimentation over a period of years one might end up with a few more. The processes that establish the wider credibility of the first ones will lend themselves to development if required.

Table 2.4   The three Sheffield University Performance Indicators

---

Academic progress
What proportion of pupils have made above average levels of progress over the relevant time period?

Pupil satisfaction
What proportion of pupils in the school are satisfied with the education they are receiving?

Pupil–teacher relationships
What proportion of pupils in the school have a good or 'vital' relationship with one or more teachers?

Answer categories for all three questions

All or most		Well under half
	About half	
Well over half		Few

THE THREE SHEFFIELD UNIVERSITY PERFORMANCE INDICATORS

In recent times we have come to recognize that there is an inverse relationship between the number of questions one chooses to ask and the quality of the evidence that can be collected in relation to each. The Sheffield Law of Performance Indicators states that 'too many questions drive out good answers'. Since 'good answers' are fundamental to the task of setting agendas for schools' further development it follows that we felt we ought to confine ourselves accordingly.

In the interests of economy, efficiency and effectiveness we have therefore restricted ourselves to the three questions listed in Table 2.4. The choice of 'academic progress' as one focus strikes us as largely unproblematic although, in the context of a national curriculum and related attainment testing in as many as ten subjects, it may be necessary to impose some restrictions.

Our second and third choices (relating to pupil satisfaction and pupil–teacher relationships) have been heavily influenced by our reading of the literature on school effectiveness.

In sum, we are arguing that a 'good' school is one where high proportions of pupils:

- make above average levels of academic progress;
- are satisfied with the education they are receiving; and furthermore,
- have formed a good or 'vital' relationship with one or more of their teachers.

We would agree with those who argue that these are not *sufficient* conditions for 'excellence'. As pragmatists we would argue, however, that it would be hard to imagine a 'good' school where these things did not happen in reasonable measure and furthermore that, where they happened frequently, the odds would be on the institution being a 'good' one. The concern that all aspects of schools' activities must somehow be brought in to complete the picture (and for justice to be done) needs to be resisted.

THE METHODOLOGY OF SCHOOL ASSESSMENTS

The cynic will ask how these assessments can be made. My answer is a brief one.

First, the technology for undertaking sophisticated analyses of pupils' academic progress is clearly largely in place. We ourselves have been involved recently in the routine application of statistical techniques whose complexity was defeating statisticians and the largest computers just two or three years ago.

And second, the assessments that are required in the other two areas (of pupil satisfaction and pupil–teacher relationships) are no more complex than those which HMI are currently making on a routine basis. If HMI can do it convincingly, then surely other experienced practitioners can as well.

The quality of a judgement rests in part on the evidence which has actually been collected in relation to it and, in part, on the way in which that evidence is marshalled to support the judgement. Having a *group* of 'judges' who are, by and large, in agreement also helps, especially if they can provide a collective articulation of the reasons why they reached the conclusions they did.

THE MISSING DIMENSION

I have argued that the complexities of the routines and practices which go to make up contemporary schooling can be reduced to just three questions about their 'quality'. Nonetheless, I would be the first to admit that something is missing. Education is about more than the mundane and the everyday. There are frequently 'lows' and there are, more occasionally perhaps, some 'highs'. When people remember their educational experiences it is often these latter 'moments' that they particularly emphasize, moments when something of significance has been learnt or experienced.

In brief, I require a fourth question or probe to cover those parts of the educational experience that performance indicators cannot reach.

Two examples of such 'moments of quality' will help to make my point. The first is an example of pupils as scientists, drawn from the archives of the Children's Learning in Science Project (Driver, 1989; Wightman, 1986).

After a number of initial activities relating to change of state, a class of 13-year-olds, working in groups, were asked by their teacher to explore and explain the properties of ice, water and steam. In particular, how precisely does ice turn into water and then water turn back again into ice?

One group starts by talking about molecules, then turns its attention to the question of bonding. They explore the idea of the bonds being somehow 'broken'. But if the bonds are broken, how are they subsequently remade?

The teacher intervenes and asks how they imagine 'bonding'.

The interactions amongst the group quicken as the pupils dig into the depths of their own understanding of scientific principles, each contributing their bit.

And then they begin to fly! Magnetism, electricity, the effects of heat on the 'vibrations' of the bonds are all raised . . . and built on.

The pace of the discussion falters. And then one of them, taking a different tack, arrives at a fundamental insight. Perhaps the force is actually 'there' all the time!

The outcome of this discussion is a considerable achievement. The pupils (13-year-olds) have brought together their knowledge that particles are in constant motion and that this motion increases with temperature with the idea of the force between particles being present all the time to explain the apparent 'making and breaking' of the bonds.

My second example is of pupils as poets. It is taken from the film *Dead Poets' Society*.

The new English teacher in a boys school has challenged a lot of his pupils' assumptions as he tries to help them value poetry for what it can say about their own lives.

On this occasion he has set them, for homework, the task of actually writing some poetry. Some find it easier than others.

The teacher asks the boys to read to the class what they have written. One boy, in love for the first time, is carried through what he might otherwise have seen as an embarrassing requirement by the strength of his feelings. He reads, he affirms himself, he feels good.

Later the teacher invites a boy, who generally lacks confidence in his own abilities, to take his turn.

He draws him to the front of the class, covers the boy's eyes with his hands and moves him round whilst, at the same time, suggesting words and phrases that evoke a brief response.

The movement quickens. The boy's responses become longer. They build to a powerful personal crescendo.

The teacher releases the boy and the spell is broken. The boy is visibly shaken but emotionally liberated; his classmates stunned, but respectful.

In these two examples we see how young people need space and stimulus if they are to fulfil the potential of their minds and their imaginations.

There's a lot in good teaching and good learning that can't be captured by a checklist or a calculator. Schools and teachers must be encouraged to identify and celebrate *their* moments of excellence.

THE ROLE OF THE CRITIC IN JUDGING PERFORMANCE

I want to conclude with some comments from Raymond Williams (1989). He is discussing the problems facing a critic who is trying to write about the modern novel. The analogy is with inspectors trying to make judgements about schools.

The critic's task is not easy. 'There's too much going on! It all looks out of control! How do I deal with it?'

The critic's first instinct is to reject so much energy, for energy is the enemy of order, and *order* is the critic's *job*. How does the critic deal with it? asks

Raymond Williams. By embracing it. Let's not *just* peddle all that tired old stuff about *standards* in the name of quality. Let's celebrate what we have and what we, as experienced practitioners, *know* is good.

REFERENCES

Cannell, J.J. (1987) *Nationally-Normed Elementary Achievement Testing in America's Public Schools: How all 50 States are Above the National Average*, Friends for Education, Daniels, West Virginia.

DES (1987) *Report by Her Majesty's Inspectors on LEA Provision for Education and the Quality of Response in Schools and Colleges in England 1986*, Department of Education and Science, London.

DES (1989a) *Standards in Education 1987–88: The Annual Report of HM Senior Chief Inspector of Schools Based on the Work of HMI in England*, Department of Education and Science, London.

DES (1989b) *The Use Made by Local Education Authorities of Public Examination Results*, Department of Education and Science, London.

DES (1990a) *Standards in Education 1988–89: The Annual Report of HM Senior Chief Inspector of Schools*, Department of Education and Science, London.

DES (1990b) *Report by HM Inspectors on Hackney Free and Parochial Church of England Secondary School*, Department of Education and Science, London.

Driver, R. (1989) The construction of scientific knowledge in school classrooms, in R. Millar (ed.) *Doing Science: Images of Science in Science Education*, Falmer Press, Lewes.

Goodlad, J.I. (1984) *A Place Called School: Prospects for the Future*, McGraw-Hill, New York.

Gray, J. *et al. Education and Training Opportunities in the Inner City* (Training Agency, Sheffield, Research and Development Series no. 51).

Gray, J. and Jesson, D. (1990) The negotiation and construction of performance indicators, *Evaluation and Research in Education*, Vol. 4, no. 2, pp. 93–107.

Gray, J., Jesson, D. and Sime, N. (1990) Estimating differences in the examination performances of secondary schools in six LEAs: a multi-level approach to school effectiveness, *Oxford Review of Education*, June.

Jencks, C. *et al.* (1972) *Inequality: A Reassessment of the Effects of Family and Schooling in America*, Basic Books, New York.

Lightfoot, S.L. (1984) *The Good High School: Portraits of Character and Culture*, Basic Books, New York.

Mortimore, P. *et al.* (1988) *School Matters*, Open Books, Somerset.

Oakes, J. (1987) Conceptual and measurement issues in the construction of school quality, The Rand Corporation, California.

Shephard, L.A. (1989) Inflated test score gains: is it old norms or teaching the test? Paper presented to the American Educational Research Association's Annual Conference, San Francisco, 29 March.

Wightman, T. (1986) *The Construction of Meaning and Conceptual Change in Classroom Settings: Case Studies in the Particulate Theory of Matter*, Children's Learning in Science Project, Leeds University.

Williams, R. (1989) quoted in D. Hare, Cycles of hope and despair, *The Weekend Guardian*, 3 June, p. 5.

This paper was delivered as an inaugural lecture at the University of Sheffield, 7 March, 1990. Slightly revised version given at the Tripartite AMA/NCB/ACC Conference on Effective Schooling, 22 March.

3

STRENGTHS AND LIMITATIONS OF THE CULTURE METAPHOR

Gareth Morgan

In an essay on the use of statistics as a basis for public policy [first] published in 1954, British economist Ely Devons drew parallels between decision-making processes in formal organizations and magic and divination in tribal societies (Devons, 1961). He noted that while organizational decision-makers would not normally think of examining the entrails of a chicken or of consulting an oracle about the fortunes of their organization or the state of the economy, many of the uses of statistics have much in common with the use of primitive magic. In primitive society magic decides whether hunting should proceed in one direction or another, whether the tribe should go to war, or who should marry whom, giving clear-cut decisions in situations that might otherwise be open to endless wrangling. In formal organizations techniques of quantitative analysis seem to perform a similar role. They are used to forecast the future and analyse the consequences of different courses of action in a way that lends decision-making a semblance of rationality and substance. The use of such techniques does not, of course, reduce risks. The uncertainties surrounding a situation still exist, hidden in the assumptions underlying the technical analysis. Hence Devons's point that the function of such analysis is to increase the credibility of action in situations that would otherwise have to be managed through guesswork and hunch. Like the magician who consults entrails, many organizational decision-makers insist that the facts and figures be examined before a policy decision is made, even though the statistics provide unreliable guides as to what is likely to happen in the future.

Devons's critique points to the exaggerated faith we often tend to place in such techniques, and hence the lack of reflection and critical awareness that accompanies their use. Like the primitive magicians, all kinds of experts are encouraged to engage in their mysterious calculations, and are allowed to preserve their credibility even when events prove them wrong. If the magician's advice proves misguided, his magic is not discredited. Failure is usually attributed to an imperfection in execution or the unanticipated intervention of some hostile force. In a similar way the technical expert is allowed to blame the model used or the turn of events, as a means of explaining why forecasts are inaccurate. The analysis is never discredited; the appearance of rationality is preserved.

Modern organizations are sustained by belief systems that emphasize the importance of rationality. Their legitimacy in the public eye often depends on their ability to demonstrate rationality and objectivity in action. It is for this reason that anthropologists often refer to rationality as the myth of modern society. For like primitive myth, it provides us with a comprehensive frame of reference, or structure of belief, through which we can make day-to-day experience intelligible. The myth of rationality helps us to see certain patterns of action as legitimate, credible, and normal, and hence to avoid the wrangling and debate that would arise if we were to recognize the basic uncertainty and ambiguity underlying many of our values and actions.

One of the major strengths of the culture metaphor rests in the fact that it directs attention to the symbolic or even 'magical' significance of even the most rational aspects of organizational life. As will be apparent from earlier discussion, numerous organizational structures and practices embody patterns of subjective meaning that are crucial for understanding how organizations function day by day. For example, meetings are more than just meetings. They carry important aspects of organizational culture: norms of passivity in the insurance company; fear and respect for unshakable facts in Geneen's intimidation rituals.[1] Even the nature of an empty meeting room conveys something about the general organizational culture, since these rooms generally reflect and reproduce the structures of interaction expected in the organization. Straight lines of chairs and note pads, each guarded by a water glass as erect as a sentry, communicate a sense of conformity and order. The friendly chaos and casualness of more informal meeting rooms extend a more open invitation to self-organization. In highlighting the symbolic significance of virtually every aspect of organizational life, the culture metaphor thus focuses attention on a human side of organization that other metaphors ignore or gloss over.

A second major strength of the culture metaphor stems from the fact that in showing that organization rests in shared systems of meaning, and hence in the shared interpretive schemes that create and re-create that meaning, the metaphor [. . .] points towards [. . .] creating organized activity by influencing the language, norms, folklore, ceremonies, and other social practices that communicate the key ideologies, values, and beliefs guiding action. Hence the current enthusiasm for the idea of managing corporate culture as the 'normative glue' that holds the organization together. Whereas previously many managers have

---

[1] Howard Geneen, chief executive of International Telephone and Telegraph (ITT), was a ruthless and intimidatory manager, whose approach, of motivation through fear, is discussed by Morgan on pp. 125–6 of *Images of Organization*, the book from which this chapter is taken.

seen themselves as more or less rational men and women designing structures and job descriptions, co-ordinating activities, or developing schemes for motivating their employees, they can now see themselves as symbolic actors whose primary function is to foster and develop desirable patterns of meaning. The results of research on organizational culture show how this form of symbolic management can be used to shape the reality of organizational life in a way that enhances the possibility of co-ordinated action.

The culture metaphor thus opens the way to a reinterpretation of many traditional managerial concepts and processes. For example, we have already mentioned how the metaphor influences our view of leadership. Traditional approaches to leadership have tended to focus on the problems of linking tasks and the people who are to perform those tasks by identifying the *behavioural* styles appropriate for different situations. The culture metaphor encourages us to reinterpret the nature of these styles to recognize the role they play in the social construction of reality. We can see that different leadership styles hinge on a question of how reality is to be defined. Authoritarian leaders 'sell' or 'tell' a reality, forcing their definition of a situation upon others. More democratic leaders let the reality of a situation evolve from the definitions offered by their colleagues, listening to what is being said, summoning and integrating key themes, and evoking and developing imagery that captures the essence of the emergent system of meaning. Such leaders define the reality of others in a more gentle and subtle way than their authoritarian counterparts, through strategic interventions that communicate key directions and sense of value, rather than by forcing people to follow their lead. Leaders do not have to lead by placing themselves in the forefront of action. They can often play a background role, shaping the all-important stage of action and the general direction that events will take but leaving choice about details to those responsible for their implementation. In viewing leadership as the management of meaning, the culture metaphor leads us to understand old styles in new ways.

The metaphor also helps us to reinterpret the nature and significance of organization–environment relations. We have already hinted at how we can understand familiar organizational concepts, rules, and procedures as interpretive schemes through which we construct and make sense of organizational reality. Equally, we can understand the way an organization makes sense of its environment as a process of social enactment. Organizations choose and structure their environment through a host of interpretive decisions. One's knowledge of and relations with the environment are extensions of one's culture, since we come to know and understand our environment through the belief systems that guide our interpretations and actions. This insight has prompted anthropologist Gregory Bateson to suggest that mind and nature are intertwined: nature renders itself visible through culture. Our understanding of nature is cultural.

This has profound implications for how we understand organization–environment relations and strategic management. For in stressing the fundamental interconnection between these phenomena we recognize that our environments are extensions of ourselves. [. . .] We choose and operate in environmental domains according to how we construct conceptions of what we are and what we are trying to do, e.g. 'be an organization in the computer industry', 'produce and sell automobiles', 'be a leader in our field', 'whip the competition'. And we act in relation to these domains through the definitions that we impose on them. For example, firms in an industry typically develop a language for making sense of their market, technology, and relations with other segments of the economy, aligning their actions in relation to the pattern of threats and opportunities which this set of interpretations makes visible. Firms organize their environments exactly as they organize their internal operations, enacting the realities with which they have to deal. Of course, the environment is not so easily controlled as internal operations. Other organizations also inhabit this domain, shaping action in accordance with *their* favourite interpretive schemes and thus influencing the environment to which others are trying to adapt and react. Environmental turbulence and change is a product of this ongoing process of enactment. Environments are enacted by hosts of individuals and organizations each acting on the basis of their interpretations of a world that is in effect mutually defined. A competitive ethos produces competitive environments. Visions of recession produce recession. The beliefs and ideas that organizations hold about who they are, what they are trying to do, and what their environment is like, have a much greater tendency to realize themselves than is usually believed.

This has considerable relevance for the way organizations should approach strategy formulation. By appreciating that strategy making is a process of enactment that produces a large element of the future with which the organization will have to deal, it is possible to overcome the false impression that organizations are adapting or reacting to a world that is independent of their own making. This can help empower organizations to appreciate that they themselves often create the constraints, barriers, and situations that cause them problems. For example, in the 1970s the American automobile industry saw the Japanese challenge as lying at the heart of their problems. A closer look at the situation would have led them to see that members of their industry had enacted the conditions that helped to make the Japanese challenge successful, e.g. by ignoring the possibility that the American market might be amenable to the idea of buying smaller cars.

A final strength of the culture metaphor is the contribution that it makes to our understanding of organizational change. Traditionally, the change process has been conceptualized as a problem of changing technologies, structures, and the abilities and motivations of employees. While this is in part correct, effective change also depends on changes in the images and values that are to guide action. Attitudes and values that provide a recipe for success in one situation can prove a positive hindrance in another. Hence change programmes must give attention to the kind of corporate ethos required in the new situation and find how this can be developed. In highlighting the fact that organization to a large extent rests in the shared interpretive schemes that inform action, the culture metaphor elevates the importance of attending to changes in corporate culture that can facilitate the required forms of organizational activity. Since organization ultimately resides in the heads of the people involved, effective organizational change implies cultural change.

The insights generated by the culture metaphor have sent many managers and management theorists scurrying to find ways of managing corporate culture. Most are now aware of the symbolic consequences of organizational values, and many organizations have started to explore the pattern of culture and subculture that shapes day-to-day action. On the one hand this can be seen as a positive development, since it recognizes the truly human nature of organizations and the need to build organization around people rather than techniques. However, there are a number of potentially negative consequences.

Persuaded by the ideas that there are good and bad cultures, that a strong organizational culture is essential for success, or that modifications to an existing culture will lead employees to work harder and feel more content, many managers and management consultants have begun to adopt new roles as corporate gurus attempting to create new forms of corporate consciousness. While many managers approach this task on the assumption that what's good for the organization will inevitably be in the interests of its employees, critics feel that this trend is a potentially dangerous one, developing the art of management into a process of ideological control. Of course, management has always been to some extent an ideological practice, promoting appropriate attitudes, values, and norms as means of motivating and controlling employees. What is new in many recent developments is the not-so-subtle way in which ideological manipulation and control is being advocated as an essential managerial strategy. There is a certain ideological blindness in much of the writing about corporate culture, especially by those who advocate that managers attempt to become folk heroes shaping and reshaping the culture of their organizations. The fact that such manipulation may well be accompanied by resistance, resentment, and mistrust, and that employees may react against being manipulated in this way, receives scant attention. To the extent that the insights of the culture metaphor are used to create an Orwellian world of corporate newspeak, where the culture controls rather than expresses human character, the metaphor may thus prove quite manipulative and totalitarian in its influence.

When we observe a culture, whether in an organization or in society at large, we are observing an evolved form of social practice that has been influenced by many complex interactions between people, events, situations, actions, and general circumstance. Culture is always evolving. Though at any given time it can be seen as having a discernible pattern, e.g. reflecting an ethos of competition or co-operation, dominance or equality, seriousness or playfulness, this pattern is an abstraction imposed on the culture from the outside. It is a pattern that helps the observer to make sense of what is happening in the culture by summarizing the sweep of history in retrospect, but it is not synonymous with experience in the culture itself. Our understanding of culture is usually much more fragmented and superficial than the reality.

This is an important point, since many management theorists view culture as a distinct entity with clearly defined attributes. Like organizational structure, culture is often viewed as a set of distinct variables, such as beliefs, stories, norms, and rituals, that somehow form a cultural whole. Such a view is unduly mechanistic, giving rise to the idea that culture can be manipulated in an instrumental way. It is this kind of mechanistic attitude that underlies many perspectives advocating the management of culture. However, from the inside, culture seems more holographic than mechanistic. Where corporate culture is strong and robust a distinctive ethos pervades the whole organization: employees exude the characteristics that define the mission or ethos of the whole; e.g. outstanding commitment to service, perseverance against the odds, a commitment to innovation, or in less fortunate circumstances, lethargy or a sense of helplessness or futility. Corporate culture rests in distinctive capacities and incapacities which, as a result of the evolution of the culture, have become defining features of the way the organization works by being built into the attitudes and approaches of its employees. Managers can influence the evolution of culture by being aware of the symbolic consequences of their actions and by attempting to foster desired values, but they can never control culture in the sense that many management writers advocate. [. . .] It pervades activity in a way that is not amenable to direct control by any single group of individuals. An understanding of organizations as cultures opens our eyes to many crucial insights that elude other metaphors, but it is unlikely that these insights will provide the easy recipe for solving managerial problems that many writers hope for.

When anthropologist Franz Boas entertained a Kwakiutl Indian from the Pacific Northwest in New York City earlier in this century, the Indian reserved most of his intellectual curiosity for the brass balls on hotel banisters and the bearded ladies then exhibited in Times Square. His attention was caught by the bizarre rather than the fundamental aspects of the culture he was visiting. His experience contains a valuable caution for those interested in understanding organizational culture, for in this sphere too attention may be captured by the hoopla and ritual that decorate the surface of organizational life, rather than by the more fundamental structures that sustain these visible aspects. In studies of organizational culture, enactment is usually seen as being a voluntary process under the direct influence of the actors involved. This view can be important in empowering people to take greater responsibility for their world by recognizing that they play an important part in the construction of their realities. But it can be misleading to the extent that it ignores the stage on which the enactment occurs. We all construct or enact our realities, but not necessarily under circumstances of our own choosing. There is an important power dimension underlying the enactment process that the culture metaphor does not always highlight to the degree possible. When this is taken into account, the culture metaphor becomes infused with a political flavour. [. . .]

REFERENCE

Devons, E. (1961) Statistics as a basis for policy, in *Essays in Economics*, Allen & Unwin, London, pp. 122–37.

4

THE CULTURE AND ETHOS OF THE SCHOOL

Derek Torrington and Jane Weightman

[*Editor's note*: This chapter is taken from a research study. The authors conducted intensive fieldwork in schools over a period of between four and seven weeks. The four examples are from sites at which they researched.]

In contrast with the traditional concept of the factory which has been dominant in most large, commercial, employing organizations, the traditional concept of the school is of a community, with the associated emphasis on ideas like ethos, spirit and individual commitment. There is concern with the process as well as with the content of the work that is done. There are people with posts of pastoral responsibility as well as those with academic responsibilities. There is discussion of the 'hidden curriculum' and a belief that the school cannot achieve its objectives unless the whole is much more than the sum of the parts.

Factory thinking [. . .] is alien, and recent use of terms like 'product' and 'customer' make most teachers wince because they run counter to the ideal of an integrated community seeking the welfare of all members. Even such a shrewd commentator as Charles Handy makes suggestions which seem to undermine the integration that most teachers regard as essential:

> the great fallacy of comprehensive education was to think that it had to be done in comprehensive institutions. Why can't they go to different places for different skills, including a work organization, with the school being the central hub, tutor-in-chief, counsellor and mentor. . . . The different bits would be smaller, more specialized institutions, language schools for instance, independently run but paid for by the local authority.
>
> (Handy, 1987, p. 521)

Teachers believe in the integration of education, with much of the emotional and intellectual development of their pupils coming from the wholeness of the school in which they are set. [. . .] We believe that teachers do not realize how much their own needs must be attended to if the integration is to be complete.

Wholeness is created and maintained by the ethos, the spirit or – in our language – the *culture* of the school. Much of the agony that schoolteachers have experienced in the era of falling rolls has come from the reorganizations that have justified the destruction of school cultures by economic expediency. Amalgamating schools is seldom successful and usually disastrous unless there is a powerful engine for growth and progress. Attaching the front of an aeroplane to the back of a train does not make a super-vehicle; it makes a nonsense. [. . .]

ETHOS AND CULTURE IN SCHOOLS

The concepts of ethos and organizational culture are very similar but there is a slight difference. Organizational culture is the characteristic spirit and belief of an organization, demonstrated, for example, in the norms and values that are generally held about how people should treat each other, the nature of working relationships that should be developed and attitudes to change. These norms are deep, taken-for-granted assumptions that are not always expressed, and are often known without being understood.

The history and traditions of a school tell one something of a school's culture because the cultural norms develop over a relatively long period, with layers and layers of practice both modifying and consolidating the norms and providing the framework of ritual and convention in which people feel secure, once they have internalized its elements.

The ethos of a school is a more self-conscious expression of specific types of objective in relation to behaviour and values. This can be in various forms, such as a formal statement by the headteacher, and in such comments as 'we don't do things that way here'.

The word 'culture' is more common in management circles whereas 'ethos' is used more often in education circles, particularly when referring to the children in the school. We are concerned with both culture and ethos but only in relation to the adults in the school, and we therefore normally use the word 'culture'.

Traditionally the culture in schools was one of high consensus, often centred on strong loyalty to a headteacher who was expected to symbolize and expound the culture of the school, rather like a monarch, through such ritual devices as social distance, taking school assembly, wearing a gown, having a veto on major decisions and running staff meetings in a magisterial way.

In the mid-1970s doubts crept in as the aims for schools became more diverse and the organization more complex. In some cases this led to increased managerialism, an interest in management for its own sake rather than as a means to an end. Through all employing organizations there is inevitably some withholding of co-operation by staff, even where they accept the authority of managers and their right to manage (Anthony, 1986, p. 41). This is, in part, because managers have an unrealistic expectation about co-operation and in part because of the limited extent to which the authority of position can be exercised. If a school culture is long established and widely accepted by staff, the authority of position may be effective. Once change becomes necessary the authority of position becomes insecure, unless the person in authority is a charismatic polymath.

It is axiomatic that schools have had to cope with a great deal of change in the last decade, but much of that change has involved teachers working in different ways, especially working more closely with each other and across the boundaries of disciplines. It would not be an exaggeration to suggest that this has been the real shaking of the foundations of recent years. Not only has it made great demands on individual teachers, it has also made inoperable a culture of consensus based solely on loyalty to the head. Debate increases as a necessary prelude to action, uncertainty becomes more commonplace, the nature of individual autonomy is being reconstructed.

It is important that those in schools should try and understand the culture they share, the extent to which it can be changed and how the changes can be made, even if the changes may be much harder and slower to make than most teachers believe.

As we have already said, culture is often not expressed and may be known without being understood. It is nonetheless real and powerful, so that the enthusiasts who unwittingly work counter-culturally will find that there is a metaphorical but solid brick wall against which they are beating their heads. Enthusiasts who pause to work out the nature of their school culture can at least begin the process of change and influence the direction of the cultural evolution, because culture can never be like a brick wall. It is living, growing and vital, able to strengthen and support the efforts of those who use it, as surely as it will frustrate the efforts of those who ignore it.

CURRENT PRACTICE – FOUR CONTRASTED CULTURES

To understand the culture of a school fully requires longer than our stays of four to seven weeks, but we feel we got under the skin of the schools by being present all day, every day of our visits. We noticed increasing levels of trust from members of staff, who talked with us very frankly and often articulated in their conversations with us feelings and attitudes that they had never previously understood.

As culture is such an individual cloak we have included four rather long examples here to demonstrate the nature of culture and ethos. The first two examples are of cultures that, in general, assist staff commitment, co-operation and self-renewal. The second two are of cultures that are rather discouraging for staff. Like all real examples, they contain inconsistencies.

Valley High: an example of staff commitment and cohesion

One of the striking features of this school is the level of staff commitment and the quality of staff cohesion. The extent of these interrelated characteristics is indicated by the frequency of and attendance at departmental and other meetings, the range of extracurricular activities, the provision of lunchtime lessons and tutorials, and the vitality of the curriculum. Not all the teachers are equally committed, but overall there are more 'keen' staff than elsewhere. As a result of attending INSET meetings elsewhere they were aware that in some way they were 'different', but they had not given much thought as to why they were so committed and worked so well together. When asked to do so they produced a range of answers which many of them had not previously considered.

The most frequent response to any question about commitment was that it had something to do with the head. Members of staff perceived him as a person who, when he was in school, was constantly involved with children and the general affairs of school life, rather than sitting remote in his office.

Many teachers commented that they could talk very easily to the head, although it was not always easy to get in to see him. He was always prepared to listen to them and took a genuine interest in their problems and plans. Most felt that, where he could do so, he had recognized their efforts with internal promotion. For his part the head professed to making his appointments 'with an eye on the future'. In this way he could be sure of having a head of department 'in waiting' in the event of a head of department gaining promotion.

Another reason for their loyalty lay in the fact that he appointed them. Only two teachers in the school predate the head, who took up his appointment in 1971. He talked about the care he took to appoint teachers with the 'right' philosophical commitment, 'outstanding candidates' with a strong pastoral orientation and potential for growth. He admitted consciously appointing people in his 'own image' and believed that he was able to select the best candidate almost intuitively.

Many of the staff had only worked in this school. Even the head was surprised to learn that 24 out of 43 full-time staff had only ever worked in this school. One of the most important reasons is that they believe in what they are doing there. Many of the staff are trapped in the school as a result of these beliefs, with the obvious disadvantages of professional narrowness, complacency and staleness.

Those staff who operate in departments meet formally at least once a week. In fact they spend almost every break and lunchtime in each others' company. This intense interaction with colleagues creates a collegial atmosphere in which the departmental curriculum is constantly under review and pressure is all-pervasive, not coming from one direction or another. If you do not work hard then you let down your colleagues as well as the children.

Most staff gain great personal and professional satisfaction from working closely with colleagues and being seen to be committed. They also feel themselves to be members of a team which is contributing to the growth of the school. Not all individuals fit into this pattern, and some departments are livelier and more cohesive than others. Nevertheless, the departmentalization of the school has helped in the development of team-oriented individuals who are generally well motivated and prepared to work hard for the department and the school.

The whole-school and inter-disciplinary meetings which operate within the school also contribute to the pattern of team building and commitment. There was less apparent inter-departmental sniping, territoriality and stereotyping than in most schools. It seems that being closeted with all your colleagues in a series of curriculum meetings, or meeting them on a regular basis to develop inter-disciplinary courses, breaks down the traditional barriers between departments and makes for greater staff cohesion and solidarity.

House staff have the opportunity of meeting each other during some afternoon registration periods and over lunch. During the course of these interactions (particularly with the head of house) they exchange ideas about how different pupils should be handled and enabled to absorb the house ethos. Conversations in the house areas at lunchtime serve to reinforce the individual's commitment to a particular way of handling children. The regular group support of other house staff and the departmental meetings help teachers maintain their belief in an enlightened approach to managing children despite the everyday pressures of the classroom.

The school is losing some of its middle-class pupils to other areas because of the zoning policy of the local authority. Teachers know they have friends amongst the councillors at County Hall but fear the drift from the smarter villages in the locality will affect their intake.

Their sixth form is barely viable and their intake down to four-entry. The staff feel unloved and misunderstood by the outside world and seem to be drawing even closer to each other for mutual support. Many talk openly of their fears for the future under a new regime because, although the head is only 48, he is not a well man and could retire early. Perhaps it is this fear which makes them want to protect him and complain that he does not get enough support from his deputies!

So here we have a school with a culture that has developed staff commitment and cohesion. This is largely due to the head, who has worked hard to develop opportunities for the staff and to take a positive interest in their work and ideas. It is also due to the stability of the staff who have grown up together in the school and have been appointed by the head 'in his own image'. Despite the risk of narrowness, and the feeling of dependence on the head that gives rise to fears of the future, the cohesion is a valuable benefit to the school and its staff. Other aspects of culture are those of mutual support within departments and cohesion through committees and the house system. These three organizational devices have become much more than means of making decisions: they have become interdependent processes by which members of staff maintain their commitment, develop fresh ideas, find emotional support, renew their understanding of the shared mission and ensure that the sum is greater than the parts.

Summerfield High: an example of how co-operation, trust, cohesion and a sense of wholeness are maintained by small things

Of all the schools visited this had the calmest, most co-operative atmosphere. The staff seemed genuinely to like the pupils – which was not always apparent among the teachers with whom we spoke in other schools. There were many extracurricular activities outside school hours, staff were very friendly and helpful to each other within school as well as at friendship/social gatherings outside school. The head and deputies were rather remote from this.

There was less expressed irritation over cover, rooming, finances, registers and duties than we found elsewhere, although there were complaints about decision-making and communication with senior management. Both children and adults were trusted. A small example of this was when two boys asked to go home at break to change for a theatre performance; permission was readily granted. A more significant example was the way in which the finance committee of department heads organized the distribution of GCSE money in the most amicable way, deciding both weightings and distribution.

As both adults and children passed each other around school they gave eye contact, smiled and said something. 'Thank you' was a common phrase in both private conversation and public gatherings.

A number of factors contributed to this atmosphere of wholeness. First, the school is organized round open-air quadrangles, so that people are constantly aware of each other. The movement of people in circles and squares rather than in lines down corridors both generates and underpins the sense of oneness. The quadrangle makes possible a feeling of community in the same way as a cloister or a courtyard. The exceptions are the headteacher, the office staff and PE staff, all of whom are located away from this set of quadrangles. PE staff made special efforts to come over to school before school started, but the headteacher remained remote.

Second, there is thoughtful use of catering facilities, with tea, coffee, toast and cereal available on arrival and at break time, provided by dinner staff in a very pleasant hall. Most children and several staff use this facility, responding positively to the civilised way in which they are treated.

Most staff came into the staffroom before the school day began to look at the cover list and to check their pigeonholes, so there was the usual brief social gathering for jokes, chat and the sense of cohesion that such occasions provide. Senior staff were rarely seen here at this time.

A block timetable enables departments to organize their own groupings of pupils, teachers and what is taught. Departmental staff are also free at the same time for meetings, with the opportunity for all members of the department to be involved in decisions. Subject groupings – such as humanities, science and craft – are relatively large, tending to increase the general level of co-operation within the school.

Academic and pastoral structures are not separated. Heads of year are subject specialists with one extra free period. By this arrangement the year heads do not become a repository for every pastoral problem. These are left for individual members of staff to handle, with the co-operation of the year head when there is some particular crisis. All the pastoral staff are located in one room to ease their interaction and exchange of information.

There are several reliable senior staff, who deal with the main day-to-day difficulties with children and variations on routines and check up on what is happening without a lot of fuss, keeping everything on an even keel. This frees other staff to try new ideas, develop their teaching and discuss longer-term changes, with the reassurance of a 'safe' environment.

Of particular interest were the position and attitudes of the senior staff. The headteacher was away for a term, although frequently mentioned by members of staff in our interviews. He and the deputies were seen as being very closely knit and rather remote from the rest of the staff. Although it may seem unsatisfactory for the senior management team to be remote, this did help to unify the rest of the staff. [. . .]

The school had frequent contact with people outside, with industry, the feeder schools, advisers, the sixth form college, college of further education and so forth, so that teachers could compare their own understanding and performance with others and have the confidence of judging themselves as doing a good job.

Summerfield High had a culture of trust and co-operation that was maintained by a number of features of school life, from aspects of established behaviour, like the smiles and 'thank yous', to aspects of the use of the buildings, like the quadrangles and the staffroom, and the sensible academic and pastoral organization. There was nothing dramatic and no overriding formula; just patient, thoughtful attention to the small things that make all the difference.

William Barnes: an example of low morale and poor self-image in a school

Low morale was indicated first by feeling among the staff that they had stagnated. The school's headteacher from 1974 until 1984 had not, apparently, allowed any new blood in or anyone out. Many staff members felt they, and many of their colleagues, had been in the school too long, many for 20 years, or their entire career. Believing they would get neither jobs elsewhere nor promotion, they faced a depressing prospect of a further 20 years without change or fresh opportunity.

A frequent comment was that the school had few signs of achievement and a bad image, due to bad pupil behaviour and poor examination results. Staff felt ignored by the LEA and advisers, and also felt that the problem of declining rolls was exacerbated by parents preferring to send their children to the neighbouring ex-grammar comprehensive school, even though reorganization was in 1974.

Some comments were made about things being sloppy and that not everyone was pulling their weight. Nothing was done properly in this view because of lack of time or poor discipline.

'Blockitis' was felt to be a problem, as people worked in one of three blocks and the only time staff came together was for ten minutes at a Monday morning meeting, which had been introduced by the present headteacher, and at half-termly staff meetings. The local joke was that you needed a passport to go to the other blocks, although several individuals explained how they, of course, did know folk throughout the school because of their jobs.

Coming from outside, we saw a different reality. Several people had been in their jobs for a long time but no more than at many other schools. The general standard of pupil behaviour and attainment seemed perfectly reasonable, compared with other schools, although not many stayed on for A-levels. There were as many cross-school operations and groupings as in many other schools. In other words, William Barnes was a perfectly ordinary, good school. So why should staff suffer from low morale?

Like many other schoolteachers, members of staff did not like the ongoing industrial action of the time. Also they were isolated from other schools because of the previous head's staffing policy, so few of them had worked in or visited other schools and had no idea of prevailing standards. The LEA had a policy of devolving autonomy, so there were very few visits from advisers. No senior member of staff had responsibility for seeing individual teachers formally about their work unless secondment or redeployment or discipline was involved.

In this school thirty-three members of staff have telephones in their classrooms, and all lessons are frequently interrupted by phone calls or by messages taken round by pupils. Most communication is done this way and we observed as many as twenty interruptions in a single lesson. There is no tradition of waiting until breaks, lunches or using pigeonholes. This means teaching is undervalued, only traditional methods can cope, and people have an excuse to give up. One example was from a teacher who said in her previous lesson a phone call was about a boy not wearing a tie and this completely disrupted her fourth-year French lesson.

Some male members of staff maintained a very heavy-handed 'macho' attitude to discipline, including yelling at children. Caning had only been abandoned in the previous year, when it became illegal. Many teachers were unable to adopt this macho approach or disliked it.

So William Barnes was a school in danger of fulfilling its own prophecy. Morale was low despite a lack of objective indicators to justify the poor self-image. Staff did not believe in themselves, each other or the children in their charge. Although they believed they had stagnated, there was no will to overcome the resultant self-doubt. The school was isolated from the educational community at large and divided within its own blocks, while the extraordinary system of communication and the reliance on 'tough' discipline militated against wholeness and any sense of caring community.

Ridley: an example of a senior management team lacking cohesion and beginning to disable a school where consensus might be expected

Recruitment of staff to this voluntary-aided school was constrained by the wish to maintain a 'Christian ethos', so producing a further variation of the normal ethos and culture theme. In addition to the normal extramural calls on the head's time, there was involvement with the Church authorities at both local and diocesan levels.

Pastoral management was through year teams, co-ordinated by heads of year and the second deputy. Heads of year had, in official guidelines for staff, an important disciplinary function. However, staff did not consistently follow those guidelines and problems arose from that failure. The generally helpful and supportive attitude at the bottom of the pastoral hierarchy was not found at the deputy head/head of year level. There was an undercurrent of antagonism directed towards the deputy, who did not receive wholehearted co-operation.

Eighteen months before the study, the first deputy head had retired and been replaced by internal promotion. The head had offered one of the unsuccessful internal candidates a new senior post of 'curriculum head' and revised the job descriptions of the deputies. The job of the curriculum head was real, but the status (Scale 4) was not a fair reflection of the work compared with that of the deputies. The one other Scale 4 teacher had, through being head of RE, accumulated responsibilities peculiar to a denominational school.

The senior management did not meet as a team during the study. The head had weekly scheduled meetings with the curriculum head and frequently met both him and the first deputy (their offices were close together). On one occasion a meeting of all three, called to discuss 'curriculum planning' as one of a regular sequence of weekly meetings on the topic, discussed matters of a pastoral nature without any note of concern that the second deputy was not present. In scheduled meetings observed between the head and the second deputy, there was a sense of minds not meeting. The head, first deputy and curriculum head made remarks critical of the second deputy and his work.

It is a small school in which everybody knows everybody else; the whole school can, and does, assemble. Its mission gives a purpose to assemblies and might have been expected to promote more unity of purpose among the staff. It is selective in a way which should generate parental support and interest. But its size means that staff challenge each other little; many staff members have been there a long time and are set in their ways. There seems to have been a peculiar bitterness during the industrial action and both the head and a union representative blamed each other for unnecessary aggravation.

The position of the second deputy was disturbing. Of foreign extraction, his command of English was insufficient for him to express himself and to understand diplomatic turns of phrase. The second deputy did not organize his time well and was inclined to unnecessary interference in the detailed work of colleagues.

The senior management seemed to be struggling. Two had only been in post for four terms and a third was widely disregarded. The head himself still felt, after several years, that he had not been accepted in 'a tightly-knit community' and was frustrated: 'We can't look to the future because of the history.'

Here was a school that ran smoothly, but did not provide the culture in which staff could review their progress and create their future. There was no openness and confidence among the members of staff, and the senior team were not able to find a way out of the collective difficulties, with one of their number being isolated by his colleagues.

CONCLUSION: CULTURE AND THE SCHOOL

The culture of the school needs to be understood because a mismatch of action and culture can produce ineffective action. The second deputy at Ridley was acting counter-culturally by undue interference in the work of colleagues who were accustomed to greater autonomy. Other members of the senior team were acting counter-culturally in tending gradually to isolate him, which was not an acceptable pattern of behaviour in the ethos of that school. At Summerfield High a tendency to isolate the senior management team from the rest of the staff appeared to increase the cohesion and trust between other members of staff.

So far we have used the word 'culture' in the singular. We find, however, a need to emphasize that each school has at least two: one for adults and one for children. The school is an integrated community, but cultural norms for children are different from those of adults, and perhaps the greatest misjudgement of the cultural match is to develop procedures, practices and behavioural expectations for adults that are only suitable for children. However obvious a point this may seem, our observations show this type of cultural mismatch to be a commonplace. A further variant is where there are separate cultural assumptions about adults in the school who are not teachers. [. . .]

The most penetrating analysis of organizational culture is by Schein (1985). He distinguishes between the ways in which an organization needs to develop a culture which enables it to adapt to its changing environment (pp. 52–65) and, at the same time, to build and maintain itself through processes of internal integration (pp. 65–83).

How do cultures change? How do they become consolidated? [. . .] The general comment of Schein is that there are primary and secondary mechanisms. The primary mechanisms are (pp. 224–37):

(1) what leaders pay most attention to;
(2) how leaders react to crises and critical incidents;
(3) role modelling, teaching and coaching by leaders;
(4) criteria for allocating rewards and determining status;
(5) criteria for selection, promotion and termination.

We note two difficulties for schools here. First, such emphasis on 'leadership' implies that a school can only succeed when led by a Great Person on whom everything depends and to whom everyone else responds (see HMI Report, *Ten Good Schools*). Second, it is too easy to confuse cultural leadership with position leadership; those who are most effective in setting the tone may not be the senior staff even though they are well placed for this.

Focusing on the Great Person as the key to school success also emphasizes hierarchical principles of organization. There are limits to what can be achieved by hierarchical means and some radical views of organizations, such as Hyman (1977), criticize all hierarchical forms of organization as preventing their members giving of their best. Organizational culture is the concern of all members and change in a culture is effective and swift only when there is wide agreement, 'ownership', concerning the change to be sought. In a school, wide agreement about important aspects of its culture seems to be best obtained, paradoxically, through a recognition and toleration of a legitimate plurality of views and styles on less central matters. In such a school, differences will not be resolved by the Great Person's exercising 'the right to manage', but through 'the collegiate approach' – discussion amongst all parties concerned.

Elevated position in a hierarchy, though possibly helpful, is not a guarantee of effectiveness in the pursuit of, or opposition to, cultural change. Many heads will have noticed profound cultural changes in their schools following the prolonged pay and conditions dispute. Despite their efforts, the changes are deep-seated because they are owned by the staff. This is an unusual example, but we know of schools where heads have been unable to effect cultural change (whether for good or ill) and of schools, often the same, where change has flowed from those in less exalted positions. 'Staffroom credibility', a combination of evident experience with persuasive personality, and patience seem to be the attributes, rather than formal positions, which help effect change.

A third difficulty is the assumption in much of the theory that the stamp of its culture leaves an identical mark across all of an organization. We refer above to a 'legitimate plurality of views and styles' as a counterweight to the Great Person. In fact, we have to go further because schools contain teams of staff, each of which will have its own culture drawing on its members' views, the nature of its subject (if a teaching team) or tasks (if a non-teaching team), its history, its location in the school and so on. A visitor walking round a school will notice different cultures in different areas; where this variety is respected across the school, the culture of the school as a whole will be quite different from that in a school where such variety is suppressed.

If we now consider Schein's secondary mechanisms for the articulation and reinforcement of culture, we see they are (pp. 237–42):

(1) the organizational structure;
(2) systems and procedures;
(3) space, buildings and facades;
(4) stories and legends about important events and people;
(5) formal statements of philosophy and policy.

This introduces a wider range of possible actions, but notice what comes last! So often we have found in practice that attempts to develop aspects of culture actually begin with formal statements of policy, or that cultural inertia is attributed to the lack of such statements.

Without a central sense of unity, schools, like all other organizations, are no more than a collection of people who would rather be somewhere else because they lack effectiveness and conviction in what they are doing. The effective school has a few central ideals about which there is a high degree of consensus and those ideals are supported and put into operation by simple rules and clear procedures. The organization that depends principally on rules for its cohesion is in the process of decay.

HMI (1977) pointed out many years ago the key to success: 'The schools see themselves as places designed for learning: they take the trouble to make their philosophies explicit for themselves and to explain them to parents and pupils; the foundation of their work and corporate life is an acceptance of shared values.' [. . .]

REFERENCES

Anthony, P.D. (1986) *The Foundation of Management*, Tavistock, London.
Handy, C. (1987) The future of work; the new agenda, *The Royal Society of Arts Journal*, Vol. cxxxv, no. 5371, pp. 515–25, June.
HMI (1977) *Ten Good Schools*, HMSO, London.
Hyman, R. (1977) *Strikes* (2nd edn), Fontana, London.
Schein, E.H. (1985) *Organisational Culture and Leadership*, Jossey-Bass, San Francisco.

PART 2:

Teaching and Learning

5

THE MANAGEMENT OF LEARNING:
Using the Information

Marten Shipman

This material has been abridged

The theme of [the book from which this chapter is taken] is that training for school management has strayed from giving priority to learning by concentrating on administration rather than the encouragement of initiatives to raise attainment. The focus on information arises from that concern. Teachers are most active around the learning they organize. That is where they can change, and have changed, the education system. But the opportunities to exert influence depend on being informed and having the motivation to take initiatives. An accelerated programme of reform imposed by central government has exhausted many teachers. Yet the Education Act of 1988 is premised on the assumption that teachers will not only implement a National Curriculum but continue to develop it.

This assumption of continuing enterprise seems macabre in many schools wrestling with the complexity of the imposed changes [in the early] 1990s. Yet development continues and the teachers still influence it where it matters: where children learn. Here the demands of the Act meet the interests of teachers. Schools are being reorganized, not just to produce a National Curriculum, locally managed, but to prepare and release information previously protected as confidential in the classroom. The 1988 Education Reform Act lays emphasis on the public availability of information as the key to raising attainment. That is where it most intimately affects teachers since they produce and use that information. The key to successful school management [is] in reconciling professional concern with information on children learning with the [. . .] demands that this information be given to parents and made public at the school level. The initiatives that have changed education have come, and will continue to come, from teachers – through their concern with learning. If these initiatives are to continue they will require a management style aimed at encouraging teachers to go on being enterprising. Keeping staff informed will be the first priority.

All service organizations, including schools, depend on those involved knowing what is going on. Further, with a National Curriculum, locally financed and requiring collaboration between staff in a school, which also gives parents and pupils information at regular intervals, closing the classroom door and concentrating on your class or your subject is a disappearing option. So is the school that keeps its attainments to itself. The demand for information from both classroom and school has [. . .] increased. More important, these two sets of information have been tied together.

Thus information is taken in this chapter as the key to the management of schools with learning as a priority. Many have of course flourished with most of the information in the minds of teachers not in filing cabinets. There it was available for use. Now the Education Act requires that much of that information is made public. It is seen as essential for parents as well as teachers. [. . .] It could even up the life chances of children. The National Curriculum has not been applied to independent schools. Parents there know just what they want from such schools. So do most of their children. That is not the case in many maintained schools outside leafy suburbs in wealthy areas. Parents and pupils need to be informed. If maintained education is to flourish, responsibilities for learning must be shared. The provision of information is the first step in that sharing. This extends from marketing schools at one end to the confidential sharing of sensitive data between teacher and parent at the other. The concern is to ensure that information, which [. . .] has to be collected to meet the requirements of the 1988 Education Reform Act, is used to increase the effectiveness of learning.

Finally, the changes in the availability of information will, like all educational developments, have unforeseen consequences. The packages of reforms introduced by the 1988 Education Reform Act [. . .] have changed the direction in which information flows. Where administrative information flowed down and academic up, the Act increased the amount available and directed much of it outside as well as around the school. That circulation of information is more typical of modern, information-based organizations than of traditional top-down hierarchies. Management will have to be alert to the possibility that the Act [is altering] the structure of schools.

THE USES OF INFORMATION

The importance of information can be seen in the extraordinary increase in the numbers earning their living by producing, processing and distributing it. IT, information technology, is the cutting edge of the sunrise industries. As those in manufacturing decrease, the number working with information has taken up the slack. Education itself is increasingly geared to produce those with the necessary skills. It is wise to be cautious about any possible 'revolution' in learning as a consequence. What is clear, however, is that we have at last appreciated that information is the key to successful management. Within organizations two uses of information can be separated. First, it enables management to control and to plan. Second, it can empower staff, putting them in a position to see what is needed and supporting them in taking the necessary action. [. . .]

INFORMATION FOR MANAGEMENT

Controlling the organization

All organizations depend on the availability of data enabling management to organize, monitor and adjust routines. In schools it is necessary to get the right teachers into the right rooms with the right children at the right time, with the right resources. It is particularly important in financial planning and will loom large in schools with local management. That is why LEAs [are] working with schools to produce performance indicators. It is why schools need to have accounting procedures. It is the substance of budgets, based on past activities and results and related to current activities and future targets. It is the subject of many books following the Education Act of 1988 (see for example Davies and Braund, 1989).

The impact of the 1988 Education Reform Act [can be] summarized [. . .] by pointing to three overlapping, interlocking packages: [one for learning, one for resources and one for politics (i.e. increased powers to governors and parents)]. Thus the information required to manage the school finances cannot be separated from the way schools are governed and the way learning is organized. The political point is clear in arrangements for local financial management. LEAs [are required to] take a strategic role, free from exercising detailed control over spending in schools. They support governing bodies with professional advice. In law the governors control spending and therefore the appointment and dismissal of staff. The amount of information required in the school to control the budget will increase (see Coopers and Lybrand, 1988). Much of this will be used for monitoring by the LEA. That monitoring is supposed to ensure that local management is delivering better education. The information for controlling expenditure is supposed to give governors and LEA indications of costs related to their effectiveness in promoting learning. The need to control spending is going to have a direct and top-down impact on the way learning is organized.

There is also a new demand for control information directly related to learning. The LEA has the responsibility to ensure, through its inspectors, that the National Curriculum is being implemented in line with the Act and subsequent Orders. Regulations spell out the information that has to be produced in schools and made public. LEAs have established arrangements for dealing with complaints about the school curriculum. Parents will be able to use these local procedures if they are dissatisfied. Once again, this is threatening to teachers used to keeping much of their information of attainments private. The amount of information for control is being increased fast.

Planning the organization

Planning in schools is complicated by the difficulties in decision-making [. . .]. Ends and means tend to get confused. Yet the school effectiveness evidence

confirms the importance of a headteacher who has clear goals for the school
and who has managed to get staff to share in striving for them. The information required is usually long term and in broader terms than control data.
Many LEAs have encouraged schools to produce plans involving review and
assessment, the specification of objectives and ways of reaching them. This is
usually a 'systems' approach, very popular in the 1970s, based on the specification of goals and feedback from evaluations of the means introduced to
achieve them. This approach has tended to go out of fashion in industry where
the plans tended to inhibit responses to fast-changing markets. But in education, such plans can indicate ways forward and keep teachers and the public
involved with the school in the picture. It is easy to mock Management by
Objectives or Programme Budgeting Systems. They did seem to be little concerned with learning and divorced from the political aspects of school life. But
they did ensure that those involved knew what was supposed to be going on.
Simplified and practical ways forward based on these are now available (see
for example Caldwell and Spinks, 1988).

School review for planning

All teachers plan ways forward. This can consist of casual discussion or thorough review. The years ahead have to be considered, even if the decision has
often been to carry on as before. But that option may now be suicidal. Even in
the 1970s, with falling school rolls and talk of accountability it was risky. That
was the time when school self-evaluation became popular. Like most innovations [of the period], this movement lost its momentum. Yet it remains influential as schools try to work out their future post-1988.

The evaluation to serve as a basis for planning ahead has several labels such
as school review, school self-evaluation and in-school evaluation. The common idea is that regular and systematic evaluations of ends and means are
essential to identify strengths and weaknesses and to act to improve the standards attained. The movement to self-evaluation reached its peak around 1980.
Like other innovations it was boosted by academics and adopted by enthusiastic schools. Over half the LEAs produced some documented scheme. GRIDS
(Guidelines for Review and Internal Development in Schools), produced by the
National Development Centre for School Management Training, received support in the Better Schools programme (DES, 1986). Yet by the mid-1980s the
momentum was lost. Turner and Clift (1985), investigating the impact of one
of the best-documented and best-known LEA schemes, found that three years
after publication fewer than half the teachers claimed to have read it or recall
it. Little or nothing seemed to have changed. The innovation faded away like
most curriculum developments in an earlier decade. But the idea of review and
planning remains.

Some LEAs managed to merge self-evaluation into ongoing practice. Leeds
developed a scheme of co-operative assessment that combined self-assessment
by staff working with LEA advisers. Oxfordshire and Brent introduced mandatory schemes. The Inner London Education Authority introduced regular

school reviews. The idea of systematically reviewing policies and practices can be found in many schools. Such reviews are always part of school management, however implicit or casual.

A weakness of most self-evaluation schemes was their denial that teachers could be held responsible for outputs. That view recurs in academic writing on self-evaluation which was critical of any attempt to assess what was learned and relate it to how schools were organized (see for example Becher *et al.*, 1981). By the end of the 1980s with Attainment Targets, regular assessments and published school results the subject of statutory orders, this view that teachers were responsible for processes not outcomes looked as academic as its origins. Self-evaluation is too valuable to jettison with the literature that restricted it. It can be a way of relating school organization to results and of checking whether the information being collected is being used effectively. The introduction of an assessment-led National Curriculum [has] meant that school self-evaluation [is] able to draw on output indicators, not only for each year group, but for the school as a whole. LEA and national comparisons [are] possible. This is a technically dubious exercise, but it [is] mandatory. Further, the 1988 Education Reform Act also increased the demand for data for accounting. Just as the Act produced a new data base on pupil attainments, so it demanded new indicators of school performance. [. . .] The data for school review has multiplied. [. . .]

Planning at the classroom level

At the centre of the information that can be used to promote learning is assessment. That serves many purposes. It is formative in providing feedback on how work is going, what is going right or wrong, where effort should be directed, how the curriculum might be changed. It is summative in showing attainment at the end of a course and providing grades for comparisons or selection, or prediction. It also emphasizes the priority of learning. If it is assessed, it is important. Every teacher knows and uses assessment for these purposes every minute of the working day. Teaching is about assessment. Some small part is recorded. The extra effort required for this means that the information should be used to obtain maximum impact from the minimum effort.

The evidence on the curriculum and its evaluation, on curriculum change and the psychology of learning [. . .] can be pulled together to guide management by the adoption of a simple model of the part played by assessment in the learning process. The evidence on the curriculum provides clues on the way

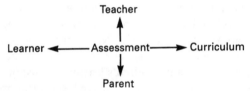

[Figure 5.1   Model of learning situation]

changes can be made to stick. The evidence on learning gives guidance on practical steps that can improve learning. The common factor in practice is assessment. The learning situation can be modelled as [shown in Figure 5.1].

[Figure 5.1] shows the central position of assessment. The information obtained informs the teacher who can then act to advise both pupil and parent, to adjust teaching style or the curriculum. It is central to matching the curriculum to the attainment of children, to sequencing work and giving it the right pace. Assessment is of course only one aspect of teaching. But it is through assessment that teachers act to support learning. It enables them to reinforce learning not only through words, but through signs, sighs and smiles. This is the most valuable kind of instantaneous feedback. Occasionally some of it is translated into comments, grades and marks on work. Some of this becomes formalized in tests and examinations, whether internal or external. Summaries are sent home to parents and discussed with children. This total body of assessment links the curriculum to the children, the learning tasks to the learner.

This view of assessment as central to learning has been reinforced by the introduction of a National Curriculum. The prominent position for assessment was not new. The Better Schools policy had specified improved assessment as essential not only for pupil attainment and teacher performance, but that of the school itself (DES, 1985b). Teachers had anticipated this demand, particularly in the primary schools, where diagnostic assessment and screening had increased in popularity. Teachers had also worked with LEA advisers to produce curriculum guidelines and materials that contained means of assessment to help children as they learned. In secondary schools this was less apparent, yet in the years up to the introduction of GCSE, graded assessment had been the fastest growing area of public examination, largely because it provided formative information. In GCSE, course work was providing feedback during rather than at the end of the courses. As the National Curriculum was introduced, guidelines for Records of Achievement were published, based on the same formative principle (DES, 1989). Formative assessment gives the information that can help learners, parents and teacher to appreciate strengths and weaknesses and work for improvement.

Bringing school and classroom planning together

[. . .] The divide between management information flowing down and information on learning flowing up [has been] an unusual and unfortunate feature of schools. By the mid-1980s the gap was being pinpointed in analyses of the school curriculum (see for example DES, 1985a). Many children were either opting out of important subjects or not covering important areas within them. After 1988, teachers still have the responsibility for ensuring that their curriculum remains broad and balanced. The National Curriculum Council has the same responsibility at national level. The assessment of the National Curriculum is supposed to ensure that children's learning is sustained and encouraged by providing information on levels achieved on Attainment Targets, thus securing continuity and matching (DES, 1988).

This consideration of learning in relation to progression through the curriculum should not be buried in the effort to get the National Curriculum and its assessment in place. It is essential to keep learning up front. Planning can not mean unthinking implementation. The National Curriculum is defined through brief Attainment Targets and Programmes of Study. It provides a framework only. The breadth and balance of the curriculum and the progression of children through it still have to be secured by teachers. Much of the planning [has] to be across the school. But it depends on information gathered first in the classroom. To ensure that each child progresses as intended takes more than the mechanical implementation of assessment. It [is] easy to tick statements of attainment achieved. The ten levels on each Attainment Target are very broad. It [is] useful to have these levels defined. But the responsibility still lies with teachers to ensure that the entitlement to a broad and balanced education is secured for individual children.

The mandatory provision of information on learning is then a burden but also an opportunity for teachers. It is a challenge to school management to use it effectively. The 1988 Education Reform Act will take a decade to implement. Even then it will need continual development, partly to rectify early mistakes, partly to respond to further social and economic change. The flood of publications will continue. It [is] essential to organize the collection and distribution of this material so that all teachers and as many governors and parents as possible know what is being proposed or imposed. Combined with information on attainments it can share responsibilities for learning. Too many children and parents have drifted along without much idea of what's going on.

The worst scenario would be for the effort to produce this information to be wasted by leaving the data in files. It would be equally wasteful to contain it within the school. Once the assessment of the National Curriculum is in place, teachers will be tracking children up ten levels on around fifty Attainment Targets. They will report summaries of this progress at the four reporting ages of 7, 11, 14 and 16. In between, the progress charted on each child can be used, not only by the teacher to help the child, but to involve the parents. They have a statutory right to receive information at the end of the four Key Stages. They will discuss this with teachers. That is a short step from encouraging them to see and discuss the detailed progress sheets on which the reporting at the end of Key Stages is based. This promises a wealth of information as a base for co-operation over learning between teacher, child and parent.

It is of course easy to ignore the technical problems in getting National Curriculum assessment into a valid and reliable form. It is an extraordinarily ambitious and technically difficult development. In the end it has to rely on teacher judgements, even if these can be guided by Standard Assessment Tasks, by in-service training and moderation meetings. The assessment tail is tending to wag the curriculum dog. Yet it is an opportunity to move beyond using assessment for planning and for control to increased empowerment and a spread of responsibility. [. . .]

Mining the data

The increase in available data as the Education Act is implemented means that there is more available to use to answer questions about children learning. Unfortunately there is less time to dig it out. Some has to be produced for LEAs. But as the National Curriculum assessments are implemented it [is not] difficult to answer some important questions about the success of the school in securing the 'entitlement' that is the justification of the National Curriculum. For example, each of the following issues could be illuminated by the tabulation of data that will have to be stored for reporting purposes.

(1) The levels achieved in specific subjects by girls and boys as they progress through school;
(2) The progress made by children from different social class or ethnic group;
(3) The impact of identifiable teaching styles, curriculum innovations, ways of involving parents, of managing the school;
(4) The resources allocated to children with special educational needs and their attainments.

Rightly, it can be objected that the indicators are crude. But teachers are going to be asked questions about such issues as parents receive more information, not only on their own children, but on the performance of the school. The school results have to be put into a context. Mining the available data helps. Over the years, time series which show changes year by year make the data more meaningful.

Organizing and reviewing the information

The collection, updating and use of information cannot be exempt from scrutiny for cost. Most headteachers take responsibility for the collection and distribution of information. That is unlikely to be possible in the future, particularly when there will be demands for financial as well as administrative and academic information. The easiest task to delegate is the collection and distribution of externally produced documents. Somebody on the staff should build up an archive of recent information on the implementation of the Education Act of 1988, for use by staff, governors and parents. It will involve keeping an eye on the educational press and sending for new publications as they appear.

The most difficult task is to co-ordinate the new information requirements with those already in existence. The Education Act has increased the amount of information required from schools. This cannot be added to that already collected without some streamlining. Hence there are several steps in the necessary reorganization. Every school has some arrangement for collecting and distributing information on the curriculum and the achievements of pupils. That working data is stored in classrooms, departments and headteacher's office. There is rarely any discussion of it as a whole. Some of it is duplicated. Some of it is collected more than once. Some of it is never used, once collected. As new demands build up it is essential to review what is collected. Demands from LEA for monitoring, from examination boards, from headteachers, for the production of Records of Achievement, for reports to parents, to careers service, references for employers, transfer information for receiving schools, for HMI and researchers need to be met, but as far as possible from data collected to meet the demands of the National Curriculum and for recording. Behind the necessary review must lie the reconciliation of management information with information on learning. That is why the whole staff have to be convinced of the need to review. Some information is jealously guarded as a source of power. Headteachers as well as those in classrooms may have to give more if the collection of information is to be made cost-effective.

REFERENCES

Becher, T. *et al.* (1981) *Policies for Educational Accountability*, Heinemann, London.
Caldwell, B.J. and Spinks, J.M. (1988) *The Self-Managing School*, Falmer Press, Lewes.
Coopers and Lybrand (1988) *Local Management of Schools*, HMSO, London.
Davies, B. and Braund, C. (1989) *Local Management of Schools*, Northcote House, Plymouth.
DES (1985a) *The Curriculum from 5 to 16*, HMSO, London.
DES (1985b) *Better Schools*, HMSO, London.
DES (1986) *Better Schools: Evaluation and Appraisal*, HMSO, London.
DES (1988) *National Curriculum: Task Group on Assessment and Testing Report*, HMSO, London.
DES (1989) *Records of Achievement*, HMSO, London.
Turner, G. and Clift, P.S. (1985) Teachers' perceptions of a voluntary LEA scheme for school self-evaluation, *Educational Research*, Vol. 27, no. 2, pp. 127–41.

6

CURRICULUM COHERENCE:
Reviewing the Quest

Penelope Weston and Elizabeth Barrett,
with Jim Jamison

[*Editor's note*: This chapter summarizes some of the main findings and implications of an NFER research study of the implementation of the National Curriculum. The authors focused on the impact of the Education Reform Act on curriculum management. They conducted case-studies in four secondary schools and twelve primary schools and a national questionnaire survey of primary, middle and secondary schools.]

Some years after the passing of the Education Reform Act [ERA] there is little sign that most schools have yet been able to construct, within the new framework, what they would recognize as a coherent curriculum, let alone the kind of holistic strategy for managing the whole curriculum which is somewhat optimistically set out in Figure 6.1. [. . .] The study showed that most senior managers were both disheartened by the disruption which ERA had brought and determined to do their utmost to safeguard the interests of their pupils. And while the struggle to meet changing statutory requirements continues, schools also have to contend with suggestions from several quarters that they are failing to meet goals set in the Act, or standards expected by professionals – especially HMI – and parents. The government-sponsored report on primary education (Alexander, Rose and Woodhead, 1992) added to the demands by setting out objectives for further improvements in primary provision.

In this [. . .] review we first want to summarize, against a background of continuing change and uncertainty, the current state of play in the 'whole-curriculum' game. What progress has there been on [. . .] coherence across all areas of the curriculum; over the age range of the school; over the 5–16 age range; and from the pupil's perspective? Next, we want to review the factors, relating to school context, resourcing or management, which seemed to make a difference to how schools were managing their curriculum in response to ERA. Thirdly, we will summarize some of the implications of this study, for

---

A holistic strategy for the whole curriculum

It was suggested that the *whole-school strategy* needs to be:

- *participative:* all the participants – staff and governors – need to feel committed to the strategy; this probably means they should be involved in shaping it;

- *scheduled:* it needs to cover short-, medium- and longer-term targets, which will all need review and adjustment;

- *coherent:* that is, managers should create structures and strategies which give due priority to the curriculum and also take proper account of resourcing and external interests (particularly parents).

It was also argued that the *whole-curriculum design* (which the strategy is intended to implement) should pay regard to a number of dimensions of wholeness:

- *wholeness across the curriculum,* for example for each year group in terms of:

   cross-curricular coverage: i.e. the coherence of subject matter (including overlap) within themes or subjects, as well as specific cross-curricular themes;

   cross-curricular process: e.g. coherence of approach on common skills, and collaborative initiatives on teaching and learning;

- *wholeness of the curriculum over time,* in terms of:

   continuity: in the schemes of work that are provided, over a term, year, Key Stage, phase and – most demanding – across phases;

   progression: i.e. the access to and take-up of the whole curriculum that is provided, by all pupils as they move through the 5–16 age range; this necessarily involves the issues of differentiation, and the formative integration of curriculum and assessment that is provided: year, Key Stage.

Figure 6.1 Strategy for coherence

curriculum managers in schools and LEAs. We will end with a brief look at future prospects for curriculum coherence at school level.

WHAT KIND OF COHERENCE?

At this point it is worth going back briefly to first principles, and reconsidering the new post-ERA learning package with which school curriculum planners have had to work. It is true that many senior managers, particularly in primary schools, recognized the value of feeling obliged, as a response to ERA, to undertake a fundamental curriculum review, within a national framework. But it also has to be said that there was surprisingly little to help those who were prepared to redesign their whole curriculum in order to enhance its coherence and commonality. The National Curriculum documents offered some common labels and organizational categories – Attainment Targets, Programmes of Study and so on – which operated across the ten subjects and began to influence other subjects outside the National Curriculum. But where were the shared elements, the core skills, concepts and knowledge, the internal scaffolding for the curriculum, from which a coherent structure could be built? Some schools and LEA staff have striven hard to identify them in the statutory subject programmes, but it is a hard task when it has to be conducted *post hoc.* By building the National Curriculum from ten separately designed subject blocks, constructed to different timetables and differing specifications, the government made the job of curriculum architects in schools infinitely more problematic. As the National Curriculum Council (1991) have pointed out, manageability has now become a key concept: 'Council will examine whether the weight of detail and the structure of programmes of study, attainment targets and statements of attainment should be rendered less complex and prescriptive.'

From the schools' perspective, the problem seems to be too much prescription on subject detail (particularly content) and too little guidance about how to fit together the demands of foundation subjects, cross-curricular elements and any other school-based curriculum requirements; in other words, too little guidance and support for coherence in the curriculum.

[In looking at] the different dimensions or aspects of curriculum coherence, [. . .] perhaps the most challenging of all is the idea of a coherent 5–16 curriculum, bridging the primary–secondary divide. [. . .] There are certain forces operating strongly against continuity and coherence of this kind, and some of them flow from other provisions of the Act, particularly on open enrolment. Schools and LEAs have demonstrated ways of promoting continuity in the longer term, but it requires patience, persistence, foresight and probably some kind of pump-priming finance. Almost as difficult is the task of securing coherence from the pupil's perspective, through a programme that fits together, relates to individual needs and offers progression over time. Part of the challenge comes from the need to integrate curriculum and assessment much more closely than has often been the case, in order to secure progression for every learner. Coherence across the curriculum was, in general, a more accessible target in primary than in secondary schools, since the plan for any one class had to cover the whole curriculum in some fashion; while coherence over time within a subject discipline came more naturally to secondary schools. Nevertheless, there were a number of case-study schools struggling with much more limited visions and objectives in curriculum planning, constrained by established structures, anomalous staffing patterns and resourcing constraints.

At the primary level, the threat to coherence was already becoming apparent in 1990–1 as schools faced the challenge of reshaping new curriculum designs based on core subjects in order to assimilate the other subject demands. Topic cycles which had been reshaped or adapted to incorporate science and technology Attainment Targets now had to accommodate all the humanities requirements, while art, music and PE were fitted in where possible or – in some cases – squeezed out. Was it the schools' curriculum organization that was at fault, or the overblown specification emerging through the statutory orders? In the view of the NCC, the structure in schools certainly needed review. 'It is unclear whether models of curriculum organization based solely on topic work . . . can be successfully adapted to meet all these new demands' (NCC, 1991). This view [was] even more specifically set out in the report on primary practice (Alexander, Rose and Woodhead, 1992). But it was also unclear to most primary schools involved in this study how nine subjects could be scheduled into a manageable curriculum for 5–11-year-olds, although the gradual transition towards a more subject-focused structure for upper primary and middle schools was evident from the study.

For secondary schools the central problem of securing coherence has taken a different form, in keeping with the contrast in curriculum culture between primary and secondary phases. The lack of an explicit common framework has made it harder to foster the mapping and sharing between subjects which could resolve the probable overload and provide some recognizable coherence for pupils. At Key Stage 4, the failure, after three years or more, to provide even the skeleton of a whole-curriculum design was, to say the least, unsatisfactory. In practice, by 1991 the majority of schools in this study had already moved to implement the spirit of the Act, and also to meet the requirements of TVEI Extension, by offering balanced science to all year 10 students, and a modern foreign language to the majority. But many were postponing further changes to their Key Stage 4 structure until the position was clarified, while some deeply resented the disruption to the carefully designed common curriculum programmes which they had developed before 1988.

Meanwhile, [the aspects of the ERA concerned with pupil learning] – including its [. . .] assessment requirements – had to be integrated with the other two elements of [the Act]: resourcing and accountability demands. Here again it was easier to spot the threats to a coherent strategy than the factors likely to enhance it. For example, the need to be accountable to parents and governors might make it even more difficult to meet the learning needs of *all* pupils, including those with special educational needs; while the pressure to fill posts in certain scarcity subjects and the need to retrain specialists in subjects outside the National Curriculum could lead to anomalies in staff status and salary levels. It has even been suggested that, in secondary schools, the outcome of financial pressures could be 'an even more rigid subject hierarchy', involving 'a steady skewing of staffing budgets in favour of the Core and Foundation subjects' (Ball and Bowe, 1992). If we take a 5–16 perspective, other obstacles to constructive integration of learning and resources have emerged, notably the discrepancy in resourcing between primary and secondary phases which results from the age-related pupil weighting formula. This in turn may reduce unacceptably the non-contact time available for curriculum planning and preparation in primary schools (Alexander, Rose and Woodhead, 1992). At the same time, the pressure to recruit pupils can further constrain efforts to build primary–secondary curriculum collaboration.

If threats to curriculum coherence can be easily identified, are there any indications that ERA has stimulated whole-curriculum thinking and management? The permanent secretary at the DES clearly felt that there were. Speaking in September 1991 he noted: 'Some might say that one of the principal gains of the National Curriculum reform process is the impetus which it has given to curriculum planning . . . [it] has increased the involvement of *all* teachers in planning and managing the curriculum across the school' (Caines, 1992). Our own study suggests that involvement of the whole staff team was more true of primary than of secondary schools, but in both phases there was evidence of renewed efforts at strategic planning, sometimes focused on the School Development Plan. Perhaps there was also greater awareness, prompted by assessment requirements, of differences between learners and their implications for curriculum design and delivery; although the gap between recognizing and meeting individual needs may be a wide one.

It seems, therefore, that there are some signs of wider participation in curriculum management, and of more recognition that plans need to be scheduled, in order to set realistic short- and medium-term targets. But in many schools the curriculum burden may still seem intolerable. How can it be eased, and the whole-curriculum game made more manageable?

COHERENCE AND DIVERSITY

Schools differ very considerably: between phases or stages, in context and in their recent history and development. These differences may affect the way their staff interpret the idea of the whole curriculum, and we might expect contrasts here in primary and secondary perspectives. Or the differences may shape the way in which schools with similar goals manage the process of realizing their aims. Thus most schools in the study had concerns about the numbers or expertise of staff in some subject areas, such as humanities (primary schools) or modern foreign languages (secondary schools). Some schools – especially those with a high proportion of 'disadvantaged' students – had more serious staffing concerns, and consequently were more worried about whether the curriculum as a whole could be implemented as they wanted. Schools with relatively new senior management teams were more upbeat about the prospects for moulding the curriculum into a coherent whole. But a heavy turnover of staff – or, alternatively, a very immobile staff with entrenched views – made it extremely difficult to build a collegial, participative approach to planning. Some primary heads tackled the problem, for the time being, by prescribing a detailed curriculum framework for all staff to follow.

Our review of curriculum managers' judgements about the factors constraining or encouraging whole-curriculum management confirmed that there were some systematic differences between the primary and secondary phases, particularly in their strategies for involving the rest of the staff team. But there was also a strong current of common concern about the manageability of the ERA initiatives. What the comments of individual heads suggested and the case-studies confirmed was how much each school's response was shaped by its own particular history and circumstances. As Ball and Bowe (1992) have suggested, 'change in the school is best understood in terms of a complex interplay between the history, culture and context of the school and the intentions and requirements of the producers of policy texts'.

They challenged what they saw as the 'assumption of commonality' among schools, that is to say the supposition that the National Curriculum, as a single national policy, would be 'implemented' by schools all 'equally able to respond, equally prepared, equally resourced'. Instead, they suggested that what was happening reflected an interplay between two complex and variable systems: national policy (which was subject to change) and the school system in which schools differed not just in their human and material resources but in how they had developed and responded in the past. Thus in addition to the expertise of their managers and teaching staff (the 'capacity' of the school), and the inherited staffing, intake, plant and facilities (the 'contingencies' with which managers were faced), schools could be seen to vary in their 'commitment' to particular curriculum patterns or cultures, and their 'history' of dealing with curriculum change.

This analysis fits rather well with the case-study schools in this study. Of course there were different challenges for schools with contrasting sets of contingencies: small versus large primaries, inner city versus rural schools, overcrowded versus undersubscribed secondaries. But it is interesting that it was the other factors – capacity, commitment and history – which seemed more likely to influence schools' approach to whole-curriculum strategy. There were several examples of new headteachers attempting to develop the school's capacity and to transform its *commitment* to certain curriculum patterns, and of the effort and time this required, in the light of the school's previous history of curriculum change.

What seems to be required, therefore, is a realistic appraisal of each school's current state of curriculum review and development, in order to help the head, staff and governors to target those aspects of curriculum coherence that are appropriate at this point in the school's history. Clearly the agenda will and should differ from one school (and LEA) to the next, but it will need to take account of the needs and capacities of each group of participants: pupils, classroom teachers, middle and senior managers, governors, LEA staff.

MANAGING COHERENCE

Allowing for the extensive differences between schools in their current capacity to manage change and to develop and sustain a coherent curriculum, what guidelines, if any, can realistically be drawn up on the basis of this study for all those who wish to develop greater coherence in the various dimensions of the whole curriculum which we have discussed? Using the terms of Figure 6.1, how might schools, with the support of the LEA move towards a holistic strategy for the whole curriculum; or prevent the disintegration of the coherence they have carefully developed in earlier years?

Within the school

First of all, does the school – staff, pupils and governors – have a shared view of where it is going? 'Effective headteachers have a vision. The vision will have at its heart the school curriculum . . . and how planning, teaching and evaluation will be undertaken in order to ensure that the aims and objectives of the curriculum are translated into pupil learning' (Alexander, Rose and Wood-head, 1992). Developing the vision, particularly in the present climate of uncertainty and pressure, may well mean changing attitudes and raising awareness over a long period.

- Senior managers can help by leading the way in developing an explicit whole-curriculum design for the school, to be implemented by stages, in accordance with a formal (but flexible) development plan.
- Developing awareness of the demands of unfamiliar curriculum areas is hard, and requires conscious effort by managers to provide appropriate opportunities for staff (e.g. by rotating subject responsibilities or promoting collaborative projects).
- Whole-curriculum planning becomes a reality when a substantial proportion of the staff appreciate the demands of subjects or age-groups outside their normal experience; and when staff in 'threatened' subjects can be incorporated constructively in new or broader teams.
- Enabling governors to share and promote the whole-curriculum vision is a major challenge, which might require a strategy of its own. It could perhaps be encouraged through a variety of staff–governor links.
- Curriculum management structures that support coherent planning can enable staff to participate more effectively, within existing time constraints, both in subject and cross-curricular deliberations.
- When the criteria for resourcing decisions are made explicit and related to whole-curriculum development planning, it may at least be possible to defend hard decisions which adversely affect certain groups within the school.
- If pupils are to be the primary beneficiaries of a more coherent curriculum, they too need to be helped to share the vision. This might include a programme of guidance from entry onwards in common principles and procedures, for classroom learning skills, assessment processes, use of resources and so on, as well as more explicit help in seeing how the elements of the curriculum fit together.
- Devising a workable strategy for whole-curriculum planning and implementation takes time – possibly several years.

Between schools

There are a number of situations in which curriculum coherence has been strengthened through collaboration between schools, but the relationship needs imaginative and careful fostering.

- Small primary schools need to collaborate in order to provide full curriculum coverage and meet all the statutory demands. Such groupings probably require additional resources and support from the LEA.
- Cross-phase families, pyramids or clusters also benefit from LEA support, but it has proved possible to develop collaboration on a school-to-school basis. Governors may have a valuable role to play in promoting links.

- TVEI-based clusters (Saunders and Stradling, 1991) illustrate the opportunities for fruitful collaboration between same-phase clusters in curriculum development.

The LEA

Although the prime responsibility for whole-curriculum planning lies with each school, this study identified a number of ways in which LEAs were able to promote greater curriculum coherence.

- Many schools welcomed a lead from the LEA through a local curriculum entitlement policy or curriculum framework documents.
- Primary schools in particular appreciated centrally provided INSET and LEA curriculum guidance materials.
- It was possible to assist all schools to improve their strategic planning through carefully targetted INSET and review by LEA inspectors.
- The LEA, which holds the prime responsibility for protecting and promoting cross-phase curriculum continuity and progression, could provide support by imaginative and flexible use of INSET resources, and by involving teachers in a variety of cross-phase development groups.
- Given the appreciation by schools of LEA support for SEN, it should be possible to encourage all schools to review their approach to differentiation and progression within a common framework of curriculum entitlement for all pupils.

LOOKING TO THE FUTURE

In this study we have tried to reflect the priorities and concerns of the schools themselves. Inevitably, it is the concerns which come over most strongly. But in most of the schools, in the national survey and in the case-study LEAs, there was a continuing, if not always explicit, debate about power. Schools often felt powerless, in the face of the continuing spate of government directives. At the same time senior managers, especially in the larger schools, were ready to use new powers under LMS to deploy limited resources in accordance with their own particular school priorities. Where is power over the curriculum going to reside in the future?

This may seem an idle question, in the light of the very considerable powers to determine the curriculum which are now held by central government. Undoubtedly, as the last of the HMI annual reports for 1990 and 1991 testify (GB, DES, HMI, 1991, 1992), schools have made considerable efforts to comply with the letter and the spirit of statutory National Curriculum requirements. Nevertheless, the government is dependent on the schools to deliver the programme, and this requires a lot more than passive compliance with regulations. At the very least, schools have the capacity to drag their feet in implementing each stage of the reform programme; more constructively, they can exercise considerable initiative in translating Programmes of Study into classroom experience, whether through decisions about the form of curriculum organization, about learning and assessment styles or about the management of staff and resources.

Schools may therefore have more control than might at first appear over the form and direction of curriculum policy and practice. In particular, it may be possible for schools to forge a new type of curriculum coherence within a statutory framework which seems in danger of eroding it, as subject disciplines continue to dispute a strictly finite territory. Much depends on the ability of senior managers to harness the energies of the whole staff team to a coherent strategy for the whole curriculum. If this strategy can, over time, embrace the needs of all pupils, integrate assessment with curriculum, allocate resources clearly but flexibly to meet changing curriculum needs and still meet statutory requirements, then schools, singly and in combination, will have created a power base that will be difficult to challenge.

REFERENCES

Alexander, J., Rose, J., and Woodhead, C. (1992) *Curriculum Organisation and Classroom Practice in Primary Schools: a Discussion Paper*, DES, London.

Ball, S. and Bowe, R. (1992) 'Subject departments and the implementation of National Curriculum Policy: an overview of the issues', *Journal of Curriculum Studies*, Vol. 24, no. 2, pp. 97–117.

Caines, Sir J. (1992) 'Improving education through better management.' In Simkins, T., Ellison, L. and Garrett, V. (eds) *Implementing Educational Reform: the Early Lessons*, Longmans in association with BEMAS, Harlow.

Department of Education and Science, Her Majesty's Inspectorate (1991) *Standards in Education 1989–90. The Annual Report of HM Senior Chief Inspector of Schools*, DES, London.

Department of Education and Science, Her Majesty's Inspectorate (1992) *Education in England 1990–91. The Annual Report of HM Senior Chief Inspector of Schools*, DES, London.

National Curriculum Council (1991) *Report on Monitoring the Implementation of the National Curriculum Core Subjects 1989–1990*, NCC, York.

Saunders, L. and Stradling, R. with Morris, M. and Murray, K. (1991) *Evaluation of the Management of TVEI(E): Clusters and Consortia. Co-ordinating Educational Change in the 1990s.* (TVEI Pathways to Implementation Series.) Employment Department, Sheffield.

7

THE NATIONAL CURRICULUM AND THE MANAGEMENT OF INFANT TEACHERS' TIME

Jim Campbell, Linda Evans, Sean Neill and Angie Packwood

TEACHING AS WORK: THE STATE OF CURRENT THEORIZING

The literature on teaching as work has had a sporadic, fragmented history, which we judge to have been not entirely helpful for understanding the changing nature of teaching, as large-scale national reforms are being implemented. There have been four strands in the literature.

1. The teacher's day

The first comprises key empirical studies in this country (Hilsum and Cane, 1971; Hilsum and Strong, 1978) which mapped out baseline data on the working days of junior and secondary school teachers. The studies were influential in dispelling the myth of teaching as a 'nine-to-four' job, primarily because they showed that a substantial proportion of working time was spent out of contact with pupils. However, the data are between fifteen and twenty years old, and there has been no systematic follow-up, although recent atheoretical surveys of teacher time spent on work (e.g. NAS/UWT, 1990, 1991; Campbell and Neill, 1990; Lowe, 1991) provide a limited basis for bringing the empirical picture up to date, particularly in respect of the 'extensiveness' of work (i.e. the overall hours spent).

2. The politics of teachers' work

A second group of studies concerns the politics and sociology of teaching. Some of these (e.g. Burgess, 1983; Grace, 1978) have contributed to our understanding of the experience of teaching in the institutional context of secondary schools. There has been international interest in the politics of teachers' work (see Connell, 1985; Lawn and Grace, 1987; Reyes, 1990) and a renewed interest in teacher professionalism and teachers' organizations (Ozga and Lawn, 1981; Lawn, 1985; Lawn and Grace, 1987; Poppleton and Riseborough, 1990). A common thesis here is of the 'deprofessionalization', 'deskilling' or 'proletarianization' of teachers, as union influence has been eroded and central control increased.

A more generalized version of this thesis, traceable to Larson (1980), emerged in Apple's (1986) book, *Teachers and Texts*, and in an analysis by Hargreaves (1991). This uses the concept of 'intensification' to argue that teachers, like other 'educated labour', are experiencing increased pressure for productivity and efficiency under late capitalism, resulting in reduced collegial relations, less time for relaxation in formal breaks, and reductions in quality of the service they provide.

We would want to link this thesis with the widely quoted work of Fullan (1982, 1991) in which it is argued that under 'imposed change' teachers will feel deskilled and lose a sense of ownership and professional autonomy in curriculum matters, whilst acquiring a sense of alienation towards the change itself.

A perspective on teachers' careers (Sikes, Measor and Woods, 1985), and in particular gender-related opportunities (e.g. Purvis, 1981; De Lyon and Widdowson Migniuolo, 1989; Skelton, 1987; Evetts, 1990), has also characterized recent work.

In so far as these studies have placed teaching as work into a central frame of analysis they are useful, but they have four substantive limitations.

First, although they refer to teaching generically, their principal concern has been secondary teaching, so that they tell us little about contemporary primary teachers' work in general, and almost nothing about the work of infant teachers. Second, there has been no attempt to build upon, extend or test the empirical baseline data established by Hilsum and his colleagues in the early and mid-1970s. This concerned mundane, but for teachers highly significant, parameters of work such as the amount of time spent, the balance of time across different components, both on and off school premises, and factors in their working conditions affecting both the realization of teaching goals and teachers' personal lives. In particular, the concentration on gender-differentiated opportunities in educational careers may have helped to distract attention from factors in the workplace of *all* teachers, irrespective of status or gender. Third, the evidence is nearly all ethnographic or based on life history, which makes for lively reading sometimes, but uncertain representativeness, always. Despite this, teacher commitment has been almost entirely neglected, with the notable exceptions of Nias's work (see below), Fullan and Hargreaves' (1991) questioning of the excessive identification of Canadian teachers with their work, and the NFER study (Earley and Baker, 1989) of teacher retention. Fourth, the statutory intrusions upon teachers' work of the Teachers' Pay and Conditions Act 1987 and the Education Reform Act 1988 have been so pervasive, recent and immediate, as to reduce the relevance of most analyses that predate them.

In particular, the local management of schools (LMS) has brought into more local focus employee–employer relations, not least through the responsibility given to governing bodies for appointment and dismissal of teachers and budget management. The detailed impact of such changes on the experience of teaching as work, workplace relations of teachers and their working conditions cannot be examined by means of macro-analyses of teacher careers and teacher–state relationships focused on the extra-school context.

3.   Primary teachers' work

The third strand is a small number of studies of primary teachers' work, the most sustained of which (Nias, 1980, 1981, 1989; Nias, Southworth and Yeomans, 1989) analysed teacher perceptions within a symbolic interactionist framework, with some discussion of the implications of the findings in a post-1988 context. Teacher satisfaction derived mainly from contact with children, and there was a marked preference for positive leadership styles from heads. Other evidence (Goodacre and Donoughue, 1983; Campbell, 1985; Taylor, 1987) revealed the changing nature of work relations, and increased occupational stress where primary teachers were adding co-ordinator roles to the conventional class teaching one. One study (PSRDG, 1987) reported stress arising from the increasing demands of primary teaching generally, a view shared by Nias. Again, none of these studies claimed representativeness for their samples. Acker's (1987) review, drawing partly upon evidence from the USA following the introduction of state-wide curriculum and testing, identified low status, low autonomy and a sense of deskilling leading to 'burn out', in an occupational culture where vocational commitment and self-sacrifice characterized women teachers. These studies, with their focus on the experience of primary teaching, its satisfactions and stresses, provide a strong conceptual framework, though it is constructed on a relatively thin empirical base.

4.   Teaching under the Education Reform Act

The fourth group relates to the work of teaching under the Education Reform Act. Two studies (Busher and Saran, 1990; Maclure and Marr, 1990) of teaching as work in the post-1987 context identified a widening definition of teaching:

> Teachers are no longer seen purely in terms of the classroom, responsible for pupil performance. They now have many other specified duties . . . including essential administration to maintain the organization of the school, attendance at parents', curriculum development and in-service meetings, as well as preparation of their lessons and marking students' work. Well understood pedagogical responsibilities have been widened to include administrative, and in some cases, managerial duties.
>
> (Busher and Saran, 1990, p. 1)

They identified three problems which they traced to the post-1987 context: the use of teachers' time; alienation from, or reduced identification with, teaching as an occupation or a career; and widespread disaffection arising from the workloads created by obligations under the 1988 Act. All three, if confirmed in other work, will have significant implications for the management of schools. Studies examining the implementation of statutory orders relating to the core curriculum and its assessment have mainly been produced by government agencies (e.g. DES, 1989a, 1989b, 1990, 1991; SEAC, 1991; NCC, 1991). They have concentrated on the work of delivering the curriculum and assessment, and have not taken account of work outside school or occupational stress.

THE NATIONAL CURRICULUM AND TEACHERS' WORK AT KEY STAGE 1: SOME FINDINGS

The above review of the literature has identified some fundamental issues, but has also illustrated the tendency for theorizing in education to run ahead of empirical data. It reveals the shortage of basic information and description to help understand the work of teachers as the National Curriculum is implemented. It raises four deceptively simple questions about the contemporary work of infant teachers about which empirical evidence is needed. They are:

(1) What is the nature of infant teaching as work under the Education Reform Act?
(2) Which factors in the teachers' working conditions hinder or help them in delivering the National Curriculum and assessment?
(3) How do teachers perceive and value infant teaching as work, and as a career, in the post-1988 context?
(4) How does teachers' work impact upon their personal, social and domestic lives?

Some answers to these questions, and their implications for management, are being developed in a series of studies at Warwick University examining the use of teacher time, drawing on records kept by teachers, questionnaires and interviews. Time in these studies is seen as the basic component in the structuring of teachers' work. The two studies (Campbell and Neill, 1990; Campbell *et al.*, 1991) that provide the data for this paper generated the following findings, grouped according to the above four questions. A summary of the statistical data on how teachers' time was spent is provided in [Figure 7.1].

1.   The nature of infant teaching

Infant teaching appears to have changed, in four ways in particular, though the shortage of baseline data referred to earlier needs to be remembered. First, it has become more extensive in terms of overall time on work. The average working week in spring term 1991, in terms of overall time, was about 55

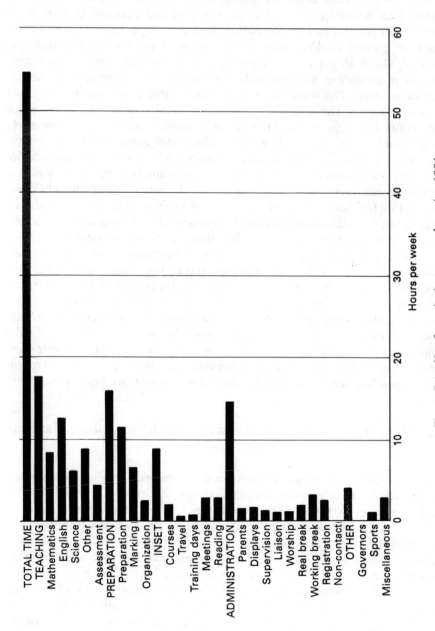

Figure 7.1   Key Stage 1: time on work, spring 1991

hours. These overall hours are similar to the NAS/UWT and Lowe studies referred to earlier (p. 77) and to the Coopers and Lybrand Deloitte study (1991), but are very high by comparison with those reported in Marsh's (1991) study of general working hours in Britain, or of women teachers within it. Second, about 58 per cent of working time was out of contact with pupils, mainly in preparing, marking and recording results, administration and in-service training. The nearest comparable figure (for junior teachers) in 1971 was 42 per cent. This suggests that a fundamental restructuring of the job is occurring. Third, the range of time spent on work was very great, between 40 hours and 76 hours per week, yet all teachers were engaged in fundamentally the same job, namely class teaching. Longer hours were not related to position-al characteristics, such as salary status or responsibility post, but were related to the personal factor of 'conscientiousness' – the hours teachers thought it was reasonable for them to be expected to work in their own time. We were not able to test the relationship between hours on work and the quality of teaching in the classroom, but the interview data show it, at best, as uncertain.

Fourth, year 2 teachers, i.e. those with at least some 7-year-olds in their class, who were involved in statutory end-of-Key-Stage assessment, were spending longer hours overall, more time on preparation and in-service, and marking and recording results, especially in their own time. The obvious dan-ger here is that the more demanding work of teachers at the end of a Key Stage will be shunned by those with choice or sought by the overconscientious; and it allows heads the power to construe it as a stick or a carrot. In either case, because of the division it may create between staff, it could corrode the fragile base in primary schools for whole-school development (see Nias *et al.*, 1989).

2. Teachers' working conditions and the delivery of the National Curriculum

The conditions under which teachers conducted their daily tasks varied consid-erably. Class size, school size and organization, the extent of collegial support, and to a lesser extent the allocation of non-contact time, showed variation without apparent logic. However, the common thread across this variation was a universal perception amongst teachers that workloads overall were un-reasonable and unmanageable even for experienced teachers; and that there was not enough time in the school day to meet all the expectations currently laid upon class teachers at Key Stage 1. This is the intensive side of teachers' work, an unwelcome complement to the extensive side outlined in the preced-ing two paragraphs. Supporting evidence appears in a range of sources (House of Commons, 1986; Whetton *et al.*, 1991; Smithers and Zientek, 1991) and is uniform. Teachers experienced the work of teaching as an enervating treadmill of hard work that rarely gave them a sense that they had achieved their goals. One of our interviewees likened it to having a running commentary at the back of her mind which was saying constantly, 'You haven't done this, you haven't done that', even though she was working flat out. To some extent infant teaching may always have been like this, as Nias (1991) argues, but the objective data from the records support the teachers' subjective sense of shortage of time. The explanation for this intensity of pressure is threefold.

First, the range of tasks now expected of primary teachers has increased, especially through the adoption of co-ordination responsibilities for all teachers. Second, the range of curriculum and assessment demands made of class teachers has increased to include science and technology, to require differentiation according to pupil capacity, and systematic assessment and recording. Third, a range of extra-classroom activities has been built into teachers' work, including meetings in and out of school for in-service training, for inter-school liaison, and for other forms of professional development. This inflation in the job specification of class teachers has not been accompanied by widespread increases in staffing to give teachers more time in the day, despite pressure for such increases from official sources such as the 1985 White Paper, *Better Schools*, and the 1986 ESAC Third Report, *Achievement in Primary Schools*. It would therefore be odd if the teachers did not feel under intense pressure. Studies of contemporary classroom organization (Bennett, 1989; Alexander, 1990) suggest there are some improvements in class management that might lead to reduced pressure. However, our early tentative evidence (Campbell *et al.*, 1991) suggests that the strategies our teachers adopted to deal with classroom pressure included making low-level demands on many children and reducing the frequency with which children were heard reading.

We would not, however, read this sense of lack of achievement, pressure and perceived inability to do the job, as supporting the theories of 'intensification', deskilling and alienation under imposed change, mentioned earlier. Our research provided us with the opportunity to test some aspects of these theories empirically, though it has to be said that the way the theories are expressed does not lend itself to the easy formulation of falsifiable propositions.

Our evidence suggests that the imposed change of the National Curriculum, far from deskilling and deprofessionalizing the teachers, was, on the contrary, seen by them as extending their skills and increasing their professionalism. In the interviews, teachers talked of the National Curriculum helping them to become better teachers, leading to improved planning of teaching and extending collaboration with their colleagues, especially in the development of whole-school approaches to the curriculum and its assessment. Moreover, the quantitative data showed the teachers implementing science for substantial amounts of time (around six hours a week on average), a dramatic increase in coverage compared to that obtaining in the pre-1988 period, and an innovation that was widely welcomed in the interviews.

3.   Teachers' perceptions of work and career

Interviews with the teachers suggested that the intrinsic satisfactions of infant teaching remain, as Nias has shown, in their interactions with pupils. However, four other aspects of work were seen as sources of dissatisfaction.

First, poor LEA in-service training and inadequate school management had led to anger amongst teachers because of the perceived waste of their time, a commodity at a premium for them.

Second, a paranoia about accountability had set in; teachers lived with a sense of fear that inspectors and parents would soon be checking up on them, and therefore had spent enormous amounts of time inventing, often at the request of headteachers, immensely detailed records and evidence of children's performance. This fear that the 'Key Stage Cops' were coming, was a figment of imagination, given the numbers of inspectors in relation to schools, but was a real influence on the way teachers saw their work.

Third, teachers saw their classrooms as less joyful places, with less attention to display, less time listening to children talk about their lives and preoccupations, on singing and painting, and following up children's spontaneous interests. This was because their work had become pressurized towards cognitive objectives, focusing on National Curriculum targets.

Finally, we found that most class teachers had lowered their career aspirations. They had been cooled out (Clark, 1961) and no longer looked for promotion to headship or deputy headship. This lowering of career ambitions may be intrinsically worrying given Maclure and Marr's (1990) identification of a growing underclass of, mainly women, teachers, but also in terms of the potential loss to the leadership of primary schools of experienced infant class teachers.

4. Impact on teachers' personal and social lives

The unmanageable workloads referred to earlier had had an impact on the personal and social lives of most teachers. We found two broad categories of teacher, which we called 'the overconscientious' and 'the sane'. The former reported that the demands of their work were causing stress personally, and putting strains on their domestic relationships. The latter, a minority, had decided that they would control the extent of interference of work in their personal lives by not taking seriously all the expectations laid upon them.

The implementation of the National Curriculum has occurred by means of a clearly defined curriculum prescription. Paradoxically the assessment arrangements were experienced by these teachers as anomic – with no clear expectations about the practical aspects of assessing and recording. The triple combination of anomie, high levels of conscientiousness, and paranoia about inspection appears to have led to teachers devoting so much time to work that they and their families were put under great stress. Part of the explanation may lie in the general occupational culture of primary teaching, but another is in the fact that the infant teaching force is almost exclusively female and therefore tends, regrettable as it may be, to carry heavy domestic responsibilities. However, the assumptions in the school workplace about work commitment are from a business model – of masculine career orientation in which work, not the family, has the prime claim on workers' time. The mismatch of this model with the reality of the women teachers' lives, where powerful claims on their time are exerted simultaneously from work (including their obligations to the needs of the children) and home, might help explain the high stress levels experienced by these teachers. It also suggests that removing the system-based obstacles to women's career advancement in primary education may be necessary but will not be sufficient, to deliver equality of career opportunity in primary teaching.

MANAGEMENT ISSUES

We have identified ten issues for the management of infant teachers' time arising from our research, and present them here in outline. We have grouped them under three headings:

(1) The use of teachers' time;
(2) The delivery of the National Curriculum;
(3) Infant teachers' work and careers.

The use of teachers' time

Pressure on teachers' time within the school day and the staffing of primary schools

The pressure the teachers were under within the school day was creating a sense of working hard but achieving little – the 'running commentary' syndrome, referred to above. Their experience was simply that they did not have time in the school day to do all the things which had to be done. We do not think that teachers can sustain this sort of pressure for very long, nor should they be expected to do so. They have a right to working conditions that enable them to do their job well. The problem is long standing and the solution has been recognized since at least 1986, when the House of Commons' Education, Science and Arts Committee's Third Report argued that primary schools could not be expected to make further improvement in standards unless they were staffed in ways that provided class teachers with some time in the school day away from their classes.

'Non-contact time', where it was available, was often snatched at the expense of other activities, such as assembly, but it was used for 'other contact', with colleagues in joint planning and review or for working more intensively with small groups of children. We think that those responsible for policy-making on staffing levels in primary schools need to give further attention, urgently, to this issue or quality and standards in learning will continue to be adversely affected. In this they would be helped by the adoption of activity-led staffing models (Simpson, 1989) rather than pupil/teacher ratios. Recent work by Kelly (1991) has shown that, using such an approach, the historic funding differentials between primary and secondary schools would almost disappear. However, if funding were to be provided, ensuring that it is used for the

Table 7.1 An example of one LEA's approach to activity-led staffing (weekly additional professional support required by each class of 27 and above 5+ pupils to meet the following needs as an absolute minimum = 3.5 hours)

1. Additional teaching in own classroom	2. Additional observation, monitoring and recording in own classroom	3. Professional support given to other colleagues in school	4. Out-of-class/school contracts
e.g.			
(i) Small-group teaching	(i) Continuous observation, assessment and recording of pupils at work according to the set criteria of the nine foundation subjects	(i) Teaching alongside a colleague to establish learning objectives and levels in cross-curricular approaches	(i) Visits to other schools: (a) to see good practice in specific curricular areas (b) to develop common criteria for moderation, especially small schools in group (c) Cross-phase observation
(ii) Meeting special needs of individual pupils with learning difficulties	(ii) Responding to parents with children having immediate problems	(ii) Working alongside a colleague to gain experience of unfamiliar areas of the curriculum, e.g. science and technology	(ii) Some INSET work
(iii) Interactive assessment and observation – listening, speaking, problem solving, etc., with individuals		(iii) Supporting a colleague as a consultant	(iii) Visiting parents
(iv) Planning the next steps in an individual pupil's programme of learning			(iv) Promoting a whole-school development plan within own school

purposes intended, and not for small reductions in class size, will raise considerable practical problems, not least in monitoring how teachers' time is used. One model of activity-led staffing used to make a bid for increased staffing is given [in Table 7.1].

Reasonable workloads

The concept of what constitutes a 'reasonable' workload for primary school class teachers is problematic. Our teachers were experiencing what they saw as unreasonable workloads. This was especially, but not exclusively, true of year 2 teachers. The objective data provide a picture of a typical working week of around 55 hours, with year 2 teachers working around 58 hours. One in five of the year 2 teachers was working an average of 68 hours a week. The time spent on work had increased since the same point in the 1990 school year, and looks set to increase further as statutory orders in new subjects are introduced.

We argued earlier that the underlying business-derived model of teachers' time in Key Stage 1 is mismatched with the empirical reality of their lives. A model of time derived from business, commerce or industry, in which the underlying assumptions are that work has a prior claim on teachers' time, both at school and at home, simply ignores the current realities. Such models also imply enthusiasm for promotion through hard work, which does not apply to the teachers mentioned above who have reduced their career aspirations. We think that the device of dividing teachers' time into directed (accounted for) and non-directed (unaccounted for and unmeasured) time has created intolerable tensions for conscientious teachers. Whilst we acknowledge the difficulties in setting ceilings for a semi-profession, the expected relationship or ratio between directed and non-directed time might be re-examined so as to indicate to teachers, and especially to heads, what could reasonably be required. Our evidence – that in the period concerned the ratio of directed to non-directed time was nearly 3:2 – might provide a starting point for discussion. We do not think that exhortation to teachers to engage in better 'time management' is anything other than a rhetoric in which the victims of unreasonable time demands are blamed for them. A particularly heavy and difficult responsibility is laid on heads in respect of year 2 teachers. Heads need to develop collegial management styles so as to share the pressures of teacher assessment through the school, rather than target them, even by default, on year 2 teachers.

Managing INSET and meetings

Our evidence shows the fundamental shift in the balance of work, with working time away from contact with pupils occupying about 60 per cent of the teachers' overall time. Much of this time is invisible to the public and needs to be brought out into the domain of public understanding, if the '9–3' image of infant teaching is to be destroyed. However, compared to time spent in contact with children, much of the other time on work was experienced as unrewarding, to put it kindly. LEAs and headteachers need urgently to develop ways of using teachers' time, in INSET and in meetings, that are efficient and product-ive (see for example, Morrison, 1990). If this does not happen, the oppor-tunities for teachers' professional development, provided by INSET and by other kinds of meetings, will not be fully realized.

Local management of schools and the use of non-teaching assistants

We found that over five hours a week of the teachers' time was spent on relatively low-level administration and welfare activities, such as registration and dinner money collection, moving children round the school, supervision at the beginning and the end of sessions, and mounting displays and assemblies. It has to be asked, and under LMS no doubt will be asked, whether this is a good use of graduate time, especially since one of the major problems for teachers is shortage of time within the school day. We acknowledge that this time is well spent in social, emotional, personal development activities but it could equally well be done by non-teaching assistants more cheaply. We do not know whether this is a practical option since many of these activities are short time spaces of three to nine minutes spread across the day, but we think it is an option that should be explored. It would shift the conception of infant teaching towards a more Euro-pean model (see Osborn, 1985), in which the focus of work is narrower but the responsibility for pupil progress is more directly accepted by teachers.

The delivery of the National Curriculum

Assessment and recording

We have shown that teachers perceived a policy vacuum or, at best, policy confusion in respect of assessment and recording. This helps explain the undu-ly complex, time-consuming and often purposeless assessment and recording activities. We think that normal expectations for recording and assessment need to be clarified. This could take the form of non-statutory guidance about what might reasonably be expected about frequency of observation of pupils, frequency of recording, numbers of pieces of pupils' work needed for a port-folio, etc., rather than DES 'guesstimates' about the hours needed for record-ing. The 1992 assessment arrangements, with extensions to both the SAT period and the TA period, appear on the surface to allow more time for the same amount of assessment and recording overall, than in 1991. However, if our analysis is correct, these proposals would lead to increased, not reduced, workloads since under them, without guidelines of the kind we suggest, teach-ers' conscientiousness would drive them to further excessive, frenetic assess-ment and recording, only over longer time-frames. If such guidance is not made available, we think headteachers and the school staff, in consultation with governing bodies, should create their own policies, bearing in mind the excessive workloads we have identified arising from practice in spring 1991.

The subversion of formative assessment

The main purpose of assessment, according to the TGAT report, was 'formative' – to help teachers identify children's achievements and to plan the next steps in their learning. Our interviews with teachers lead us to believe that they have largely excluded the formative purpose from their thinking about assessment, which was dominated by concerns to achieve a 'summative' purpose, i.e. to allocate pupils fairly to levels in ways that could provide a basis for comparison between pupils, classes and schools. This has happened partly, of course, because of the time when we were conducting the research, during spring term when teacher assessment has to serve a summative purpose, following the decision that most Attainment Targets would not be assessed by SATs. In addition, there has been a drift towards the end of the Key Stage in assessment and recording because the statutory arrangements are largely concerned with this period. There needs to be an attempt to reclaim the formative purpose of assessment and to redress the balance of assessment activities so that they are spread across the whole of the Key Stage. The advantages would be that the burdens of year 2 teachers would be lightened and that teachers would not feel that the formative approach to assessment, which they found attractive and worthwhile, had been discredited.

Class size and class management

The teachers had classes ranging from those with 20 pupils to those with 35 pupils. There may be good reasons for such variations but, nonetheless, they mean that different conditions under which the National Curriculum and assessment are being implemented do not obviously bear direct comparison. From our pilot study (Campbell and Neill, 1990) about 25 pupils was a threshold beyond which questionnaire responses showed that class size became the most serious obstacle to delivering the curriculum. This figure was confirmed to us in our interviews. The Audit Commission has arrived at a threshold of about 30 pupils. Whilst we accept that class size is a crude measure – it ignores the age range and the existence of support teachers, assistants, etc. – we think that schools should develop a policy on class size that takes account of the demands of the National Curriculum and assessment. Moreover, central and local government policy-making on teacher supply needs to take account of the large proportion (1 in 5) of primary classes over 30 pupils. To restrict the policy discussion to analysis of pupil–teacher ratios ignores the realities of large classes since the pupil–teacher ratio has only an indirect relationship to class size.

Moreover, in order to implement National Curriculum and assessment, the teachers were adopting two class management strategies in which they did not believe, and which they thought would lead to lower standards. The two strategies – increasing pupil independence in matters of classroom routines while setting 'low input' tasks, and hearing children read less frequently than they thought desirable – were designed to free-up teachers' time in classrooms to engage in detailed observation and recording of groups and individuals. We do not know whether the teachers' views that these strategies would lead to lower standards, especially in reading, will be borne out from future evidence, but the teachers' perceptions need to be taken very seriously. If the only way that very experienced infant teachers can deliver the core curriculum and assess it is by setting most pupils low-level tasks to keep them busy and by hearing them read less frequently than previously, the cost of the core curriculum and assessment might be high. The findings in the SEAC evaluation of the pilot SATs were congruent with the views of our teachers. When, over 1992–3, the other foundation subjects come in, teachers will be put under even greater pressure to adopt such strategies for class management. Changes in assessment arrangements, reducing the targets assessed by SATs, will not solve the problem since they will not remove obligations on teachers to assess the attainment targets concerned. They simply transfer it to teacher assessment.

The core and foundation: breadth and balance

We were able to show that, although the teachers were implementing the core subjects, the other foundation subjects and RE were being delivered for the equivalent, at most, of about fifteen minutes a day. Most of these subjects, e.g. art, music, PE and movement, and technology, are time consuming since they are practical activities. It is difficult to believe that reasonable time was being devoted to these subjects, given the understandable concentration upon the core. The delivery of the broad and balanced curriculum, as defined in the Act, seemed in question in 1991. As the statutory orders in the other foundation subjects come in, the pressure on time and teachers is likely to increase. The manageability of the whole curriculum is now *the* key problem. A management concern in this period should be to negotiate or provide INSET for the whole curriculum, or for integrated approaches to aspects of it, rather than, or in addition to, training focused on single subjects.

Infant teachers' work and careers

Teacher retention and promotion

We argued in 1990 (Campbell and Neill) that the fundamental shift in the structuring of teachers' work, outlined above, would lead to teachers leaving the profession. The reason we advanced was that the parts of the job that teachers found attractive and satisfying – contact with children – comprised, relative to other parts, a small proportion of time. Our argument was not directly supported, but we did find that almost all the teachers had lowered their personal ambitions. They no longer saw promotion to deputy head and head as attractive because of the legal, moral and administrative responsibilities attached to the posts. If this view is widespread in the profession as a whole, two consequences follow. First, there is a time bomb in the supply of high-quality leadership in infant schools and departments because it will become even more difficult than at present to fill headships and deputy headships. Secondly, where these are filled, it may often be by people who have relatively low commitment to children's interests and high commitment to administration and public relations. They may, more often than not, be men. We are not sure that this will be a benefit to infant schools. Ironically, if the policy of rewarding good teachers for remaining in the classroom were to be taken seriously and implemented widely, it would reinforce this possibility.

The trap of conscientiousness: implications for management

Personal commitment, 'conscientiousness', rather than salary position, was associated with long hours on work. We originally used the term 'conscientiousness' to imply the possibility of 'overconscientiousness', i.e. conscientiousness to a fault. We think that many teachers in Key Stage 1 were having to, or choosing to, spend so much time on work in the spring term 1991, that the virtue of their conscientiousness must be called into question. They saw it as damaging their personal lives, their health and, ironically, the quality of their pupils' learning and relationships with them. Conscientiousness had become counterproductive. We do not think that this state of affairs is intentional but heads and governors will need to help teachers limit the time they spend on work.

Teachers can, of course, take control themselves; they need not be so conscientious, though this will be difficult because of their training into an occupational culture in which a high value is placed on vocational commitment. But, if the demands on time are actually absurd, conscientious teachers need not simultaneously take all of them seriously. Headteachers have a role in both resisting outside pressure to do everything at once and in not making more demands upon teachers than are necessary. Records in five different formats, for example, or in daily checklists, or in Records of Achievement format, all of which we found being asked of teachers, are not statutorily required. LEAs and governing bodies should examine their staffing formulae, using activity-led models to find ways of improving staffing levels.

We acknowledge that headteachers have *de facto* responsibility for the management of the school and have to satisfy themselves and their governors that their management style is effective. Part of this is a general responsibility for the way teachers' time is used. If the position argued earlier is accepted, three general points about the relationship between teachers' time and headteacher style need to be made.

First, heads will need to 'service' class teachers in the sense that they will need to monitor and prioritize documents from outside, prevent or reduce interruptions, and unplanned changes, and generally avoid the waste of teacher time that currently is permitted.

Secondly, the vast majority of primary teachers are women with, though we run the risk of sexism by saying it, heavy domestic responsibilities. Their personal time, as opposed to their institutional time, may often be structured differently from that of male teachers. Lengthy, unpredictable after-school meetings, twilight-hour training courses and other activities that assume somebody else is carrying domestic responsibilities, are predicated on unrealistic assumptions, however regrettable the situation may seem. Formal training days and other provision, well planned in advance, perhaps at the weekends rather than in the evening, may be a more amenable use of their time for professional and career development. Models of time management, even towards the end of the twentieth century, ought to be based on accurate consideration for the personal time of the (largely) female workforce, not upon other, possibly masculine, assumptions about personal time.

Third, time management is a potentially dangerous concept in practice. Faced with absurdly demanding expectations, class teachers who do not meet them all effectively should not be made to feel that the reason for not meeting them is their failure to manage their own time properly. This would be to blame the victim. The answer, as we have argued above, is either to reduce the demands or to staff primary schools in ways that enable the teachers to gain the satisfaction of doing their work well. Heads and governors might note that the two are not mutually exclusive options.

Finally, the national political context is also influential. Central government might wish to take into account the experience of Key Stage 1 teachers so far, and consider the implications for its reforms over the next few years as further subjects come into statutory orders, and as statutory orders affect Key Stage 2. The teachers supported the reforms and had achieved much in attempting to make them work. But we do not think they will be able to sustain permanently the heavy workloads and high levels of stress that they see as necessary to make the reforms work. It is probable that *some* reduction in time will be made as teachers get used to the changes. However, it is difficult to envisage the full National Curriculum (as opposed to the core curriculum) and assessment being effectively delivered if the working conditions of primary teachers are not improved. By far the most pressing improvement in conditions is time in the school day, and the most obvious way of securing that improvement is to press for staffing levels in primary schools to be increased. The purpose would be to support class teaching, not reduce class size, and the funding would need to be earmarked. Without such improvement the reforms are unlikely to succeed.

REFERENCES

Acker, S. (1987) Primary school teaching as an occupation, in S. Delamont, *The Primary School Teacher*, Falmer Press, Lewes.

Alexander, R. (1990) *Teachers and Children in PNP Classrooms: Evaluation Report 11*, University of Leeds.

Apple, M. (1986) *Teachers and Texts*, Routledge & Kegan Paul, New York.

Bennett, N. (1989) Classroom-based assessment: the National Curriculum and beyond, *Proceedings of the Second Annual Conference of the Association for Study of Primary Education*, Bristol Polytechnic.

Burgess, R. (1983) *Experiencing Comprehensive Education*, Methuen, London.

Busher, H. and Saran, R. (1990) Teachers' morale and their conditions of service. Paper delivered at the *Annual Conference of BEMAS*, Reading University.

Campbell, R.J. (1985) *Developing the Primary School Curriculum*, Holt Rinehart & Winston, London.

Campbell, R.J. and Neill, S.R. St J. (1990) *1330 Days*, AMMA, London.

Campbell, R.J., Evans, L., Packwood, A. and Neill, S.R. St J. (1991) *Workloads, Achievement and Stress*, AMMA, London.

Clark, B.R. (1961) The cooling-out function in higher education, in A. Halsey *et al.* (eds.) *Education, Economy and Society*, Free Press, New York.

Connell, R. (1985) *Teachers' Work*, Allen & Unwin, Sidney.

Coopers and Lybrand Deloitte (1991) *Costs of the National Curriculum in Primary Schools*, NUT, London.

De Lyon, H. and Widdowson Migniuolo, F. (eds.) (1989) *Women Teachers: Issues and Experiences*, Open University Press, Milton Keynes.

DES (1989a, 1989b, 1990) Series of reports called: *The Implementation of the National Curriculum in Primary Schools*, Summer 1989, Autumn 1989, Summer 1990.

DES (1991) *Assessment, Recording and Reporting*, HMSO, London.

Earley, P. and Baker, L. (1989) *The Recruitment, Retention, Motivation and Morale of Senior Staff in Schools*, NFER, Slough.

Evetts, J. (1990) *Women Teachers in Primary Education*, Methuen, London.

Fullan, M.G. (1982) *The Meaning of Educational Change*, Teachers' College Press, New York.

Fullan, M.G. (1991) *The New Meaning of Educational Change*, Cassell, London.

Fullan, M.G. and Hargreaves, A. (1991) *What's Worth Fighting For? Working Together for Your School*, Ontario Institute for Studies in Education, Toronto, Canada.

Goodacre, E. and Donoughue, C. (1983) *LEA Support for the Language Postholder in the Primary School*, School of Education, Middlesex Polytechnic.

Grace, G. (1978) *Teachers, Ideology and Control*, Routledge & Kegan Paul, London.

Hargreaves, A. (1991) Teacher preparation time and the intensification thesis, *Annual Conference of the American Educational Research Association*, Chicago, Illinois, 3–7 April.

Hilsum, S. and Cane, B.S. (1971) *The Teacher's Day*, NFER, Windsor.

Hilsum, S. and Strong, C. (1978) *The Secondary Teacher's Day*, NFER, Windsor.

House of Commons – Education, Science and Arts Committee (1986) *Third Report: Achievement in Primary Schools: Vol. 1*, HMSO, London.

Kelly, A. (1991) Activity-led models of staffing, British Education Research Association Annual Conference, Nottingham, 1991.

Larson, S.M. (1980) Proletarianisation and educated labour, *Theory and Society*, Vol. 9, no. 1, pp. 131–75.

Lawn, M. (ed.) (1985) *The Politics of Teacher Unions*, Croom Helm, London.

Lawn, M. and Grace, G. (eds.) (1987) *Teachers: The Culture and Politics of Work*, Falmer Press, Lewes.

Lowe, B. (1991) *Activity Sampling*, Humberside County Council, Hull.

Maclure, M. and Marr, A. (1990) *Final Report: Teachers' Jobs and Lives*, ESRC Contract R. 000231257.

Marsh, C. (1991) *Hours of Work of Women and Men in Britain*, EOC, HMSO, London.

Morrison, M. (1990) Managing time for professional development, *CEDAR Report 7*, University of Warwick.

NAS/UWT (1990) *Teacher Workload Survey*, NAS/UWT, Birmingham.

NAS/UWT (1991) *Teacher Workload Survey*, NAS/UWT, Birmingham.

National Curriculum Council (1991) *Report on Monitoring the Implementation of the National Curriculum Core Subjects: 1989–90*, NCC, York.

Nias, J. (1980) Leadership styles and job satisfaction in primary schools, in T. Bush *et al.* (eds.) *Approaches to School Management*, Harper & Row, London.

Nias, J. (1981) Commitment and motivation in primary school teachers, *Educational Review*, Vol. 33, pp. 181–90.

Nias, J. (1989) *Primary Teachers Talking*, Routledge, London.

Nias, J. (1991) Principles, priorities and plans – professional tensions on a school journey, *ISATT Conference*, Amsterdam, September.

Nias, J., Southworth, G. and Yeomans, R. (1989) *Staff Relationships in the Primary School*, Cassell, London.

Osborn, M. (1985) Teachers' conceptions of their professional responsibility in England and France. Occasional paper, University of Bristol, School of Education.

Ozga, J. and Lawn, M. (1981) *Teachers' Professionalism and Class*, Falmer Press, Lewes.

Poppleton, P. and Riseborough, G. (1990) Teaching in the mid-1980s: the centrality of work in secondary teachers' lives, *British Educational Research Journal*, Vol. 16, no. 2, pp. 105–22.

Primary Schools Research and Development Group (1987) *The Primary School Teacher: A Profession in Distress*, University of Birmingham, School of Education.

Purvis, J. (1981) Women and teaching in the nineteenth century, in R. Dale *et al.*, *Education and the State*, Vol. 2, Falmer Press, Lewes.

Reyes, P. (ed.) (1990) *Teachers and their Workplace*, Sage, California, USA.

SEAC (1991) *Key Stage 1 Pilot 1990: A Report from the Evaluation and Monitoring Unit*, SEAC, London.

Sikes, P., Measor, L. and Woods, P. (1985) *Teacher Careers: Crises and Opportunities*, Falmer Press, Lewes.

Simpson, E. (1989) *Review of Curriculum-Led Staffing*, NFER, Windsor.

Skelton, C. (1987) Primary teaching: women's work, men's careers, *Annual Conference of BERA*, Manchester Polytechnic.

Smithers, A. and Zientek, P. (1991) *Gender, Primary Schools and the National Curriculum*, NAS/UWT, Birmingham.

Taylor, P. (1987) *Expertise and the Primary School Teacher*, NFER/Nelson, Windsor.

Whetton, C. *et al.* (1991) *A Report on Teacher Assessment*, SEAC, London.

White Paper (1985) *Better Schools*, HMSO, London.

PART 3:

Managing Resources

8

LOCAL MANAGEMENT OF SCHOOLS:
An Introductory Summary

Christine Gilbert

This material has been abridged

Local management of schools [LMS] must be judged on how far it enables the whole education service to respond to the needs of *all* pupils in the locality. All are entitled to attend the local school, to receive an education which responds to their needs and allows them equality of opportunity. Before they embark on LMS, it is vital for schools to clarify and articulate their educational philosophy as the basis of their School Development Plan. This shared understanding should then inform decisions about priorities, responsibilities and activities within the school. Such development planning commits the school to improvement and to constructive competition against itself rather than against the neighbouring school.

Substantial power is devolved to school level by LMS, but the issue of exactly who is to be involved in decision-making must be an area of keen debate for governors and teachers. Viewed positively, LMS offers the opportunity of running schools more democratically so that greater delegation entails greater participation in decision-making. This would lead to more explicitly shared plans for the school's development and for the local management of the school's resources. The staff of a school are its most important resource and their commitment to decisions made is likely to be of major significance in ensuring effective implementation. Pupils too might be included in discussions of where the school is going. Such 'ownership' of plans would give the school a clearer and more unified sense of purpose and direction and reduce the stress felt in such a time of educational change.

The two major components of these [. . .] managerial powers and responsibilities are *financial delegation* and *staffing delegation*. Based on a formula devised by each LEA, LMS delegates the school's financial budget to governors. This is a major financial responsibility. At the same time, LMS delegates related managerial authority and responsibility for staff. Such financial and staffing delegation is intended to enable governing bodies and headteachers to deploy their resources in accordance with their own needs and priorities and to make schools more responsive to parents, pupils, the local community and employers. The rest of this chapter outlines the extent of financial and staffing delegation so that governors and teachers are aware of the main aspects of this [. . .] responsibility and power.

School's delegated budget share

[. . . The school] is free to decide exactly how the money is to be spent. Given that it will need to meet the costs of items such as:

- staffing,
- internal building repairs and maintenance,
- cleaning,
- books, stationery, equipment,
- postage and telephones,
- rates and rent,
- energy, and
- examination fees,

freedom to spend will be marginal, but [. . .] still important.

However, management of the school's budget share is about much more than managing the school's money. As indicated earlier, LMS implies a coherent approach to the whole management of the school; budgeting should therefore be an integral part of the planning and decision-making process. The budget is simply a way of costing and laying out the plans. The governing body will also be able to decide, with due regard for value for money, when and where to place contracts for goods and services. [. . .]

Budget preparation

Budget preparation leads to the presentation of a document indicating planned spending under various headings known as *budget heads*. There are several ways of tackling such preparation and although these do not always fit neatly into discrete categories, some understanding of the general approach followed is useful for governors and staff.

Approaches fall into three general classifications. These are ascribed a number of different names, but Knight (1989) offers the clearest:

- the pragmatic approach;
- the limited-plan approach; and
- the full-plan approach.

Also described as traditional (or incremental) budgeting, *the pragmatic approach* starts with the previous year's allocation of resources and updates it for any anticipated changes in, for example, planned activities, prices, or the total money available. This approach tends to preserve previous spending patterns because planned expenditure is based on historical and current practice. It is easy to operate as it fits in with existing school organization. It is likely that, while gaining experience, most schools will approach LMS in this way during their first year. The danger of this pragmatic approach is that it encourages too ready an acceptance of historical costs, and thus change becomes difficult. It does not fit easily with the notion of an integrated and coherent management strategy as reflected in the School Development Plan, where resource allocation is linked to the achievement of the school's aims and priorities.

The School Development Plan emphasizes a rational approach to decision-making by encouraging schools to focus on a limited number of priorities and devise action plans to implement and evaluate these. A *limited-plan approach* uses the historical budget as a foundation and then costs the priorities – that is, those elements of the School Development Plan which focus on desirable change. [. . .] This approach does indeed encourage more effective planning. However, as it diverts resources from historical and current expenditure items and therefore continuing provision, it is essential that it rests on the establishment of carefully planned priorities which are important to the school's development.

The practice of limited planning can be extended to include all the school's activities. Based again on the School's Development Plan, such a *full-plan approach* attempts to use a decision-making model for budget preparation which proceeds in a highly rational and ordered sequence. Zero-based budgeting is probably the best known aspect of this rationalist approach. The view of school management on which this rests was set out by Coopers and Lybrand (1988) and is advocated by the LMS Initiative (1988):

Management is a cyclic process which involves:
- identifying objectives;
- planning how to reach them;
- preparing and matching the financial plan and budget;
- controlling execution of the plan;
- monitoring and evaluating achievement and expenditure;
- varying the plan;
- reporting achievement.
The preparation and control of the financial plan or budget is an integral part of the process of management.

This approach recognizes continuing activities as part of the School Development Plan, but forces justification of them each year. The budget is therefore set up anew each year. There seems to be no experience of such an approach in the UK. Caldwell and Spinks (1988) describe an Australian school which established such a model over a number of years.

Although this approach has much to commend it in terms of logic and rationality, by requiring justification of every activity and expenditure item it places an enormous workload on schools at a time when they are already overwhelmed. Commitments do exist from year to year and constant re-evaluation is impractical and might prove more destructive than constructive. The reality of the process of change is that it is conducted in context. However, this approach would be entirely appropriate when establishing a new school for instance.

Whatever approach to budget preparation is used, it should be discussed with governors and staff. Governors have responsibility for agreeing the school's budget plans. There should be a collective understanding of the issues, so that the judgements involved in decision-making can be well informed.

Budget format

Schools can organize their budgets in any form to suit this purpose, but it is likely that each LEA has already suggested a format which follows traditional conventions. A common format enables LEA monitoring and evaluation to be carried out more easily. However, a flexible and effective information system should allow schools to organize data to suit not only their own operational needs, but also LEA needs.

Items of expenditure are likely to be classified under headings such as:

- Employee
  —teachers;
  —supply teachers;
  —welfare assistants;
  —administrative and clerical staff;
  —technicians;
  —librarians;
  —cleaners;
  —caretakers;
  —midday supervisors.
- Premises
  —building maintenance;
  —grounds maintenance;
  —gas;
  —electricity;
  —water;
  —rates;
  —cleaning supplies.
- Transport, e.g.
  —car allowances;
  —minibus costs.
- Supplies and services, e.g.
  —books;
  —stationery;
  —equipment;

—postage;
—telephones;
—examination fees;
—recruitment.

Although they are likely to be far fewer, items of income – for instance, lettings – are also likely to be identified in any budget format. When preparing budgetary estimates of income, schools should take attendant costs – for instance, caretaking, heating, lighting, wear and tear with lettings – into account.

Budgetary control

Each school's delegated budget share will be cash limited, which means there will be a specified amount to spend regardless of inflation. Schools will therefore have to plan for possible alterations in price and salary changes throughout the year. Regular budgetary control reports should be able to show for each item:

(1) The budget total for the year;
(2) Expected expenditure to date (i.e. taking account of planned increases or seasonal spending – for example, teacher salary increases, more expenditure on advertising in April and May);
(3) Committed expenditure to date (i.e. spending committed, but bills not paid);
(4) Actual expenditure to date (i.e. bills already paid);
(5) Differences, or variances, between (2) and (3).

Governors and teachers do not need to be able to work these out, but they should be able to understand how the figures were reached and what such a budgetary report means. It would not be sensible for anyone other than staff with specific responsibilities in this area to get weighed down in mechanical details such as costing the specific details of any aspect of the school's plans. However, members of the school community should have enough skill and confidence to be able to analyse and query budgetary data such as the regular statements which should be produced by the headteacher. The latter should play a leading role in ensuring these statements are understood by governors and staff.

STAFFING DELEGATION

The staffing responsibilities given to governing bodies with delegated budgets are an integral part of LMS. They apply to both county and voluntary-aided schools although the extent of change for the latter is less marked as the governing body was already the official employer of most staff at the school.

Local management of schools transfers powers over personnel and staffing matters from LEAs to the governing bodies of schools which have delegated budgets. This gives them the major role in making decisions about the most important school resources. Although the LEA remains the employer of the staff in the school, the governors take on extensive powers over staffing and responsibilities under employment law. These new powers of the governing bodies apply to teaching and non-teaching staff, to part-time and full-time staff and to temporary and permanent staff alike. They also affect those – such as special-needs teachers or welfare assistants – who hold posts at the school but are not funded through the delegated school budget. They do not, however, apply to school-meals staff (unless provision for this area has explicitly been delegated to the school), or peripatetic staff attending the school on an irregular part-time basis.

Although LMS sees LEAs transfer much of their powers, authorities still have a key role to play as the principal source of advice on the complexities of employment law and on fair procedures for appointment, discipline, grievance and dismissal. The framework of support so established might well lead to a partnership between schools and LEAs which gives more effective support to those working within the institution. Chief education officers (CEOs) retain certain rights over consultation and advice but governing bodies have a new role in relation to setting staff numbers (the school staffing establishment); appointment of staff; and dismissal and discipline of staff.

Setting staff numbers

Once a school has a delegated budget, an LEA will no longer be able to decide on just how many staff the school employs. For most schools this represents a marked change from previous practice. The governors have power to decide the school's complement – that is, how many people should work at the school and at what level. They may wish, for instance, to change the balance between teaching and non-teaching staff. Such decisions should rest on the needs of the school as outlined in the School Development Plan. These needs will have to take into account factors such as the governing body's statutory responsibility for implementing the National Curriculum and the points about employment rights made later. Given the pressures of open enrolment, governors will also want to protect the school's image and credibility by establishing a responsible complement of teachers and acceptable class sizes.

The governing body therefore, will have the responsibility for determining a staffing plan for both teaching and other staff in the school. The LEA may offer advice about essential staffing levels and a model establishment figure given curricular demands and the size of the school's budget, but the governors have the ultimate decision-making power. The DES guidelines (DES, 1988) indicate that governors should seek the advice of the headteacher on staffing issues such as this.

Pay and conditions of service

Local management of schools also entails the delegation to schools of various powers over pay and conditions. Governing bodies will still be subject to the local and national agreements enshrined in existing staff contracts. However, should these agreements conflict with governors' statutory responsibilities the latter will take precedence. So, for instance, the responsibility of governing bodies for disciplinary and grievance procedures overrides previous local and national agreements. Employment law provides employees with a range of rights including the right not to be unfairly dismissed, the right not to be subject to discrimination on the grounds of race or sex, and the right for women to receive the same pay as men if employed to do the same work or if the work is considered to be of equal value.

Teachers' pay and conditions are legally fixed by law [. . .] and set out in successive annual documents. Once a school has a delegated budget governors have discretion over the award of incentive allowances to teachers and over acceleration up the main scale. *The Chilver's Report on School Teachers' Pay and Conditions* (Chilver, 1990) pointed towards far-reaching changes which give governing bodies considerable discretionary powers to enhance the salaries of individual teachers.

Good practice in staff planning

The strength of a school rests on its staff. Good working relations are essential: the more effective the staff, the more effective the quality of teaching and learning. The headteacher has a major role to play in encouraging governors to adopt a response to the staffing responsibilities of LMS which values people and ensures the successful development of the school. Such a response involves sharing information with staff and involving them in decisions, some of which have budgetary implications. Care should be taken to develop clear and effective channels of communication and decision-making structures which involve all employees. [. . .]

It also entails the preparation of a staffing plan as an important component of the School Development Plan [. . .]. Such a plan would analyse current and future staffing needs in terms of the whole school, teams within the school, and individuals. It would then suggest ways of meeting these needs in the short and long term so that the quality of the staff could be maintained and developed. Planning would be likely to highlight the need for an effective staff development policy so that existing staff were able to contribute more actively to the implementation of the School Development Plan and thus to the changing needs of the school. Such a policy should make the school more self-aware, responsive and adaptable. It would enable staff to know what was expected of them, to have professional support and encouragement and opportunities provided for future improvement.

Governors might find it useful to receive a regular report from the headteacher outlining the current staffing situation and its match with existing needs. Such a report would also include some reference to priorities for the future including those for the staff training and recruitment necessary to realize the School Development Plan. The LEA's training programme, for both teaching and non-teaching staff, should support the school's development programme. It should be a product of dialogue and partnership with the school and should seek to develop the service as a whole.

CONCLUSION

Local management of schools was introduced to allow schools to decide for themselves how best to spend money to meet their pupils' needs. Schools are increasingly positive about the opportunity for greater self-management offered by LMS. By encouraging a shared and coherent approach to planning and decision-making, LMS could be a means of enabling schools to concentrate more collaboratively on the quality of learning. A clear and agreed School Development Plan, which has the needs and interests of children at its core, should inform all major resourcing decisions. Such a plan allows schools to manage themselves more democratically and to keep the curriculum as the major focus.

The worry is not so much the idea of self-management as the fear that the size of the budget will not allow schools to manage effectively. Critics of LMS have seen it as a way of bringing about education cuts without blame being ascribed to either local or central government. Governing bodies must develop strategies for co-operation across LEAs which enable them not only to share some resources, but also to apply greater pressure on decisions about the size of the education budget. Indeed, the many benefits of schools working together within an LEA should underpin each school's plans.

The real danger of LMS is that it will encourage schools to go down individual and isolationist paths. This will lead to the breakdown of a coherent local system of education which seeks to meet the needs of the whole learning community. Schools will be poorer if the co-operation of the past is destroyed by the competitive ethos underlying LMS. Strong and creative relationships between schools and within an LEA result in a richness of educational provision which could not be achieved by each school going its own way.

REFERENCES

Caldwell, B.J. and Spinks, J.M. (1988) *The Self-Managing School,* Falmer Press, London.

Chilver (1990) *Third Report of the Interim Advisory Committee on School Teachers' Pay and Conditions,* 30 January 1990, HMSO, London.

Coopers and Lybrand (1988) *Local Management of Schools: A Report to the DES,* HMSO, London.

DES (1988) *Education Reform Act: Local Management of Schools Circular 7/88,* DES, London.

Knight, J. (1989) *Local Financial Management in Schools: Training Materials,* Longman Group, Harlow.

LMS Initiative (1988) *Local Management of Schools: A Practical Guide,* LMS Initiative, London.

9

COUPLING FINANCIAL AND CURRICULUM DECISION-MAKING IN SCHOOLS

Rosalind Levačić

As schools have become responsible for managing the bulk of the resources which they utilize they have acquired more of the features which in general characterize productive organizations. For instance, pupil-driven formula funding and more open enrolment make schools more like the general run of organizations in their dependency on their external environment. Although state schools operate in a highly regulated market environment, in that they cannot alter the price received for educating a pupil nor amend the specifications of the National Curriculum, financial delegation gives them greater control over their resources, in particular over materials, equipment and staff.

Organization theory has focused on two essential but potentially antagonistic structural features of organizations – differentiation and integration (Pugh and Hickson, 1989, pp. 45–7). In order to operate effectively an organization needs to engage in task specialization and hence has subunits differentiated by function. In the primary school the major differentiation is by class unit, in secondary schools by subject department: both forms of differentiation are curriculum oriented. The enhanced management responsibilities brought about by recent legislative changes have reinforced a further differentiation – that between the class and subject teachers, and those in the 'senior management team', all or some of whom are primarily involved in budget management.

However, in order to operate effectively an organization also has to co-ordinate its differentiated subunits. The extent of differentiation and the consequent integration required for effective operation is contingent on the nature of the organization's external and internal environment (Lawrence and Lorsch, 1967). This chapter is concerned with developing this analysis in relation to the integration between financial and curriculum decision-making in schools with fully delegated budgets. It draws upon evidence from twelve schools whose implementation of local management of schools was studied over the period 1991 to 1992 by means of observing meetings, interviewing teachers and governors and reading documents.

THE CONCEPTS OF COUPLING AND INTEGRATION

The concept of integration between financial and curriculum decisions is akin to that of 'coupling' analysed by Weick (1989) specifically in relation to schools. According to Weick coupled events retain their separate identity but are responsive to each other. He depicts schools as organizations in which many events are not coupled. For example, specific educational aims may be publicly espoused by the headteacher but not put into practice by the school's teachers. I start with the basic premise that a school's curriculum and its finances are separate entities. Schools have a lot of experience at curriculum management but much more recent and limited experience of budget management. There are situations in which one will of necessity respond to the other – a severe budget cut must impact on the curriculum; but a budget increase need not affect it, while the curriculum can be changed without its effects on the school budget being made apparent, as when one subject teacher is replaced by another. But in ensuring that a budget cut does least damage to the curriculum, or that available funds are allocated in relation to curriculum priorities requires a deliberate coupling of financial and curriculum decision-making.

While the main thrust of this chapter is that a reasonable degree of coupling between financial and curriculum decision-making is necessary for effective resource management, it must be borne in mind, as Weick (1989) points out, that integration is not costless since it increases organizational complexity.

Coupling and rationality

The importance of coupling financial and curriculum decision-making derives directly from the general thrust of recent changes in the financing and management of schools towards greater rationality – a stronger emphasis on relating means to specific ends. The external environment of schools is being fashioned by political efforts at making public sector organizations more accountable for adding value to the resource inputs they acquire. Schools are expected to adopt a rational approach to resource management by planning the use of resources so as to achieve observable educational outcomes. For example the local management of schools circular (DES, 1988) states:

> It will be for the governing body, together with the headteacher, to develop and carry out a *management plan* for their school within the general conditions and requirements of the LEA's scheme. In developing such a plan, governing bodies will need to take account of the full range of their responsibilities for the management of schools, including those on the curriculum and admissions set out in the Act.
>
> (DES, 1988, p. 6)

In preparing and implementing schemes, LEAs, governing bodies and headteachers will need to have regard to the relationship between schemes of local management and their respective curricular duties under the Education Acts.

(DES, 1988, p. 35)

Within the education profession itself there is now a greater emphasis on rational approaches as seen in the school development planning movement (Hargreaves and Hopkins, 1991) and in the popularity of Caldwell and Spinks (1988), though the former book has little to say on the financial aspects of development planning. The key to a more rational approach to resource management must be integrating financial and curriculum decision-making since the curriculum is made up of the processes by which schools strive to achieve their intended educational outcomes. If educational priorities are to drive the budget rather than the other way round, it follows that financial and curriculum decision-making must be coupled.

ORGANIZATIONAL DEVICES FOR COUPLING

The general organization literature singles out a number of devices that are used for integrating differentiated subunits, such as paper systems, committees or teams representing different functions, managerial hierarchies and direct managerial contact by individuals who act as integrators. In the educational context, Weick cites Glassman's (1973) proposition that the degree of coupling between two areas depends on the extent to which they share variables in common. Applying these ideas to the financial and curriculum decision-making, coupling would occur to the extent that the two

- serve the same set of aims and priorities;
- utilize the same set of information;
- share the same decision-making cycle;
- are undertaken by the same set of decision-makers;
- are perceived in the same way by staff with different functions, in particular by senior managers and governors on the one hand and by the rest of the staff on the other.

The integrating devices used by schools to link financial and curriculum decision-making mirror those of organizations in general:

- Committees and working groups on finance, staffing and curriculum staffed by individuals with different functional responsibilities;
- Paper systems to communicate information between committees and individuals;
- Integrating individuals, in particular headteachers, deputies and key governors who are involved in both financial and curriculum decision-making and who are in continuous contact with a wide range of members of the school community.

As already noted, coupling financial and curriculum decision-making is an inherently rational endeavour. The key features of the rational approach to decision-making are themselves closely allied to the integrative devices listed above. These features are (Carley, 1982):

- Determining and communicating a set of collective and shared aims for the organization and securing agreement on current priorities;
- Gathering and analysing information on the alternative means by which aims can be achieved;
- Selecting the course of action which is judged to be most effective in achieving the organization's priorities.

While these three features belong to an ideal rational model of decision-making, they still serve as a guide for what is required in order to strengthen the links between curriculum and budget decision-making. These are clear aims and priorities, information gathering and analysis and the decision-making capacity to link curriculum goals and priorities to financial constraints and opportunities.

OBSTACLES TO FINANCIAL AND CURRICULUM COUPLING

Before examining in more detail how schools deploy these integrating devices and attempt to develop a rational approach to financial and curriculum linkage, I would like to consider the major obstacles to achieving such coupling.

Inflexibility is one such problem. Even if a school manages to produce a good curriculum plan, it is unlikely to be achievable with the staff expertise and accommodation currently possessed. It will take some time for staff development and new appointments and buildings alterations to be undertaken, even if these resource changes can be afforded.

Another common problem is uncertainty both about externally imposed changes in such matters as the curriculum, pupil assessment and staff management as well as about future funding. LEAs usually cannot announce school budgets till very close to the beginning of the new financial year because of uncertainty about the amount of funding they are permitted by central government. In addition, schools often do not know the precise amount carried over from the previous financial year until well into the summer term.

A third factor – and one which undermines the rational model – is that financial and curriculum issues are influenced by a wide variety of people with different interests and values. The greater the differentiation of values and interests the more likely it is that decisions are reached by negotiation and compromise in order to resolve conflict rather than by the rational selection of means which best achieve collective goals.

Fourthly there is lack of time for exchanging views, sharing experiences, developing good information and for participatory decision-making. Lack of staff commitment to these activities has essentially the same effect as lack of time but obviously requires a different solution.

The last problem in my list is inadequate information. This stems from a combination of uncertainty and lack of time, resources and commitment for producing management information.

GENERAL STRATEGIES FOR OVERCOMING OBSTACLES TO FINANCIAL AND CURRICULUM COUPLING

Before moving on to considering decision-making structures for financial and curriculum coupling, I woud like to review some general strategies for overcoming obstacles to such coupling, illustrating them with some specific examples from the schools studied.

An essential factor in ensuring that educational aims and priorities drive the budget has to be establishing and communicating a clear view of the school's broad educational philosophy and aims which is shared by most staff and informs decisions at all levels. Because educational aims are usually couched in general terms it is often easier to agree these than the more specific priorities for short- to medium-term action. However, such agreed priorities are especially needed when difficult choices have to be made because of lack of resources. Financial decisions can only be made to serve to educational aims and objectives when these underpin curricular decisions for which the financial implications have been made explicit.

A good example of a School Development Plan which unfolds from general educational aims to specific resource management objectives with clear financial implications is provided by Glory Farm, a 5–11 primary school with 450 pupils. The school developed its first plan in 1986, starting with a survey of views from a range of stakeholders – governors, staff, parents and members of the outside community with an interest in the school. A second plan was produced in 1989 by staff and governors, a shortened version of which is reproduced in Table 9.1, with my italics emphasizing the resourcing aspects of the plan.

The process of agreeing aims, objectives and priorities through meetings of staff and governors enables governors to learn about curriculum issues while staff become more aware of governors' financial concerns. It enables governors to make or approve budget decisions with a much better appreciation of the educational purposes underlying the budget plans. A clear set of aims, long-term goals and short- to medium-term priorities provide consistent criteria for responding to the uncertainty created by unexpected externally generated changes and for overcoming resource inflexibility by seizing upon opportunities for moving in the desired direction as they arise. For example, as unplanned underspending on various budget heads materializes in the course of the year these can be vired to meet previously identified priorities rather than building up a surplus to carry forward to the next year which leaves money unutilized and may convey to politicians the message that schools are generously funded.

For effective curriculum and resource management, staff need to be both motivated and co-ordinated. Standard methods of co-ordination are hierarchy

Table 9.1 Glory Farm School Development Plan

General principles underlying the objectives of our development plan

(i) The absolute need for the school community, especially the governors and staff, to have a shared vision for the school and its children.
(ii) *'Monies' will be devolved to individuals and teams for expenditure purposes, having agreed an overall budget strategy, with priorities.*

Staff and staff development objectives

(1) To *achieve, within the limitations of the school's budget, the following priorities:*
　　(i) *to improve pupil/teacher ratios, or at least maintain present average levels;*
　　(ii) *to develop and improve levels of non-contact time;*
　　(iii) *to maintain ancillary support, at least, in line with the county formula (i.e. 1 hour to 4 pupils) and to seek improvements;*
　　(iv) *to follow the DES 60 per cent upper limit for allowance posts.*
(2) To maintain and develop, in the light of the evaluation exercise, the school's staff development policy, giving special attention to area and staff review meetings and mutual support of staff through co-operative partnerships, consultancy, age-group co-ordinators and mentors for inductees.

Premises objectives

(1) To achieve best use of the remodelled building and new extension.
(2) To develop the environment adjacent to the 'temporary' classrooms.
(3) To develop closer links with the two schools sharing the site so as to secure a well-maintained and secure site.
(4) To maintain all parts of the buildings to the highest possible standards within budget constraints.

Curriculum development objectives

(1) To prepare and agree policy documents for all core and foundation subject areas which will include aims, objectives, teaching approaches, resources and schemes of work and be compatible with National Curriculum requirements.
(2) To further develop, agree and implement policy and procedures for assessment, profiling and recording.
(3) To ensure continuity and progression throughout all age-groups.
(4) To communicate the above to parents.
(5) To *resource the curriculum needs of our school to the highest level possible, giving priority to:*
　(i) *developing central resources for science, music, PE/games, library, artifacts and teacher resources;*
　(ii) *ensuring good class-based resources, especially fiction books and equipment;*
　(iii) *achieving at least one Nimbus computer per class with appropriate software, plus an extra administrative computer.*

---

or committee decision-making by majority voting, both of which can be de-motivating for those who feel disempowered by them. Establishing shared views on aims and priorities is an alternative integrating device as individual staff can then be trusted to act on their own discretion in order to further collective goals without the need to obtain prior approval from senior members of the hierarchy or from a committee of colleagues.

A second strategy is improving management information and staff motivation by generating ideas from staff and encouraging them to put these into practice. There are a number of ways in which this can be done. One is to have a key policy-making group which goes well beyond the senior management team. In primary schools it is possible to do this with whole-staff meetings but in secondary schools working parties or committees are needed. At one school studied, High Storrs, the new head had established a curriculum and staff development advisory committee comprised of heads of faculty, the senior management team, and two governors and open to all staff.

School reviews and audits are a very useful way of establishing what staff think are current priorities. At High Storrs, for example, the headteacher ascertained staff opinion about the strengths and weaknesses of the school through a GRIDS (Guidelines for the Review and Internal Development of Schools) questionnaire. GRIDS is an approach to school self-evaluation which includes a school audit of its strengths and weaknesses. For the audit a list of issues is developed and staff are asked to indicate for each whether it is a strength, a weakness or is satisfactory and whether or not it would benefit from review. The top five items which High Storrs staff picked out as benefit-ting from specific review were:

- Staff and pupil facilities, which some described as 'appalling' and 'squalid';
- Staff development and INSET procedures;
- Care and maintenance of the school premises;
- Provision for children with special needs, particularly the poorly motivated lower-ability pupils;
- Staff teaching loads.

The key issues emerging from this survey were subsequently discussed at INSET and other staff meetings. The GRIDS information was supple-mented six months later by a two-page 'Development Plan Questionnaire' sent to heads of department. This asked them to project over the next three years the major curriculum changes they envisaged being necessary in their areas, and to specify the staffing, INSET, accommodation and materials resourcing implications of these changes. The major priorities thus identi-fied were:

(1) Changes to the curriculum
    (a) in order to implement the National Curriculum, particularly with re-spect to the cross-curricular themes, IT and technology;
    (b) to develop a curriculum more suited to lower-ability pupils and to cater for a wider range of ability and interests in the growing sixth form;
(2) Staff development to support curriculum changes, particularly as they had received little INSET in the past;
(3) Improvements in the quantity and quality of books and equipment (most departments complained of a severe shortage of textbooks);
(4) Increased specialist accommodation;
(5) Improvements to the general appearance of the school by redecorating it, renewing furniture (some of which dated from prewar days) and under-taking repairs.

These priorities were then addressed by the senior management team and the governors in the budget decisions taken over the next three years as the school benefitted from a rising roll and budget delegation.

Another tactic is to create an environment which encourages individual or small-group initiatives whereby teachers use resources they are allocated according to their own priorities and develop networks to obtain further resources from outside the school. In this kind of internal environment the head and senior management team do not attempt to centralize management information but economize on information by leaving it dispersed amongst the staff. Staff are motivated to generate and utilize information rather than to just gather it and signal it up the management hierarchy for centrally co-ordinated action. Thus coupling between financial and curriculum decision-making is sought at individual staff level rather than just through central co-ordination.

An essential element of curriculum and financial coupling is adequate information about the financial implications of curriculum decisions. Particularly when the budget is tight, curriculum decisions have to be taken in the light of their resource costs, and budgets need to be planned in order to ensure that the most urgent curricular priorities are met. For example, one head of modern languages expressed considerable concern that as the decision to offer a second language to year 7 and 8 pupils and to extend language provision to all pupils in years 10 and 11 was about to come on stream, the resources needed had not been costed and allocated when planning the change. She found that in order to have an additional language teacher she had to give up foreign assistants, because the school budget could not afford both and that there was not enough departmental allowance to buy new textbooks both for the second year 7 language and for the less able year 10s who needed a different text from that currently used. However, taken to the other extreme, only implementing curriculum changes which a school had precisely costed and was certain it could afford would stifle many such developments. Once a change has begun to be implemented there is then greater pressure to find the necessary resources.

Downes (1991a, p. 20) warns that 'An accurate understanding of the costs of curriculum development should be available to all involved throughout the discussion process otherwise a great deal of time can be wasted and the frustration level increased.'

He gives a basic formula for calculating the annual cost of a teaching period per week as:

$$\frac{\text{Average annual salary cost of a teacher}}{\text{Contact ratio} \times \text{number of periods a week in the school timetable}}$$

To this should be added ancillary staff costs and materials according to curriculum area. By carrying out this kind of calculation Hinchingbrooke School estimated that given their current resourcing levels, 'simply to implement the basic requirements of the National Curriculum, we would need to see the age-weighted pupil unit increase by 3.45 per cent more than inflation' because of the switch to more science and technology which are taught in smaller classes and require more materials, equipment and ancillary staff (Downes, 1991b).

These general strategies for countering the problems of integrating financial and curriculum decision-making can inform more detailed consideration of decision-making structures for achieving such coupling.

BUDGET DECISION-MAKING: CENTRALIZED AND DECENTRALIZED PROCESSES

The case-studies and more casual observation indicate that budget decision-making in schools is divided into two main areas of concern:

(1) The whole-school budget. This is the province of the senior management team, narrowly or broadly defined, with a varying degree of input from governors. Typically governors, both on finance subcommittees and on the full governing body, approve budget decisions recommended to them by the headteacher or senior management team.

(2) Curriculum support expenditure or those items covered by the old term 'capitation' or departmental allowances in secondary schools. Here there is much greater involvement of teaching staff in determining the allocation of this sum and in recommending to governors what its amount should be.

Curriculum support expenditure

The method of allocating curriculum support expenditure can range from highly centralized to quite decentralized. I would classify a centralized system as one where decisions about how to spend money are made by the school collectively whereas under a decentralized system they are made by individual teachers, particularly curriculum co-ordinators or heads of department. A centralized system of collective control on how the money is spent is often exercised by approving bids for specific purposes made by budget holders. Those granting approval can be limited to the headteacher only, or can be broadened to include the entire senior management team, a mixed teacher–governor committee, a committee of all heads of department, an elected committee of staff or, in a small school, all staff. Bids can be invited from any interested budget holder or from all designated budget holders. While the former makes bid selection easier by reducing the number of bids, at one case-study school where this had been introduced for additional capitation, it limited the diffusion of understanding about how the bid system worked and led some heads of department to feel that 'shouting loudest' was the key to successful bidding.

In a decentralized system monies are allocated to departments or individual teachers as budget holders on the basis of a formula, relating to pupil periods taught, age of pupils and with additional weightings for practical subjects. The formula may be the product of one or many minds, but the decisions on how to spend the money once allocated by formula are left to individual budget holders to determine. A few headteachers have advocated a highly decentralized model where money for ancillary staff and even teaching staff is allocated to departments. This model is in essence LMS translated to the school level.

There are arguments for and against centralized and decentralized approaches which need to be balanced in deciding which is the best combination to adopt. Centralized approaches encourage whole-school priorities to be addressed whereas decentralization encourages the pursuit of sectional interests. The expenditure needs of different curriculum areas change year by year and this cannot be reflected in a formula but must be a matter of annually judging the relative importance of curriculum area bids. Also bidding ensures that budget holders assess their expenditure needs carefully and make a convincing case as well as promoting the exchange of information across different areas of school.

Points in favour of decentralization are that:

- The decision process for determining allocation is less time consuming once a formula is agreed.
- Class teachers or departments are better informed of their own priorities than a central group of decision-makers. This can be extended to argue that virement across staffing and non-staff budgets is therefore better done at departmental level.
- Decentralized resource allocation is better at motivating and empowering staff who control subunit budgets than a centralized system which controls what they can do more carefully.

One interesting finding among the case-study schools was that class teachers were more favourably inclined towards local management of schools in the three larger primary schools than in the small primaries or the secondary schools. Larger primary schools have a big enough budget to give some flexibility while the staff are not too many to be all involved in budget discussions. The allocation of teacher roles according to class rather than subject department and the need for most staff to have specific curriculum responsibilities means that most teachers can become budget holders, unlike secondary schools where budget holding is usually restricted to senior teachers and heads of department. This form of decentralization was observed in the three larger primary schools where all the teachers, either individually or in small teams, were allocated a budget to buy all they needed in the way of classroom materials and books. Headteachers still retained a central role. For instance at Glory Farm the headteacher, while he considered that he gave the staff greater freedom than before LMS to determine purchases, exercised considerable influence in determining the size of class and curriculum area allowances. Curriculum co-ordinators put in bids and the head's and deputy's subsequent recommendations were discussed at a staff meeting and at the governors' curriculum subcommittee where they were approved.

Whole-school budget decision-making

Evidence from the case-study schools and elsewhere indicates that class teachers and even most heads of departments do not expect or wish to participate in preparing the whole-school budget. They like to be kept informed. Headteachers and senior management teams often see their role as gatekeepers who filter out information which is liable to change or which would worry staff, a practice noted by Wallace (1992).

In contrast to their role in budget decision-making, teachers are much more likely to participate in curriculum decision-making. Since this has implications for expenditure on staff, material resources and premises, teachers thereby become involved in the processes which establish the priorities to which the school's budget planning group works. However, if curriculum issues are discussed without the financial implications being made explicit teachers are unaware of these linkages. Teachers, by virtue of past culture and practice, are not attuned to looking out for the financial aspects of the curricular decisions and activities in which they are involved and therefore need to have such information explicitly presented if they are to appreciate the cost implications of educational decisions. This lack of financial awareness is probably less marked in primary schools because they have much less differentiation of staff by subject specialism and so have readier access to a common set of information. Also the financial implications of curriculum developments are usually more limited in primary schools as they do not normally require changes in specialist staff, apart from additional incentive allowances for curriculum responsibilities and targetted INSET. Because secondary schools are larger and have greater differentiation by subject, coupling financial and curriculum decision-making is a more complex task than in primary schools.

Schools which claim to ensure that the curriculum drives the budget have at the centre of their decision-making structure a curriculum planning committee on which sit SMT and heads of faculty. Sometimes governors are included and some are committees with open membership. The link between curriculum and finance is forged by the headteacher or members of the SMT who belong to the finance committee as well. In primary schools, particularly smaller ones, such a formal structure for the teaching staff is unnecessary since curriculum development can be done in meetings of the whole staff and the links with financial planning made by the head or deputy. However, primary schools of all sizes still need a structure for enabling governors to deal with curriculum and financial issues and for bringing together staff and governors. So to get the curriculum to drive the budget a school requires:

(1) A decision-making structure which integrates (couples) the key management areas of curriculum, finance, staffing and external relations;
(2) A management information system which makes explicit the financial implications of alternative curriculum arrangements;
(3) An annual cycle of review, planning and implementation, which appropriately sequences curriculum and financial decisions.

A key aspect of the decision-making structure, particularly for larger schools, is the committee structure which is examined below. Committees need to be supplied with appropriate information and the frequency and timing of their meetings is crucial in establishing an effective annual cycle of review, planning and implementation. The disjunction of the academic and financial years has proved to have advantages for operating this cycle. The curriculum planned for the next academic year is discussed in the previous autumn term, and finalized in the spring term. Staffing and staff development requirements and the need

Table 9.2   Main functional areas and stakeholders represented on school committees

Main functional areas	Main groups with an interest
Curriculum	Senior management team
Finance	Governors
Staff	Heads of faculty/department, curriculum co-ordinators
Premises	
External relations	Heads of year/house
Pupil welfare	Class teachers
	Ancillary staff
	Pupils
	Parents

for materials, equipment and buildings work are then established in time to determine budget setting in March and April. Because of the lag in budget information it is just as well that the summer term's resource needs are already set by the current academic year's requirements and that adjustments in budget plans and curriculum changes due to unexpected variations in pupil numbers can then be made in time for September.

CRITERIA FOR DESIGNING COMMITTEE STRUCTURES FOR FINANCIAL AND CURRICULUM COUPLING

In creating their committee structures schools reflect their solution to balancing the advantages of specialization by function with the concomitant loss of integration caused by functional differentiation of the committees. The main functional areas covered by committees are shown in Table 9.2. The other key consideration is the balance of representation on committees of the different stakeholders, listed in the second column of Table 9.2. I have listed them in declining order of importance (in terms of frequency of representation and influence on decision-making) which I have impressionistically observed from the sample of committees studied.

The committee structure in terms of specialization of committee by function and the representation of stakeholder interests in its membership reflects the balance struck between differentiation and integration. As well as function and membership other key aspects of the committee structure are the decision-making powers of the committees *vis-à-vis* each other, the reporting linkages between them, and the frequency, timing and sequencing of their meetings. In judging how to select and combine the various elements of the decision-making structure for curriculum and financial linkage a number of criteria need to be considered.

(1) The functional areas should be integrated so that the repercussions of each on the others is taken account of in making decisions.
(2) There should be a broad representation of different interests to ensure potential conflicts are resolved, adequate information is obtained and final decisions are widely supported.

Table 9.3 Criteria for judging the effectiveness of a decision-making structure: mutual consistency and inconsistency

	Integration of functions	Broad participation	Economize on time	Decisiveness	Good information	Accountability
Integration of functions		consistent	inconsistent		consistent	consistent
Broad participation			inconsistent	potentially inconsistent	consistent	
Economize on time					inconsistent	
Decisiveness						consistent
Good information						

(3) Decision-making should not be too time consuming. It should not demand too much of governors' and staff time and should be expeditious.

(4) Decision-making should be decisive; i.e. the outcome of the process should be clear decisions which are widely understood.

(5) Decisions should be based on good information. This depends on the expertise committees can draw upon and the time available to gather and analyse data.

(6) Accountability for decisions should be clear so that those making them are aware that they are responsible for the resulting outcomes.

Inevitably some of the criteria are mutually inconsistent so that the appropriate balance must be a matter of judgement. Table 9.3 indicates which criteria are likely to be mutually consistent and so reinforce each other or mutually inconsistent and therefore require trading off against each other. Blank cells indicate no clear relationship either way. For instance one could argue that accountability is improved by breadth of participation because a wider range of people become responsible for the decisions made. On the other hand when large groups take decisions it is easy for individuals to feel that responsibility cannot be pinned on them personally.

A major tension in designing a decision-making structure is that the integration of functions and the breadth of participation and quality of analysis which successful coupling requires, are time consuming and organizationally complex, in contrast to decision-making by a few, small specialist groups.

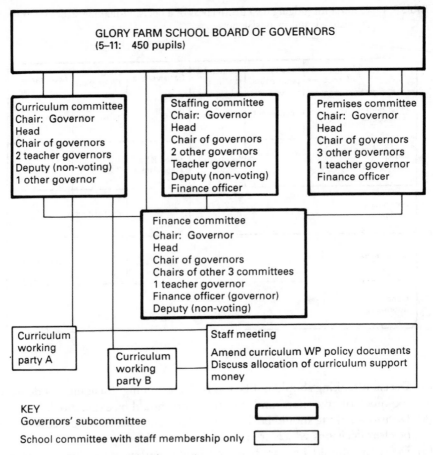

Figure 9.1 Glory Farm School committee structure

EXAMPLES OF COMMITTEE STRUCTURES

Schools resolve the issues of committee structure design in different ways, depending on the weight they give to the different criteria listed above. The committee structures of Glory Farm and High Storrs Schools shown in Figures 9.1 and 9.2 illustrate two approaches to this.

Glory Farm School, in Figure 9.1, has four governor subcommittees. The curriculum, staffing and premises committees are each allocated a part of the development plan (shown in Table 9.1) to execute and monitor together with the associated budget heads. The finance committee plans the school budget, receiving bids from the other three committees and puts the plans to the governing body for discussion and final approval. Thus accountability for the different aspects of the School Development Plan is allocated to specific committees while integration between school objectives and the budget is addressed by giving each committee part of the budget to oversee. Integration is

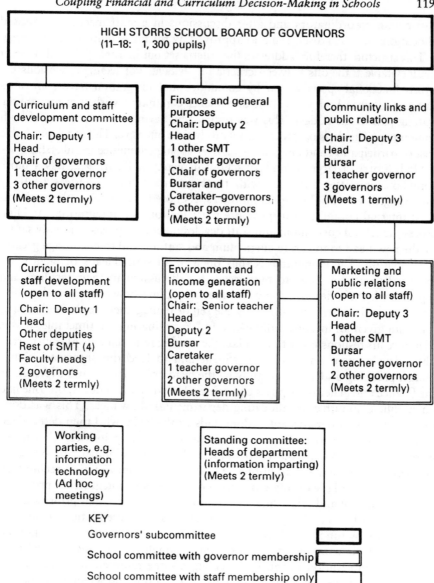

Figure 9.2   High Storrs School committee structure

also achieved through the pivotal roles of the headteacher, who is a member of all the committees, and the chair of governors who sits on most of them. Involvement of staff is achieved in various ways. Working parties on specific curriculum areas are set up to develop curriculum policies. Their initial policy papers are amended after thorough discussion in staff meetings and then go to the curriculum committee for further discussion and approval. Care is taken to allocate curriculum support funds in line with current curriculum priorities. This is done mainly by the head and deputy in response to bids for money from curriculum co-ordinators and after discussions in a staff meeting. Proposed allocations are then discussed and approved by the curriculum subcommittee.

This structure therefore addresses the criteria set out in Table 9.3, and some of the inevitable trade-offs between criteria are evident. For example, tensions between functional specialization by committee and integration have sometimes surfaced as when both the staffing and finance committees wished to prepare the staffing part of the budget. This was resolved by having a joint meeting of both committees. The decision process is relatively time intensive. This is the inevitable cost of participation and integration via overlapping committee membership.

High Storrs, a large secondary school depicted in Figure 9.2, has a more complex committee structure with three governor subcommittees partially mirroring three school-based committees. As noted earlier, secondary schools need internal committees to promote participation and integration. At High Storrs the school curriculum and staff development group was expressly set up by the new head to integrate curriculum and staffing and to encourage greater participation. The committee is thus open to all staff. Heads of faculty are expected to attend so as to take issues for discussion to their faculties and report back staff views to the committee. Coupling between curriculum and finance was done almost entirely by the senior management team, with one of the team given an incentive allowance for co-ordinating the timetable. It was therefore his responsibility to calculate the staffing requirements of each curriculum development and each department and to feed this information into budget planning undertaken mainly by the head and a deputy and overseen by the finance and general purposes committee. Unlike many schools, this one had no specific committee for allocating departmental allowances. This was done through heads of department making bids to the SMT who then determined allocations using a formula plus judgements on current priorities. Allocations were then discussed at the curriculum and staff development or heads of department meeting. An additional *ad hoc* fund for information technology was given to the IT working party to allocate so as to integrate IT provision across the school and relate financial allocations to educational priorities.

Both Glory Farm and High Storrs are examples of differentiation of committee structure by function which presents the associated problem of integrating the work of the committees. A contrasting, though less common model is to resolve the integration problem by having a large representative policy and planning committee which deals with all the functions and which is supported by functionally specialized working parties. (Churchfields School, featured in OU (1993) Module 1, unit 2 and TV1, is one such example.) The proponents of this model believe that the relative unwieldiness of such a large and wide-ranging committee is more than made up for by the advantages of integration and breadth of participation.

CONCLUSION

Coupling financial and curriculum decision-making is not an easy undertaking but it is quite feasible with careful reflection and time to develop the processes and structures required. One of the most common problems in achieving coupling is lack of experience and awareness in tracing out the resource implications of curriculum developments – the different kinds of resources needed, their cost and the required sequencing over time. The analytical capacity to do this needs to be developed, as noted by Downes (1991a, 1991b).

Not surprisingly, the chief integrators are the members of the senior management team who undertake curriculum and financial coupling largely informally. This means that the appreciation of how coupling occurs is restricted to the SMT or even to one or two of its key members. Governors in the schools observed have on the whole not demonstrated much understanding of the curriculum decisions underlying the budget plans proposed by the SMT which they discuss and usually approve with little modification. For example, governors are presented with a budget plan giving the totality of spending on teachers' salaries rather than being shown what parts represent changes in staffing due to specific curricular and organizational changes. Governors are usually unfamiliar with curriculum issues and so lack confidence in this area, in contrast to their frequent expertise on premises costs and purely financial matters on which they therefore concentrate. Because governors are most at home with financial issues and teachers with curriculum matters, coupling where it does occur, is largely restricted to members of the senior management team. While this may be perfectly adequate for effective resource management, especially when time is in short supply, the quality of governor involvement and teacher participation in policy decisions can only be enhanced by developing their appreciation of financial and curriculum coupling.

ACKNOWLEDGEMENTS

ESRC grant R000 232234 funded most of this work. I would also like to thank all the case-study school staff and governors participating in the research for their co-operation and Ron Glatter for comments on an earlier draft. Any factual or interpretive errors are my responsibility.

REFERENCES

Caldwell, B. and Spinks, J. (1988) *The Self-Managing School*, Falmer Press, Basingstoke.

Carley, M. (1982) Analytic rationality, in A.G. McGrew and M. Wilson (eds.) *Decision Making: Approaches and Analysis*, Manchester University Press, pp. 60–6.

DES (1988) *Education Reform Act: Local Management of Schools*, Circular 7/88, DES, London.

Downes, P. (1991a) Costing the curriculum, *Managing Schools Today*, Vol. 1 no. 3, pp. 20–21.

Downes, P. (1991b) The big sting, *Managing Schools Today*, Vol. 1 no. 4, pp. 30–1.

Glassman, R.B. (1973) Persistence and loose coupling in living systems, *Behavioural Sciences*, Vol. 18, pp. 83–98.

Hargreaves, D.H. and Hopkins, D. (1991) *The Empowered School*, Cassell, London.

Lawrence, P.R. and Lorsch, J.W. (1967) *Organizations and their Environment*, Harvard University Press, Cambridge, Mass.

Open University (1993) *Managing Schools: Challenge and Response* (Course E326), The Open University, Milton Keynes.

Pugh, D.S. and Hickson, D. (1989) *Writers on Organizations* (4th edn), Penguin Books, London.

Wallace, M. (1992) Flexible planning: a key to the management of multiple innovation, in N. Bennett, M. Crawford and C. Riches (eds.) *Managing Educational Change*, Paul Chapman, London.

Weick, K.E. (1989) Educational organizations as loosely coupled systems, in T. Bush (ed.) *Managing Education: Theory and Practice*, Open University Press, Milton Keynes, pp. 118–30.

10

COSTING THE CURRICULUM

Peter Downes

One of the most exciting aspects of the development planning process is the implementation of a curriculum improvement. It might be the creation of smaller classes, the introduction of new options or a new grouping policy. It represents a challenge for heads, deputies and governors on curriculum and finance committees because of the difficulty of costing the effect of the changes, both in the short and long term.

The conventional advice on school development planning is that we should decide on our curricular priorities (involving discussion with academic planning committees, heads of faculty/department) and then seek the financial resources to carry them out. My message in this chapter is that an accurate understanding of the costs of curriculum development should be available to all involved throughout the discussion process, otherwise a great deal of time can be wasted and the frustration level increased.

The three main areas to be considered are teaching staff, non-teaching staff and books/equipment/materials costs. As the staffing costs are proportionately

[Table 10.1   Example profile of teaching staff costs at a large comprehensive school]

SNS scale point	No. of teachers	Salary level	Full year cost
10	57	£17,523	£ 998,811
9	10	£16,431	£ 164,310
8	7	£15,339	£ 107,373
7	1	£14,517	£ 14,517
6	8	£13,695	£ 109,560
5	6	£12,873	£ 77,238
4	5	£12,051	£ 60,255
3	3	£11,502	£ 34,506
2 & 1	0		
TOTAL	97		£1,566,570

the greatest, it is essential to get these as accurate as possible. I suggest the following steps.

Work out the average cost of a teaching period. This can be done by ignoring the salaries of heads and deputies, and the cost of incentive allowances, and by concentrating on the profile of teaching staff on the Standard National Scale. An example from a large comprehensive school (head, 3 deputies and 97 teaching staff) might look like Table 10.1.

To this total must be added the on-costs (national insurance and superannuation) – the LEA finance team should be able to provide the correct figure. Alternatively you will be able to work it out from the most recent print-out. The exact percentage will depend on the distribution of staff across the age range; for the school in this example the relevant figure was 15.3 per cent, giving a total of £1,806,255.

This school has a 20-period week and operates on a 0.8 contact ratio (including head and deputies) so the number of taught curriculum periods is 101 × 20 × 0.8 = 1,616. The total shown above is divided by 1,616 to give the cost of a teaching period in the academic year 1991–2, i.e. £1,118 (December 1991 price base).

The next step is the difficult one because you have to estimate what the staff profile will be in September 1992 where you are proposing to introduce curriculum changes. You can take one of two approaches.

(1) you can assume that no teacher will leave and therefore everyone will 'drift' up the incremental scale. You simply repeat the exercise described above, moving everybody up by one point. This will give you the maximum cost for each teaching period, in the above example £1,143.

(2) you can estimate the likely 'turnover', i.e. the amount by which the unit cost will go down by the departure of older members of staff to be replaced by those younger and therefore lower down the incremental scale.

It is possible that the LEA will give you a guideline figure based on trends over the recent past; indeed, some LEAs deduct a small figure from their base budget every year in the expectation that 'turnover' will take place. My cautious advice would be to take a figure just slightly lower than the 'worst-case scenario', i.e. hardly anyone leaving, perhaps something like £1,140 in the example given.

You can now begin to do some costing of the curriculum changes you are proposing but remember that, in the financial year 1992–3, the increased (or decreased) curriculum will only have a financial effect for 7/12ths of the financial year (September to March). The real cost of curriculum changes in the 1992–3 financial year will therefore be £665 per taught period.

The teaching staff costs are the major factor in deciding on a change but the ancillary non-teaching staff costs should also be borne in mind. If the growth area is science, for example, you will already know how much you spend on technical assistance relative to the number of taught pupil periods in the science faculty. A simplified example might look like Table 10.2.

Table 10.2 gives a total of 4,756 taught units of science in a week. If the technical support runs currently at, say, 80 hours, every unit gets notionally

[**Table 10.2**   An example of a breakdown of taught pupil periods in the science faculty]

Year 7:	300 pupils take science for 2 periods per week =	600 units
Year 8:	280 pupils take science for 2 periods per week =	560 units
Year 9:	260 pupils take science for 3 periods per week =	780 units
Year 10:	290 pupils take science for 4 periods per week =	1,160 units
Year 11:	256 pupils take science for 4 periods per week =	1,024 units
Year 12:	86 students take science for 4 periods per week =	344 units
Year 13:	72 students take science for 4 periods per week =	288 units

one minute of support. If the average cost of the ancillary staff (with on-cost) is £5 per hour, every unit costs 8p.

You can quickly work out the cost implications of a curriculum change involving more or less ancillary support; you may well decide that they are so small relative to the teaching staff costs that they can be ignored but I would argue that it is unreasonable to make major curriculum changes without considering the knock-on effect on all aspects of the school.

A similar process of unit cost analysis can be applied to the money allocated for books, equipment and materials. Divide the amount allocated to a department by the number of pupil periods taught to obtain a unit cost (you may have already devised a weighting system to take account of the different costs of pupils of different ages). Depending on the subject, the figure may typically be between £2 and £5 per pupil/taught period.

With these figures in mind, the financial impact of curriculum change can be considered during the planning period, usually September to December, for the following September implementation. When you receive the provisional budget from the LEA in January/February, you will then be well placed to know to what extent you can fund the changes you want to make.

The process has, of course, assumed level funding from year to year, i.e. a stable age-weighted pupil unit value. It serves to highlight how important it is for LEAs to allow for the full effect of inflation. It is crucial that, at the same time as we beaver away at the detailed scrutiny of our in-school costs, we do not lose sight of the need for continued pressure at national level to ensure proper funding for education. In the excitement of picking our way through the undergrowth of LMS and planning, we must retain a vision of the overall shape of the wood!

11

INTERFACING FINANCE

James Kennedy

Many people still view [local management of schools] LMS as a chore, if not worse. They see financial management as distracting attention from the quite separate concern of schools with curricular and pastoral matters.

LMS does involve some drudgery, but financial management comes into its own when it is made to serve curricular and pastoral planning instead of distracting from it. The key is to mesh together financial and educational decisions, rather than seeing them as belonging to separate compartments.

The process can be illustrated by a simple example, taken from a recent Audit Commission report (HMSO, 1991) (the situation described does not relate to any particular real school but we are confident from our work in schools that it is realistic). After discovering that there are deficiencies in pupils' learning in science, a school notes:

- its teachers lack confidence in teaching science;
- pupils show less motivation in science work than in other areas;
- science equipment is deficient;
- some classrooms have no water supply.

The school identifies a series of actions to respond to the deficiencies. For each action, it identifies the associated resource requirements and attaches a priority rating. The result is a table such as Table 11.1. Starting from concerns in the area of teaching and learning, the school has arrived at statements about resources in a form which can feed in usefully to financial decision-taking.

The statements in Table 11.1 are demands for resources. The other key financial question is the availability of funds. At one level the answer to this question is easy. The funds available to a school are its revenue allocation (together with any capital allocation, but schools have little discretion over the use of their capital allocations).

Table 11.1 Every possible action is developed into resource and budget implications

Action required	Resource requirements	Budget implications	Priority
1. All teachers to make written plans for their science teaching	Variable – depending on the amount of time teachers currently devote to planning	Possible loss of time for other preparation	1
2. Release science co-ordinator to support colleagues	Three hours per week of teacher time for one term	£530	2
3. Science specialist to come into school to work with staff for one day	One of the school's closure days and the specialist's fee	£150 for the fee	2
4. New science equipment	Purchase of suitable equipment and storage	£200	3
5. New reference books	Purchase of 200 books	£180	3
6. Review science teaching guidelines	*n* hours of science co-ordinator's time	Possible loss of time for other preparation	1
7. To secure a water supply for classrooms which currently lack one	Plumbing work and materials	LEA capital or substantial funds from LMS budget	2
8. Bristol exploratory excursion	Intensive supervision	Parents to come too	3

ALLOCATING REVENUE

In practice, the revenue allocation is not a very helpful estimate of the funds available to a school because there is a substantial chunk of expenditure which schools have no options about. There have to be teachers for the classes; the rates have to be paid; the school has to be cleaned. [. . .] Many schools therefore start their financial planning from what remains of the funding allocation after the deduction of the expenditure necessary to maintain current commitments. To this is often added an estimated sum corresponding to any funds realizable through efficiency saving such as improved energy management. The trouble with this second estimate is that it goes too far the other way. It underestimates the scope for a school to exercise choice. While it is generally accepted that pupils need to be assigned to teaching groups and that teaching groups need teachers, there is considerable choice in the organization of teaching groups and of teachers.

To get at a realistic estimate of the funds over which a school can take decisions, we developed for primary schools the concept of a school's base budget. This concept is based on the guiding principle that the base budget should prejudge as few ways of meeting the needs of pupils as possible. We described the concept in detail by reference to a hypothetical school called Vincent Square School.

For 1990–1, Vincent Square School had an allocation of £232,300 for the 220 pupils on its roll. Certain elements of expenditure clearly form part of the base budget: items such as the unavoidable running costs of the premises, midday supervision, support for the governing body and administrative supplies. We postulated that for Vincent Square School these would pre-empt about £39,000. That is the easy bit; what about teaching staff? We plumped for the funds necessary to employ sufficient teachers to ensure that no class has more than 30 pupils, plus 0.3 full-time equivalent (fte) of a teacher to release the headteacher for 1.5 days a week. For Vincent Square School this means 8.3 fte teachers.

This baseline inevitably incorporates some arbitrariness but it is not as arbitrary as may at first appear. The figure of 30 for the maximum class size is widely regarded as the threshold of acceptability in primary schools. And there are many primary classes with more than 30 pupils, including some mixed-age classes. There are also primary headteachers with as little as 1.5 days of non-contact time per week.

Taking teacher staffing and other unavoidable costs together led to a base budget for Vincent Square School of £190,000, leaving over £42,000 for the exercise of discretion (which does not imply that the £42,000 is available to buy frills – this point cannot be emphasized too strongly). The school may decide that it wishes to use its discretion to meet needs such as those identified and costed in Table 11.1. It can also contemplate:

- teaching groups smaller than 30 throughout the school;
- splitting of classes to narrow the age and ability ranges within classes;
- provision of withdrawal teaching for pupils who need it;
- team teaching;
- staffing to fulfil administrative functions, probably including appointment of clerical staff and of teachers to free the headteacher from teaching.

For example, the school could decide that curriculum development called for three teaching posts to have incentive allowances assigned to them and for there to be two days a week of extra teaching time to make possible such practices as team teaching and the observation of one teacher by another. This might lead to an addition to the base budget of:

- 0.4 fte of a teacher;
- 1 × B incentive allowance;
- 2 × A incentive allowances.

If the school has started by calculating its base budget, it can consider all claims on the discretionary funds together and decide priorities by reference to pupils' needs, without taking for granted any current practices which commit expenditure. It can then go on to map out a spending plan which fully integrates curricular and pastoral aims with actual funding.

Implementation of the spending plan raises one serious snag, a snag which can face any organization reviewing its activities systematically. The chosen expenditure pattern is likely to be rather different from the current one. In particular, the implied staffing establishment, both teaching and non-teaching, may be rather different from current staffing. The school is then faced with the

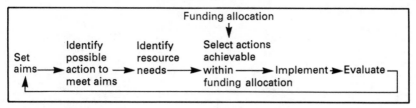

Figure 11.1 Spending plan

issue of how and how much to change its staffing. This is not straightforward because reductions in any category of staff can be painful. So a compromise may be arrived at between the sought-after staffing and current staffing. In that case the value of identifying a planned expenditure pattern starting from the base budget is that the school knows the starting point of its compromise as well as the current situation which it is compromising with. And there are cases where a combination of good fortune and management decisions can match the actual expenditure closely to the expenditure pattern the school is after.

I have by now referred to most of the steps shown in Figure 11.1. The importance of evaluation is becoming well acknowledged in the education service but it is worth stressing in this context the importance of evaluation against success criteria determined in advance of a management decision. [The term 'success criterion' is taken from Hargreaves *et al.* (1989).] By the time a management action has had time to take effect, the purposes which lay behind the action may have been modified or even superseded. But it is still worth evaluating the effects of the action against the original success criteria, to assess the effectiveness of the decision process.

Figure 11.1 looks as if it could have come out of a management textbook intended for general use in industry or elsewhere in the public service. This is no accident. A systematic management process has a lot to offer a school – so long as it is rooted firmly in the realities and concerns of school life.

REFERENCES

Hargreaves D.H., Hopkins, D., Leask, M., Connolly, J. and Robinson, P. (1989) *Planning for School Development. Advice to Governors, Headteachers and Teachers*, December, DES, London.
Audit Commission (1991) *Management Within Primary Schools*, February, HMSO, London.

12

ASPECTS OF MANAGEMENT INFORMATION SYSTEMS

David Lancaster

This material has been abridged

INTRODUCTION

Local management of schools is developing with a recognition of assumptions that:

- schools should plan;
- resources should be allocated to support plans;
- managers should be accountable for the achievement of plans.

Each of those assumptions has implications for the information which is available to support planning, resource allocation and the monitoring and controlling of the implementation of plans.

It has rapidly been recognized that the information base which is needed in schools is not narrow but broad, and does not relate solely to financial information but is more wide ranging. The Coopers and Lybrand report (1988) referred to the need for schools to have 'financial and administrative accounting systems'. Only a short time later, in Circular 7/88 [DES, 1988] that phrase had been superseded by the term 'information systems'. That difference of emphasis is important. It reflects the recognition of the increasing importance of information as a resource to be managed in a school. That recognition is consistent with developments in organizations outside the education sector. Indeed, it has been claimed (Stonier, 1983) that information is the major resource in post-industrial economies.

That implies that organizations need to develop strategies for managing information as a strategic resource consistent with strategies which are developed for managing the other major resources such as people, premises and finance.

In attempting to manage information as a resource many organizations are turning to formal management information systems. A management information system (MIS) has been defined as 'a network designed to provide the right information to the right person at the right time at minimum cost' (Schoderbek, Kefalis and Schoderbek, 1985).

The concept of an information system hinges on the distinction between data and information. Data can be regarded simply as isolated facts, whereas information is the meaning derived for the user from data. So, information is data with value in a particular situation. But what is data to one teacher in the school may be information to another, what is data for the headteacher today in relation to one problem may be information tomorrow in relation to a different problem.

In schools there are three main purposes of using information which have become more prominent in the context of local management of schools:

- for planning purposes;
- for monitoring and control purposes;
- for communication purposes.

Each of those uses raises managerial issues which need to be addressed in schools, and each will be discussed here in turn.

HOW INFORMATION SYSTEMS CAN HELP SCHOOLS PLAN

Planning is one of the management functions which currently has a higher profile in schools than has been the case in the past. The planning function rests upon the systematic use of information.

A significant way in which information systems and information technology are influencing planning in a number of schools is by the use of spreadsheets. A spreadsheet can be thought of as a large sheet of paper on which are ruled many columns and rows dividing the sheet into a number of rectangular cells. Each of the cells can be used to store a figure, a label or heading, or a formula. A spreadsheet is used in some schools as an aid in curriculum planning. So, in the various columns we could store information about each of the year groups in the school, and in the rows information about each of the areas of the curriculum. The cells in the spreadsheet matrix could then be used to represent the number of timetable periods per week allocated to each of the curriculum areas for each of the year groups, the row totals would represent the number of teaching periods per week in each of the subjects and the column totals the number of teaching periods per week required from each of the subject teams. Another part of the same spreadsheet could be used to derive teacher contact ratios, average class sizes, etc.

The spreadsheet could then be used in a curriculum feasibility study to address questions of the 'what would happen if . . .?' type. For example, what would happen to the teacher contact ratio or the pupil/teacher ratio if the number of groups in year eleven French was decreased, or if the number of teaching periods allocated to science in year nine was increased? Such a modelling approach can be used either for planning the curriculum on a one-year timescale, or as part of a longer-term plan for addressing the effects on the curriculum provision of, for example, likely changes in school roll.

The combination of a spreadsheet program for modelling with a computer graphics facility to produce diagrammatic output in addition to tabular results from the model can provide feedback to the planners in the school on the effects of their planning assumptions in a very powerful way. The requirements of the National Curriculum are likely to make such curriculum modelling prominent again, and to encourage planners within schools to consider curriculum changes not only incrementally but also using the same 'zero-based' approach which may be used for financial budgeting. Local management of schools may result in a curriculum model being translated in a further stage from time or teaching periods as a currency to a costing of the curriculum in financial terms.

A second example of spreadsheet use for planning is in the area of budget modelling. Different cost items of the school, for example teacher costs, clerical staff costs, heating and lighting, equipment, consumables, etc., could be scheduled on a month-by-month basis and related in total to the budget of the school, and that budget model again used in planning to answer 'what if?' questions and evaluate in cost terms the desirability of making changes in the recent proportions of funds allocated to different areas of the school's activities.

HOW INFORMATION SYSTEMS CAN HELP SCHOOLS IN MONITORING AND CONTROL

Planning and monitoring and control are closely related. There is limited use in planning if the implementation of the plans derived is not monitored. Conversely, monitoring and control systems operate in a vacuum in the absence of information from a planning process indicating the performance to be monitored. [. . .] That may demand an information system which can collect, process and report on the performance indicators used, whether those indicators have been generated within the school or from outside. Here, the distinction made above between data and information is particularly relevant. The use of performance indicators depends not on the production of large amounts of raw data but the generation from that raw data of relevant information. That implies processes of aggregation of data (for example the calculation of averages and other measures which can produce figures which are representative of the mass of data from which they were produced), filtration of data to eliminate irrelevant data, and the transformation of data, such as the calculation of ratios, for example a pupil/teacher ratio.

The introduction of LMS brings with it particular requirements for the monitoring of financial information. In many small schools, particularly primary schools and small secondary schools, the main application, at least initially, is using a microcomputer simply for processing daily transactions and monitoring receipts, payments and balances outstanding. But, particularly in larger schools, the initial aim is not restricted to bookkeeping but is to use such information technology for management accounting purposes in rather more sophisticated ways to monitor financial performance against budgets. The LMS Initiative (1988) manual recommends that financial information should be produced on a monthly cycle incorporating:

- budgets and expected expenditure to date;
- actual expenditure and commitments;
- forecasts of out-turn expenditure and variances (differences between budgets and out-turns);
- resource allocation allowances;
- transactions processed;
- balances of allocation brought and carried forward.

In developing an information system for the local management of schools, or in each school using a system which has been designed for user flexibility, it is necessary to consider which of those kinds of information are needed only on a whole-school basis and which would be beneficial additionally on a departmental basis. [. . .]

In developing information systems for monitoring and control purposes in schools it is useful to reflect on a number of principles of control systems design:

- pyramid reporting arrangements;
- management by exception;
- graphic presentation.

Pyramid reporting arrangements

Not all people who need information about a particular aspect of the school's activities need information in the same level of detail. A year leader, for example, is likely to need relatively detailed information about a specific year group, the headteacher perhaps less detailed information about each year group but information about each of the year groups, the governors less detailed information still, and the LEA summary information using a particular performance indicator. The principle of data aggregation to produce information is clearly relevant in this example.

Management by exception

Instead of reporting data in detail it is often useful to report information only on aspects of organizational performance which in some way is exceptional; that is normally interpreted to mean areas in which organizational performance differed substantially from that which was planned or budgeted. Management by exception is a particular example of the use of data filtration to produce information.

Graphic presentation

Information presented graphically (by the use of bar charts, pie diagrams, etc.) can usually be assimilated much more easily than that which is presented only in tables or figures.

HOW INFORMATION SYSTEMS CAN HELP SCHOOLS COMMUNICATE

The Education Act of 1988 has been stated to be a piece of legislation which has resulted in school decision-making being more managerial and perhaps less consultative. It nevertheless implies, and requires, a substantial commitment to the communication of information, particularly to parents and to governors. But information systems can be used to make information more readily and widely available within the organization also, and the culture of schools implies that teaching staff will expect such information systems to be used to disseminate information more widely amongst teaching staff, and to involve teachers in the decision-making process and in monitoring the outcomes of decisions.

It is widely accepted that the documents produced in both primary and secondary schools for communicating with parents, governors and other groups have in the past been of an insufficiently high quality. The facilities for word-processing, and in some cases desk-top publishing, available as standard features on the systems being introduced into schools for local management enable such documents easily to be produced to a much higher standard. Those improvements are, of course, merely cosmetic but in a climate in which schools need to be more aware of their external communications they are not insignificant.

COMPUTERS IN INFORMATION SYSTEMS

The above discussion on information systems applies equally to those which use a technology of pen and paper and those which use a technology in which computers are prominent. Even tools such as spreadsheets which have come to be associated with computers do not require such technology; indeed the term spreadsheet refers to the sheet of paper on which accountants laboriously carried out analyses before the availability of computers.

But there are a number of reasons why computer-based information systems offer particular advantages in comparison with manual systems in the local management of schools. It has long been recognized that computers can be very efficient in information-processing activities which have particular characteristics:

- when extensive searching and sorting of data is required;

- when different people need access to the same or similar data;
- when there are repetitious but well-defined tasks.

More recently, computers are increasingly being used for activities with other characteristics:

- when 'what if?' decisions are needed (modelling applications);
- when text needs to be processed (word-processing);
- when information needs to be circulated quickly to a number of people (electronic mail).

But, although the *principles* of information systems design can be implemented with a variety of technologies, the efficiency of those technologies varies enormously, and at present it is unlikely that a school management information system other than one which is computer based would be introduced. But not all aspects of information processing in schools will be computerized. Even for those which are not computerized (perhaps particularly for those which are not) information systems concepts remain relevant.

When existing information-processing systems are being evaluated, or when computer-based information systems are being introduced to replace manual systems, the opportunity should be taken to reassess information management in the school. The distinction between datalogical and infological perspectives on information systems change made by Methlie and reported by Wilson (1984) is particularly relevant:

> The datalogical perspective regards the existing data flows as satisfactory representations of the information needs in the organization. The aim of the change task is to find more efficient ways of processing the existing data. A common solution is to computerize manual procedures and data files. The benefits of this approach are primarily of the cost-savings type. This perspective is the traditional computer application view and is still common in current systems work. The infological perspective of information systems design looks at the organization as an information processing system. Thus communication and control aspects are in focus. Information is the knowledge, communicated between individuals and groups, needed to perform the tasks. The focus of this perspective is to find an effective information system for the whole or part of the organization to which the information is to give service.
>
> (Wilson, 1984, pp. 193–4)

MIS FOR LMS IN RELATION TO OTHER ASPECTS OF COMPUTERIZED SCHOOL ADMINISTRATION

The context in which computer-based information systems are being introduced into schools for local management of schools is different from that in which they entered schools during the last decade for a variety of school administration tasks. Then the context was usually one of first-time users. Now it is typically that of a system for local management of schools following one for general school administration. Local management of schools brings with it the need to handle a number of new administrative tasks relating to budgeting and other financial matters, but further needs also, deriving from pupil assessment and associated Records of Achievement, the recording of teacher participation in in-service education and training, records supporting pupil admissions and voting lists of parents, and so on. Nevertheless, new systems are not being introduced in a vacuum. There is a need, therefore, for the two systems to relate to each other and not simply be two isolated independent sets of applications. That puts an onus on the developers of systems for local management of schools to ensure an element of integration, and that management information systems meet all the administrative needs of schools, not merely those relating to school finance.

As a result of the introduction of computerized administration in schools there is now a greater appreciation of the training needed when a new computer system is brought into a school, and the need for office accommodation which is secure. Similarly, the need to address the issues of who the users of the system will be, and the allocation of use for particular applications by teachers and by office staff is recognized. [. . .]

THE EFFECTS OF USING COMPUTER-BASED INFORMATION SYSTEMS FOR THE LOCAL MANAGEMENT OF SCHOOLS

Typically, in the use of computer systems in new application areas, a number of initial effects are manifest, and further long-term effects emerge. [. . .]

It is generally accepted that computers can be used either to restrict information by removing the need for information processing and analysis to be delegated, or can be used to facilitate the dissemination and communication of information. Although the truism that 'information is power' is generally accepted, the organizational culture of schools and the ethos of professionalism is such that there is an expectation that relevant information will be shared with staff. The use of information technology in planning, and monitoring and control makes that expectation more easy to meet. Particularly in the planning area, for example in the use of models such as those discussed above, it becomes easier to enable staff to participate in the planning process by enabling assumptions to be shared and the effects of particular decisions to be addressed before those decisions are implemented.

But there is a particular feature of the development of computer-assisted systems for local management of schools which is likely to be significant in the effects of the use of those systems. Most of the systems used for local management of schools are developed not by schools themselves on a one-by-one basis, which would clearly be inefficient. They are mainly developed by local education authorities in consultation with schools. The fact that all or many schools in a local education authority are using identical systems, probably with a facility for the transmission of information between the schools and the LEA can have both detrimental and beneficial effects. It raises questions about the 'ownership' of information, and enables the comparison of performance between schools on a scale not previously possible, and may encourage the use of performance indicators on which data can readily be collected and processed rather than on areas which are more easily justifiable but for which information is not easily obtainable. Teachers have generally been wary of quantified inter-school comparisons. The extent to which such comparisons will be accepted in schools depends directly on the particular performance indicators which are utilized. But the fact that inter-school comparisons can be processed more easily than in the absence of a standardized information system brings such issues more prominently on to the educational agenda. Conversely, in addition to obvious efficiency savings, it makes communication between the LEA and schools much easier, and also facilitates communication between schools within the same LEA; indeed, a number of the schemes incorporate for that purpose electronic mail facilities which have been welcomed by the user schools.

In addition to the effects on the school as a whole and its external relationships, particularly with the LEA, the introduction of a computer system may have effects, possibly unanticipated, within the school, especially on people's jobs. Although it is unlikely that school management information systems will result directly in major changes in job numbers, there are potentially effects on the distribution of job tasks which may need to be monitored. For example, it is necessary to ensure that a manifestation in a number of schools of the introduction of computerized administration systems is not repeated. In several schools some jobs, such as the production of pupil lists, which were previously carried out by clerical staff, moved out of the school office and were processed by teaching staff who had computer expertise. That is a major waste of the schools' most valuable resource and must be avoided as information systems for the local management of schools are implemented. Similarly, headteachers and other senior staff of schools need to ensure that they use information systems and financial systems to assist them in their core activity of delivering effective learning rather than being diverted from that purpose and managing the school to too great an extent on the basis of the outputs of an information system, however sophisticated that system may be.

CONCLUSION

The management functions of planning, monitoring and control, and communications which have always been important in schools have become more prominent with local management of schools. Each of those managerial funtions rests on the use of information which is relevant, accurate and current. The provision of such information to support decision-making within the school is vital to the success of local management of schools. That implies that the provision of relevant and usable management information systems, and the addressing in each school of the issues identified above is, in turn, vital to the success of local management in both primary and secondary schools. [. . .]

REFERENCES

Coopers and Lybrand (1988) *Local Management of Schools: Report to the DES*, DES, London.

DES (1988) *Education Reform Act: Local Management of Schools* (Circular 7/88) DES, London.

Stonier, T. (1983) *The Wealth of Information*, Methuen, London.

Schoderbek, P.P., Kefalis, A.G. and Schoderbek, C.G. (1985) *Management Systems: Conceptual Considerations*, Business Publications, Plano.

LMS Initiative (1988) *Local Management in Schools: A Practical Guide*, CIPFA, London.

Wilson, B. (1984) *Systems: Concepts, Methodologies and Applications*, Wiley, Chichester.

PART 4:

Staff and Leadership

13

LEADERSHIP

Hedley Beare, Brian Caldwell and Ross Millikan

Outstanding leadership has invariably emerged as a key characteristic of outstanding schools. There can no longer be doubt that those seeking quality in education must ensure its presence and that the development of potential leaders must be given high priority.

Setting aside legend and anecdote, there was by the early 1980s a surprisingly narrow base of knowledge to guide practice. Theories of leadership, often resulting from painstaking empirical research, rarely excited the practitioner and even more rarely shaped practice. Indeed, several of those theories were difficult to explain in language which could be understood by practitioners or even agreed upon by scholars. However, there is now a far richer body of knowledge winning the confidence of scholars and practitioners alike. This has been achieved with more expansive, multidisciplinary study of organizations and leaders rather than what had become an increasingly narrow focus on a small number of measurable variables in research conducted within the framework of a single field of inquiry. Leaders, aspiring leaders and others with an interest in leadership can now proceed with much greater confidence than was the case a decade before.

The purpose of this chapter is to describe and illustrate the major features of what is now known about leadership in a way which should provide a guide to action in the school setting. Emphasis is given to the broader, emerging view although attention is given to some products of the earlier 'theory movement' which, while of limited utility, are nevertheless part of the larger picture. Prominent in this larger picture is vision in leadership: outstanding leaders have a vision for their schools – a mental picture of a preferred future – which is shared with all in the school community and which shapes the programme for learning and teaching as well as policies, priorities, plans and procedures pervading the day-to-day life of the school. The major part of the chapter is devoted to ten generalizations about leadership which have emerged from recent studies. Illustrations in the school context are offered in each instance. The final section of the chapter gives special attention to description and illustration of vision in leadership and the ways in which vision may be articulated. [. . .]

Consistent with a pattern of school governance emerging in several countries and which is the preference of the authors, most illustrations of the actions of leaders assume a high level of school autonomy or 'self-management' where, among public schools or a system of private schools, there is significant and consistent decentralization to the school level of authority to make decisions related to the allocation of resources, with resources defined broadly to include knowledge, technology, power, *materiel*, people, time and money. This decentralization tends to be administrative rather than political, with decisions at the school level being made within a framework of local, state or national policies and guidelines, while the school remains accountable, [. . .] to a central authority for the manner in which resources are allocated.

LEADER AND LEADERSHIP DEFINED

A useful starting point is to clarify the concepts of 'leadership' and 'leader'. The large number of meanings which may be discerned in print and in everyday use is often a source of concern. It seems that each scholar and practitioner has a different personal opinion. The view taken here is that there is no one 'correct' meaning and that differences in definition reflect different contexts as well as different perspectives.

Dubin (1968, p. 385) saw leadership as 'the exercise of authority and the making of decisions' while Fiedler (1967, p. 8) considered the leader to be 'the individual in the group given the task of directing and co-ordinating task-relevant group activities'. According to these definitions, principals, headteachers and other senior staff who have formal authority by virtue of their appointments are leaders and may exercise leadership. Dubin and Fiedler offer a view which is constrained by the source of power (authority), scope (task-relevant) and function (decision-making, directing, co-ordinating). Stogdill (1950, p. 4) had a broader context in mind when he defined leadership as 'the process of influencing the activities of an organized group toward goal setting and goal accomplishment'. While this view includes the contexts envisaged by Dubin and Fiedler, it acknowledges that people without formal authority may exercise leadership. The source of influence or power may be their expertise, or their capacity to bring rewards or benefits, or their capacity to apply sanctions, or their personal qualities which make them liked or respected as people. Such leadership may emerge in many contexts in a school and may involve people other than the principal and senior staff.

Stogdill's view also included the setting of the goal itself as well as the influence of activities associated with the accomplishment of the goal. This aspect of leadership is important in effecting change. Lipham (1964, p. 122) focused exclusively on change when he defined leadership as 'the initiation of a new structure or procedure for accomplishing an organization's goals and objectives'. In this view, a principal will not be a leader at all if activity is limited to the maintenance of existing means and ends. Management rather than leadership may be a more appropriate description of such an activity.

More recent attempts to explain the concept of leadership penetrate more deeply than 'the organization' and the activities associated with goal setting and goal accomplishment. Attention now is also given to meanings and values. Pondy (1978, p. 94), for example, considers that the effectiveness of a leader lies in 'ability to make activity meaningful . . . not to change behaviour but to give others a sense of understanding of what they are doing'. The exercise of leadership by the principal thus involves making clear the meaning of activity in the school by posing and securing answers to questions such as the following. What are the purposes of our school? How should we as teachers work with students to reflect our purposes? What should be the relationship between our school and its local community?

To Greenfield (1986, p. 142) 'leadership is a willful act where one person attempts to construct the social world for others'. He suggests that 'leaders will try to commit others to the values that they themselves believe are good. Organizations are built on the unification of people around values' (*ibid*, p. 166). Greenfield challenges us to think of leaders in terms very different from those in the traditional view. For example, debate on a school's discipline policy may be seen as a contest of values reflecting different beliefs about 'what ought to be'. Those representing each set of values are leaders in that debate. The outcome of the contest is reflected in the words of the policy. The principal may be a leader in debate and, once policy is determined, becomes a leader in another sense. The policy is presented to all parents and students as an expression of the values of the school and an attempt is made to build commitment to that policy: an attempt to bring about 'unification of people around values' and to 'construct the social world for others'.

An example of each definition of leader and leadership can thus be found in the school setting. Whereas earlier definitions focused on the exercise of formal authority related to the setting and accomplishment of goals, more recent perspectives invite us to consider at a deeper, more personal level what actually transpires when decisions are made and people try to make sense of their work. Concise definitions and descriptions are difficult, if not inappropriate. As Duke (1986, p. 10) observed, 'Leadership seems to be a gestalt phenomenon; greater than the sum of its parts.'

LEADERSHIP TRAITS AND THEORIES: PART OF THE PICTURE

Studies until the late 1970s and early 1980s yielded useful but limited information about leaders and leadership. Attempts to identify the traits of leaders led to a relatively small list of attributes to guide the selection process. A quarter-century of careful research focused on two dimensions of leadership behaviour, generally concerned with tasks and people, with some measure of success in determining which particular behaviours or styles are the more effective in different situations. Some findings of these earlier studies are summarized here, with brief illustrations of their utility in the school setting. Attention is then turned to the larger picture which emerged in the 1980s.

TRAITS OF LEADERS

Studies in the first half of the century compared the physical and psychological characteristics of leaders and non-leaders. An analysis of many of these studies by Stogdill (1948) found little consistency in their findings. The search for traits in leadership continued, however, with different approaches to measurement and an effort to distinguish among leaders on the basis of their effectiveness. Analyses of these later studies by Stogdill (1974) revealed a number of traits which consistently characterize more effective leaders. These include:

- sense of responsibility;
- concern for task completion;
- energy;
- persistence;
- risk-taking;
- originality;
- self-confidence;
- capacity to handle stress;
- capacity to influence;
- capacity to co-ordinate the efforts of others in the achievement of purpose.

While these characteristics may be used with a relatively high degree of confidence in the selection and development of leaders, they are but a small part of the picture and provide little to guide the day-to-day activities of leaders in the school setting. More detail was added as attempts were made in the 1950s and 1960s to develop theories of leadership.

THEORIES OF LEADERSHIP

Some major findings of the 'theory movement' in leadership are briefly summarized here. Details may be found in books which deal in comprehensive fashion with this movement as far as its contribution to knowledge in educational administration is concerned (see, for example, Hoy and Miskel, 1987).

   Research has consistently revealed the importance of two 'dimensions' in describing the behaviour of leaders. These behaviours reflect a concern for accomplishing the tasks of the organization and a concern for relationships among people in the organization. It is generally accepted that both kinds of behaviour are required for successful leadership. Attempts to develop theories have involved the careful study of situations in which leadership is exercised, acknowledging that there is no one best way to lead in all situations, but that in any particular situation one approach to leadership may be more effective than another. The challenge has been to identify particular attributes of leadership and circumstances which are important in establishing these situational contingencies. Two well-regarded contingency theories (Hersey and Blanchard, 1982; Fiedler, Chemers and Mahar, 1977) are summarized briefly, with illustrations of their utility in the school setting.

Hersey and Blanchard (1982) proposed in their situational theory that leadership behaviour should be varied according to the maturity of subordinates or followers. The situation in this theory is thus defined by maturity, with two dimensions proposed: professional maturity and psychological maturity. There are also two dimensions of leadership behaviour: task behaviour, in which the leader emphasizes or specifies the task; and relationship behaviour, in which the leader invests time in developing good interpersonal relationships with and among the group. The theory proposes four general types of leadership behaviour, each of which is appropriate to a particular level of maturity. With increasing maturity, the leader should move through styles designated 'telling' (high task, low relationship); 'selling' (high task, high relationship); 'participating' (low task, high relationship); and 'delegating' (low task, low relationship).

Application of the Hersey and Blanchard theory calls for a highly personalized approach to leadership behaviour. In the school setting, for example, there may be high variability among staff in terms of maturity so that different behaviours will be required for different people. Particular members of staff may have different levels of maturity for different tasks. Furthermore, maturity levels will change from year to year as staff acquire professional and psychological maturity.

Surprisingly, the Hersey and Blanchard theory has not been subjected to rigorous validation. However, its propositions are intuitively well received and have become the focus of widely used management training programmes. The capacity carefully to diagnose maturity levels of staff and then to select matching leadership behaviour according to these propositions would appear to be a worthwhile addition to the repertoire of the school leader.

To understand the contingency theory of leadership formulated by Fiedler (see Fiedler, Chemers and Mahar, 1977, for more detailed explanation and illustration), we need to distinguish between leadership style and leadership behaviour. To Fiedler, leadership style is an innate, relatively enduring attribute of our personality which provides our motivation and determines our general orientation when exercising leadership. Leadership behaviour, on the other hand, refers to particular acts which we can perform or not perform if we have the knowledge and skills, and if we judge them appropriate at the time (this is the sense in which leadership behaviour is used in the Hersey and Blanchard theory).

Fiedler found that task-motivated leaders (those whose primary, driving motivation is to ensure that the task at hand is addressed) tend to be best suited to situations which are either highly favourable or highly unfavourable according to the extent to which tasks are structured, where there are good leader–member relations and when the leader has position power. Relationship-motivated leaders (those whose primary, driving motivation is to ensure that there are good relations with and among members of the work group) are best suited to situations which are moderately favourable on these dimensions. The Fiedler theory has implications for matching leaders to situations and for encouraging leaders to modify their situation where possible to ensure consistency with style. These applications rest on such fine distinctions, and represent such a small aspect of all that must be considered, that the theory seems unlikely to have major impact, despite its validation through research in a variety of settings.

Hodgkinson summed up the theory movement in leadership as embodied in what he judged to be the finest of its products:

> I am prepared to acknowledge that the general productive effort of this type of research, particularly as it is embodied in Professor Fiedler's work, yields us the best theory we have to date in the domain of psychological discourse. I would suspect, however, a paradox. The closer such theory approaches the truth, the more incomprehensible it will become.
>
> (Hodgkinson, 1983, p. 200)

A DECADE OF STUDY: THE LARGER PICTURE

Retaining for a moment the metaphor of a picture, it seems that attention for some twenty-five years or so was turned to just one part of the scene (leadership behaviour, narrowly defined on two dimensions) which was then studied through a series of lenses with increasing power in terms of their capacity to discern detail, resulting in the precison of theories such as that offered by Fiedler. There seemed to be little impact on practice as the result of such efforts. Then followed a decade of study in which observers, in effect, stepped back and examined the whole picture, or at least a much broader canvas of activity, in an effort to describe and explain what makes organizations and their leaders successful. The outcomes do not yet constitute a new theory in the strictly scientific sense, but the generalizations which have emerged seem to hold much greater promise for shaping practice. They are intuitively well received by experienced practitioners, and have a richness and vibrancy which inspire action to a larger extent than the findings of earlier attempts to develop theories of leadership.

EMERGING GENERALIZATIONS

Emerging from these studies are several generalizations which can shape leadership in schools where excellence is valued. Ten are offered here, with acknowledgement of their source in the literature described above. A summary

Table 13.1 Generalizations and illustrations reflecting recent advances in knowledge about leadership

Generalization	Illustration
1. Emphasis should be given to transformational rather than transactional leadership	Principal takes action to change community attitudes towards school
2. Outstanding leaders have a vision for their organization	Principal envisages school as a learning centre for whole community
3. Vision must be communicated in a way which secures commitment among members of the organization	Principal seeks commitment of teachers in devoting time and energy to change community attitudes towards school
4. Communication of vision requires communication of meaning	'Community' is metaphor for school; principal rewards related teacher activities
5. Issues of value – 'what ought to be' – are central to leadership	Principal has strong commitment to equity in terms of access to schooling
6. The leader has an important role in developing culture of organization	Principal involves members of community in all ceremonies at the school
7. Studies of outstanding schools provide strong support for school-based management and collaborative decision-making	School policy is determined by group representing parents, teachers, students and community at large
8. There are many kinds of leadership forces – technical, human, educational, symbolic and cultural – and these should be widely dispersed throughout the school	Planning for the various programmes in school carried out by teams of teachers, each having its own leader
9. Attention should be given to institutionalizing vision if leadership of the transforming kind is to be successsful	The vision of the school as a learning centre for the community is reflected in goals, policies, plans, budgets and activities
10. Both 'masculine' and 'feminine' stereotype qualities are important in leadership, regardless of the gender of the leader	Principal is sensitive and caring about personal needs ('feminine' stereotype); principal fosters competitive, team approach in raising school's academic standing ('masculine' stereotype)

with brief illustration is contained in Table 13.1. Guidelines and further illustrations are provided in the next section[. . .].

1. Emphasis should be given to transforming rather than transactional leadership

This important distinction was made by James McGregor Burns (1978) in his study of leadership and followership. According to Burns, leadership is transactional in most instances, that is, there is a simple exchange of one thing for another: jobs for votes in the case of a political leader and the electorate; a congenial working atmosphere and security in return for keeping central office, parents and students happy in the case of a principal and teaching staff. The transforming leader, while still responding to needs among followers, looks for potential motives in followers, seeks to satisfy higher needs, and engages the full person of the follower. The result of transforming leadership is a relationship of mutual stimulation and elevation that converts followers into leaders and leaders into moral agents (Burns, 1978, p. 4).

The transforming leader may motivate citizens to make new commitments to help those in need (Mother Teresa) or to achieve a breakthrough in civil rights (Martin Luther King Jr) or to achieve independence (Mahatma Gandhi). The principal who is a transforming leader may secure substantial commitments of time and energy from teachers in a drive to change attitudes of students and parents to school in a community where previously there were low levels of achievement and little value was placed on education. Illustrations of this thrust in transforming leadership are contained in Table 13.1.

2.   Outstanding leaders have a vision for their organizations

Providing a vision was one of four strategies or themes in the study by Bennis and Nanus (1985) of ninety transforming leaders in a variety of settings. A vision is

> a mental image of a possible and desirable future state of the organization
> . . . as vague as a dream or as precise as a goal or mission statement . . . a
> view of a realistic, credible, attractive future for the organization, a condition that is better in some important ways than what now exists.
>   (Bennis and Nanus, 1985, p. 89)

The vision of Martin Luther King Jr was captured in his stirring 'I have a dream' speech on the steps of the Lincoln Memorial in Washington. The vision of John F. Kennedy concerning space exploration was precise: a man on the moon before the end of the decade.

The importance of vision is a recurring theme in studies of excellence and leadership in education. The vision of a transforming principal may be a dream expressed in written form as 'Our school will be a learning centre in the community, where every child will enjoy coming to school and will acquire the basic skills, and where parents and other members of the community can engage in educational programmes for their personal improvement and enjoyment.' This vision is illustrated in Table 13.1. The vision may, alternatively, be a more precise statement of mission: 'Our students are presently performing far below those in schools in comparable social settings on tests of basic skills; we aim to come in the top ten among these schools on system-wide tests of achievement.'

3.   Vision must be communicated in a way which secures commitment among members of the organization

Bennis and Nanus highlight the compelling nature of what is involved:

> Their visions or intentions are compelling and pull people toward them.
> Intensity coupled with commitment is magnetic . . . [Leaders] do not have

to coerce people to pay attention; they are so intent on what they are doing that, like a child completely absorbed in creating a sand castle, they draw others in. Vision grabs.

(Bennis and Nanus, 1985, p. 28)

Starratt (1986) includes the same requirement in his theory of leadership, emphasizing that the shared vision must pervade day-to-day activities. One facet of this theory is that 'the leader articulates that vision in such compelling ways that it becomes the shared vision of the leader's colleagues, and it illuminates their ordinary activities with dramatic significance'. In a school, for example, a vision of high levels of self-esteem for every child in a community marked by severe disadvantage requires the shared commitment of all teachers. This commitment must shape every interaction of teacher and student; every word and every action must reflect that vision. Vaill (1986) coined the term 'purposing' to describe what is required of leaders in helping to achieve commitment. Purposing is 'that continuous stream of actions by an organization's formal leadership which have the effect of inducing clarity, consensus and commitment regarding the organization's basic purposes' (Vaill, 1986, p. 91). One can imagine the very careful attention to 'purposing' in a school where the achievement of self-esteem is part of the vision, since that achievement is dependent on 'clarity, consensus and commitment' among the staff as they carry out their 'ordinary activities'.

4. Communication of vision requires communication of meaning

According to Bennis and Nanus (1985, p. 33) 'the management of meaning, [the] mastery of communication, is inseparable from effective leadership'. In reviewing the significant changes which have occurred over a decade of study in leadership, Sergiovanni asserted that

At the heart of these changes is the view that the meaning of leadership behaviour and events to teachers and others is more important than the behaviour and events themselves. Leadership reality for all groups is the reality they create for themselves, and thus leadership cannot exist separate from what people find significant and meaningful.

(Sergiovanni, 1987, p. 116)

Particular attention has been given in recent years to the use of metaphors and symbols in the communication of meaning. Spoken and written words have always been regarded as important in the sharing of purposes and intentions, but the choice of metaphors takes on special significance, not only in expressing a vision but also in shaping the climate of the school and the meaning of ordinary activities. Some of the metaphors employed in describing a school are familiar: factory, hospital, family, community, war zone, or even a prison. The student is portrayed, respectively, as a worker, patient, family member, young citizen, soldier or prisoner. Teachers may be seen as factory supervisors, doctors, parents, community leaders, sergeants or warders. There will be debate and conflict about the choice of metaphors since they reflect values and views about the nature of people, society, schooling and education. Gaining consensus and commitment to the particular metaphors which will shape the ordinary activities of the school is thus an important concern for the principal and other leaders in the school.

Symbols are also important for the communication of meaning by leaders. A recent study of the management of symbols by school principals led Kelley and Bredeson (1987, p. 31) to describe symbolic leadership in terms of integrated messages 'communicated through the patterned use of words, actions and rewards that have an impact on the beliefs, values, attitudes and behaviours of others with whom the principal interacts'. The principal who seeks commitment among teachers to a vision which includes raising the levels of self-esteem will give careful thought to words, actions and rewards. For example, verbal interaction with students will be characterized by praise and encouragement. The principal will choose to attend and, where appropriate, participate in a wide variety of activities involving students with low levels of self-esteem. The presence of the principal will communicate to teachers, students and parents that these activities are valued. Rewards will come in the form of praise and encouragement of teachers who use similar words and engage in similar activities.

5.   Issues of value – 'what ought to be' – are central to leadership

Greenfield (1986, p. 166) asserted that 'organizations are built on the unification of people around values. The business of being a leader is therefore the business of being an entrepreneur of values.' For transactional leadership, where there is a simple exchange between leader and followers ('votes for jobs'), these values will be what Burns (1978, p. 426) called modal values or values of means such as honesty, responsibility, fairness and the honouring of commitments. For transforming leadership, where the pursuit of higher goals calls for full engagement and commitment, he suggests that the leader must be more concerned with end values such as liberty, justice and equality (Burns, 1978, p. 426).

Much of the principal's work will involve transactional leadership. The aforementioned values of honesty, responsibility, fairness and the honouring of commitments are a basic requirement if the support of teachers is to be gained. If excellence is the goal, then transforming leadership and associated end values are needed. Excellence, however conceived, is itself an end value and, along with other end values, will be the subject of debate. Sergiovanni *et al.* (1987, p. 7) recognized this when, writing in the American context, they stated that 'at the heart of educational policy debates are four widely held but conflicting values: equity, excellence, efficiency and liberty'. Similar debates occur in other countries. Managing conflict over basic values will be as much part of the principal's role as it will be of leaders at local, state and national levels. For example, the value of excellence, conceived in terms of high levels of achievement in a relatively narrow range of academic studies, may conflict with the value of equity, conceived in terms of access to a range of educational programmes for all students, regardless of social and economic circumstance. Alternatively, substantial investment in resources with the intention of achieving excellence and equity might conflict with the value of efficiency. These conflicts, however resolved, will be followed by leadership acts designed to achieve what Greenfield (1986, p. 166) described as the 'unification of people around [these] values'.

6. The leader has an important role in developing the culture of the organization

[. . .] As with the management of meaning, 'cultural leadership' has emerged as a major theme in studies over the last decade. Indeed, generalizations offered thus far are all embodied in the special attention which is accorded this aspect of leadership. While acknowledging that technical and managerial conceptions have their place, Sergiovanni believes that

> Cultural leadership – by accepting the realities of the human spirit, by emphasizing the importance of meaning and significance, and by acknowledging the concept of professional freedom linked to values and norms that make up a moral order – comes closer to the point of leadership.
>
> (Sergiovanni, 1987, p. 127)

The opportunities for cultural leadership in the school may be briefly illustrated. While definitions of culture are as varied as the definitions of leaders, there is general agreement that shared values and beliefs lie at the heart of the concept. There is also agreement that the extent to which values and beliefs are shared cannot be easily measured or directly observed. We can only rely on what Deal (1987, p. 6) called 'tangible cultural forms' or Sathe (1985, p. 17) described as 'manifestations of culture' in making inferences about culture in an organization.

Deal listed six tangible cultural forms, each of which can be developed by the principal: shared values as reflected in shorthand slogans ('we care for every child in this school'), heroes in the life of the school or in society at large who embody the values which are held to be important ('former teacher Beth Hanson visited the home of every child she taught in twenty years of service'), rituals in the form of repetitive activities in which shared values are experienced ('new students are made welcome each year at a party where they are served by teachers'), ceremonies where values and heroes are highlighted and celebrated ('every child has the opportunity at least once each year to be recognized in some way at the Monday morning assembly'), stories illustrating, for example, where values and heroes triumphed in adversity ('the principal recounted to beginning teachers how Beth Hanson visited the parent of one of her students, the father, who was in prison at the time'), and cultural networks of people ('gossips, spies, storytellers') who in a variety of ways serve to protect the ways things are done.

7. Studies of outstanding schools provide strong support for school-based management and collaborative decision-making within a framework of state and local policies

While acknowledging that much research remains to be done, Purkey and Smith (1985, p. 355) believe that existing research on school effectiveness 'is sufficiently consistent to guide school improvement efforts based on its conclusions'. They offer a model for creating an effective school, with implications for school leadership among its thirteen elements. One strategy for the development of school culture is the adoption of collaborative planning and collegial relationships. Another in the same vein is school-site management wherein

> The staff of each school is given a considerable amount of responsibility and authority in determining the exact means by which they address the problem of increasing academic performance. This includes giving staffs more authority over curricular and instructional decisions and allocation of building resources.
>
> (Purkey and Smith, 1985, p. 358)

These recommendations are consistent with those of scholars such as Theodore Sizer and John Goodlad following their respective studies of schooling in the USA. Sizer (1986, p. 214) believes that one 'imperative for better schools' is to give teachers and students room to take full advantage of the variety among them, a situation which 'implies that there must be substantial authority in each school. For most public and diocesan Catholic school systems, this means the decentralization of power from headquarters to individual schools.' Goodlad (1984, p. 275) proposed 'genuine decentralization of authority and responsibility to the local school within a framework designed to assure school-to-school equity and a measure of accountability'. He noted that 'the guiding principle being put forward here is that the school must become largely self-directing' (Goodlad, 1984, p. 276).

School-based management calls for approaches to school leadership which encourage and support high levels of collaboration among teachers and, where appropriate, parents and students.

8. There are many kinds of leadership forces – technical, human, educational, symbolic and cultural – and these should be widely dispersed throughout the school

Symbolic and cultural aspects of leadership have been a feature of recent studies as reflected in most of the generalizations offered thus far. However, other aspects which have been part of more traditional perspectives must also be sustained. Sergiovanni (1984, p. 6) provided a useful classification of what he called 'leadership forces', each of which 'can be thought of as the means available to administrators, supervisors and teachers to bring about or preserve changes needed to improve schooling'. Technical leadership forces include the capacity to plan, organize, co-ordinate and schedule. Human leadership forces include building and maintaining morale, encouraging growth and creativity and involving people in decision-making. Educational leadership forces include the capacity to work with staff to determine student needs and develop curriculum and to provide supervision.

The technical, human and educational aspects of leadership in the Sergiovanni classification encompass the task and relationship dimensions of leadership behaviour used in earlier attempts to develop theories of leadership. Sergiovanni suggested that these three forces alone may ensure an effective school but, if excellence is desired, symbolic and cultural forces should also be evident.

It will be rare for a single leader such as the principal to exercise all of the leadership forces. Consistent with evidence of benefit from collaborative approaches, Sergiovanni (1987, p. 122) suggests that highly successful leaders recognize the importance of 'leadership density' which refers to 'the extent to which leadership roles are shared and the extent to which leadership is broadly exercised'. There will thus be many leaders in an excellent school.

9. Attention should be given to institutionalizing vision if leadership of the transforming kind is to be successful

This generalization takes up implications of those listed previously that point to the importance of what Burns called 'transforming leadership', with the principal having a vision for the school, and being able to articulate that vision in such a way that others become committed to it and day-to-day activities are imbued with its meanings and values. It is necessary, of course, that the vision be sustained or 'institutionalized', with its meanings and values embedded in the culture of the school. Starratt (1986) combined all of these perspectives in a simple, eloquent model for leadership as the 'communal institutionalizing of a vision':

- The leader's power is rooted in a vision that is itself rooted in something basic to human life.
- That vision illuminates the ordinary with dramatic significance.
- The leader articulates that vision in such compelling ways that it becomes the shared vision of the leader's colleagues, and it illuminates their ordinary activities with dramatic significance.
- The leader implants the vision in the structures and processes of the organization, so that people experience the vision in the various patterned activities of the organization.
- The leader and colleagues make day-to-day decisions in the light of that vision, so that the vision becomes the heart of the culture of the organization.
- All the members of the organization celebrate the vision in ritual, ceremonies and art forms.

This model may be shaped further by other generalizations related to collaborative decision-making as well as to density of leadership and the variety of leadership forces (technical, human, educational, symbolic, cultural). The principal may work with others to establish the vision for a school. The principal should work with others to implant the vision in the structures and processes of the school, something that calls for the technical and human skills of policy-making and planning. The making of day-to-day decisions in the areas of curriculum and instruction in a manner which reflects the vision will call for density of the educational leadership force; that is, a number of teachers will be leaders as the purposes, policies and priorities of the school are reflected in the various areas of the curriculum and in approaches to teaching and learning.

10. Both 'masculine' and 'feminine' stereotype qualities are important in leadership, regardless of the gender of the leader

The shortcomings of research and theory on the basis of their limited focus on males has been documented (Shakeshaft and Nowell, 1984). A cultural bias toward leadership by males is also evident, with Burns (1978, p. 50) noting that 'femininity has been stereotyped as dependent, submissive and conforming, and hence women have been seen as lacking in leadership qualities'. Burns believed that 'male bias is reflected in the false conception of leadership as mere command or control'. He sees promise of a shift in bias as other conceptions of leadership take hold, especially those which deal with the relationship between leader and followers. An examination of this relationship was central to his own study of leadership which led to the important distinction between transactional and transformational leadership. Burns concluded that as 'leadership comes properly to be seen as a process of leaders engaging and mobilizing the human needs and aspirations of followers, women will be more readily recognized as leaders and men will change their own leadership styles'.

Some valuable insights on this issue were provided by Lightfoot (1983) in her investigation of 'the good high school'. She described her studies as 'portraits' because 'I thought it would allow us a measure of freedom from the traditions and constraints of disciplined research methods, and because I thought our work would be defined by aesthetic, as well as empirical and analytic, dimensions' (Lightfoot, 1983, p. 13). This approach enabled her to capture aspects of leadership which may have eluded the researcher who employed a more constrained methodology. She found that the six principals in her investigation, all of whom were male, were stereotypically male in some respects (images included 'the raw masculinity of the coach', 'the paternalism of the father-principal', 'the imperial figure'). Yet, she observed, 'in all cases, the masculine images have been somewhat transformed and the arrangements of power have been adjusted. In the most compelling cases, the leaders have sought to feminize their style and have been aware of the necessity of motherly interactions with colleagues and staff'. Lightfoot concluded that the 'people and context demand a reshaping of anachronistic patterns':

The redefinition includes softer images that are based on nurturance given and received by the leader; based on relationships and affiliations as central dimensions of the exercise of power; and based on a subtle integration of personal qualities traditionally attached to male and female images.

(Lightfoot, 1983, p. 333)

While the need for further research is evident, a generalization which acknowledges the importance of both masculine and feminine qualities in leadership can be offered with confidence. It seems especially relevant to leadership in a shift toward more autonomy for schools, with school-based management characterized by collaborative approaches.

VISION IN SCHOOL LEADERSHIP: GUIDELINES AND ILLUSTRATIONS

The final section of the chapter provides guidelines and illustrations of three generalizations related to vision in school leadership:

- Outstanding leaders have a vision for their organizations (see generalization no. 2 above).
- Vision must be communicated in a way which secures commitment among members of the organization (generalization no. 3).
- Communication of vision requires communication of meaning (generalization no. 4).

In most instances, these guidelines and illustrations are for the school as a whole, with the principal as leader. The same guidelines and similar illustrations may be developed for units within the school and their leaders.

THE NATURE OF VISION

Bennis and Nanus considered vision in broad terms to mean

A mental image of a possible and desirable future state of the organization . . . as vague as a dream or as precise as a goal or mission statement . . . a view of a realistic, credible, attractive future for the organization, a condition that is better in some important ways than what now exists.

(Bennis and Nanus, 1985, p. 89)

Some writers such as Block (1987) would prefer to distinguish between a vision, a mission and an objective, but the broader view is adopted here. It is acknowledged, however, that the term 'vision' as it now appears in the literature on leadership has the same or similar meaning as has been usually ascribed to words like 'goal'. Sheive and Schoenheit (1987), for example, wrote about vision and leadership after interviewing twelve educators, including five principals, who were widely regarded as leaders. These interviews began with a question which asked about the leader's goals as an educator, after which the subject was asked 'Is your vision, then, to . . .?' (Sheive and Schoenheit, 1987, p. 96). In this chapter we are not ascribing to the term 'vision' any special characteristic which has recently been discovered, although we accept its usefulness in describing a 'mental picture' which is shaped by one or more goals.

The study by Sheive and Schoenheit is a useful starting point for providing illustrations of visions for schools. Those interviewed shared two kinds of vision, one related to their own organization and the other to the world beyond their own organization; the former embodied a vision of organizational excellence, the latter centred on the issue of equity and was concerned with 'righting a wrong'. It would seem that the specific vision for the school is shaped in part by a more general vision which reflects some basic values and beliefs held by the leader. This is consistent with the model for leadership proposed by Starratt (1986) which suggested that 'the leader's power is rooted in a vision that is itself rooted in something basic to human life'. At the broadest level, these basic values and beliefs seem to fall into constellations which are often in conflict. These 'competing visions' in society as a whole were described by Sowell (1987).

Roueche and Baker (1986) obtained 'profiles of excellence' of 154 schools selected in the 1983 National School Recognition Program in the USA and found that principals tended to have visions not only of a preferred outcome but also of the process of change through which that outcome would be attained. Processes of change include preferred approaches to teaching and learning as well as preferred approaches to the management of change. As with vision related to outcomes, preferences in terms of process reflect different values and beliefs held by the leader. Both kinds of vision – process and outcome – seem to include what Sergiovanni and Starratt (1983, p. 227) described as the leader's 'educational platform', a set of assumptions and beliefs which 'deal with the way children and youth grow, with the purposes of schooling, with the nature of learning, with pedagogy and teaching, with educational programmes, and with school climate'.

GUIDELINES – 1

Drawing together this research and writing, we offer the following as a guide to the nature of vision for a school:

- The vision of a school leader includes a mental image of a possible and desirable future state of the school.
- The vision will embody the leader's own view of what constitutes excellence in schooling.
- The vision of a school leader also includes a mental image of a possible and desirable future state for the broader educational scene and for society in general.
- The vision of a school leader also includes a mental image of a possible and desirable process of change through which the preferred future state will be achieved.

- Each aspect of the vision for a school reflects different assumptions, values and beliefs about such matters as the nature of humankind; the purpose of schooling; the roles of government, family and church in schooling; approaches to teaching and learning; and approaches to the management of change.
- There will be competing visions of schooling reflecting the many, often conflicting differences in assumptions, values and beliefs.

ILLUSTRATION – 1

The following is an example of one leader's vision for a school, illustrating each of the elements listed above.

Ruth Griffiths has been appointed principal of a high school in a lower socio-economic area of the city. The school buildings are becoming dilapidated because of their age as well as from increasing vandalism. Parents and other members of the community rarely visit the school. Ruth would like to see a quite different scene in five years. She has committed herself to stay for five years and would like to assemble about her a staff which will develop a similar commitment. She wants to create a school in which children can take pride and which parents and others will visit regularly and support. She acknowledges that student achievement may never be as high as that in more favoured areas but she is convinced that most of the children can do well and can enjoy their schooling. She has the same view for education in general, believing that the quality of life for all will be enhanced if this can be achieved. Ruth Griffiths believes that it is possible for all parents to be involved in the school in a variety of ways, including direct involvement in their children's learning and in the planning and implementation of change. She would especially like to engage the many businesses and industries in the community in a major effort to improve the school. She believes in a partnership of government, community, home and school since all have an interest in what the school accomplishes for its students, each of whom should be able to make a contribution to the community at large at the same time as being satisfied and challenged as an individual. Ruth expects that curriculum and instruction should reflect the needs and interests of all children but that high expectations can be pursued with consistency and enthusiasm. She acknowledges, however, that her views are different from those of many of her teachers who believe that little more can be expected of the school than is being achieved at present.

The term 'vision', as we have illustrated it above, is not describing a new phenomenon in leadership. It is simply attaching a label to the sort of dream or constellation of goals or scenarios that form in the mind of everyone from time to time. What we now know is that these form readily in the minds of leaders who succeed in transforming their organizations. Before progress can be made, however, the leader must succeed in communicating that vision in ways that secure commitment among others.

COMMUNICATING THE VISION

[. . .] Here are some guidelines, with brief illustration, of what is not only a necessary first step but also a continuing requirement, namely communicating the vision in ways which are likely to gain the commitment of others.

SYMBOLIC LEADERSHIP

A simple presentation, both rational and eloquent, to a meeting of staff, or a carefully constructed discussion paper for distribution to staff prior to such a meeting, are useful contributions but constitute only a narrow range of leadership behaviour. Among the generalizations which have emerged from recent studies of leaders was the importance of symbolic leadership and the communication of meaning, especially through the use of metaphor, and it is to acts of symbolic leadership that the principal should turn in an effort to communicate a vision for the school. The definition of symbolic leadership offered by Kelley and Bredeson (1987) is a useful starting point for developing some guidelines. They described symbolic leadership in terms of integrated messages which 'are communicated through the patterned use of words, actions and rewards that have an impact on the beliefs, values, attitudes and behaviours of others with whom the principal interacts' (Kelley and Bredeson, 1987, p. 31).

GUIDELINES – 2

This view of symbolic leadership, and the recognition that it is the meanings others attribute to actions rather than the acts themselves which are significant, produces guidelines like the following:

- Words, both oral and written, are important for effective communication of vision, giving particular attention to metaphors which describe what is preferred, especially in relation to people, behaviours and relationships.
- Vision can be communicated through actions which, quite separate from any words which might accompany them, can communicate meaning in very powerful ways – the way the school leader dresses, how the school leader arranges an office and greets visitors, events which the school leader chooses to attend, people with whom the school leader is seen to associate, ceremonies which the school leader decides to conduct, and how the school leader allocates time during the school day.
- Vision can be communicated through rewards. What words and behaviours of others the school leader chooses to reward and in what manner will readily convey a picture of what is preferred. These rewards may be bestowed on students, members of staff, parents and other members of the school community and may come in the form of simple words of thanks or praise as well as through the granting of some privilege or favour.

- It is important for the school leader to demonstrate consistency among these elements of symbolic leadership and be consistent over time with different people in different circumstances. It is also important for others in the school to see consistency between these acts of symbolic leadership and what they discern as the personality and underlying motives and values of the leader.

ILLUSTRATION – 2

The view of a preferred future by Ruth Griffiths, a recently appointed principal of an inner-city high school, was offered as an illustration of a vision for a school. What follows here are illustrations of how elements of that vision might be communicated through words, actions and rewards.

- *Element of vision*: 'Ruth Griffiths sees a school in which all children can take pride.'
  Words: Ruth Griffiths openly articulates to staff and students her commitment to improving the condition of the school buildings.
  Actions: Ruth Griffiths rescinds a previous decision to paint and repair the wing of the school where her office is located and arranges for the work to be done instead on two common rooms used by the students.
  Rewards: Ruth Griffiths encourages students to make their own improvements in their common rooms and classes. She secures funds and donations from local business to upgrade the facilities used by students.

- *Element of vision*: 'Ruth Griffiths would especially like to engage the many businesses and industries in a major effort to improve the school.'
  Words: Ruth Griffiths arranges invitations to speak at meetings of the Chamber of Commerce for herself, a parent, a teacher and a student. The benefits of close links between school and community are stressed. Metaphors such as 'community' and 'partnership' are used here as well as in meetings of staff and in communications with parents.
  Actions: Ruth Griffiths attends seminars organized to promote local business and asks to be invited to management seminars for leaders in the community. She invites a highly regarded business executive to speak at a staff seminar on trends in the use of technology.
  Rewards: Ruth Griffiths ensures that the seminar involvement of staff and business is noted in newspaper accounts. She makes favourable comment on each occasion staff develop these and similar linkages.

These examples illustrate just two elements in the vision for the school offered by Ruth Griffiths. Since there are several elements in that vision, it is evident that there is a rich array in the repertoire of symbolic acts available to the principal. This aspect of leadership will demand time and energy, requiring a sharing of leadership in what Sergiovanni described as 'leadership density' in the distribution of leadership forces. Over time, however, this commitment by the principal will become the shared commitment of staff and others in the community, setting the stage for 'institutionalizing' the vision in the structures and processes of the school. [. . .]

SUMMARY

Our purpose in this chapter has been to demonstrate how recent advances in knowledge about leadership can contribute to the achievement of excellence. Earlier views about the nature of leadership itself were rather constrained and superficial, tending to emphasize the exercise of formal authority in achieving the goals of the school. This view gave way to recognition that leadership involves influence and that many who are not formally designated as such may serve as leaders. More recently, we have gained a deeper appreciation of leadership by examining the relationship between leaders and other members of staff, noting the importance of meanings which are derived from leadership acts.

So theories of leadership have provided only a small part of the total picture. We know, for example, that it is important for leaders to give attention to two dimensions: accomplishment of the tasks at hand, and establishing good relationships with and among members of staff. So-called 'contingency theories' offer refinements which are helpful but are somewhat narrow in their potential for application and impact. For example, the situational theory of Hersey and Blanchard reminds us of the importance of varying leadership behaviour according to the maturity of staff for the task at hand; the more mature in a personal and professional sense, the less directive and more participative the leader should be. Fiedler's contingency theory tells us that the relatively unchanging, somewhat innate aspects of our leadership style make us better suited to some situations than to others.

However, it is the larger picture which has resulted from leadership studies of the last decade which will prove most helpful to the leader who wishes to make a contribution to excellence in the school. It seems that emphasis should be given to transforming rather than transactional leadership, with the intent being to change attitudes and bring about commitment to 'a better state' which is embodied in a vision of excellence for the school. We know that outstanding school leaders have such a vision and that they succeed in communicating it in a way that secures the commitment of others in the school and its community. The most important aspect of communication is the meaning it conveys. So it is important for the school leader to decide on the meanings which are intended and then to choose acts which will ensure the intended outcome. Leadership is concerned with gaining commitment to a set of values, statements of 'what ought to be', which then become the heart of the culture of the school. Gaining this commitment can be achieved in a number of ways, especially with collaborative approaches to decision-making and with placing at the school level high responsibility and authority for making decisions related to the allocation of resources in the school. We know that there is a variety of what Sergiovanni called 'leadership forces' – technical, human, educational, symbolic and cultural – and all should be present and widely dispersed in the school ('leadership density') if excellence is to be attained. Having a vision and securing commitment to that vision is just the starting point. That vision must then be 'institutionalized' so that it shapes the everyday activities in the school. All of these approaches call for masculine and feminine qualities of leadership, regardless of the gender of the leader.

This chapter also contained some guidelines and illustrations for forming and communicating a vision. The vision should be concerned with a possible and desirable future state for the school, should embody a view of excellence and a view of a preferred future for education and society in general, should incorporate a picture of the process of change through which the vision for the school will be achieved, and will reflect different assumptions, beliefs and attitudes which are basic to life and education. There will be competing visions of what is preferred, reflecting a variety of assumptions, beliefs and values. In communicating the vision, the school leader should use a wide range of symbolic leadership acts, broadly classified as words, actions and rewards, with consistency in their use being important. [. . .]

REFERENCES

Bennis, W. and Nanus, B. (1985) *Leaders*, Harper & Row, New York.
Burns, J. M. (1978) *Leadership*, Harper & Row, New York.
Deal, T.E. (1987) The culture of schools, in L.T. Sheive and M.B. Schoenheit (eds.) *Leadership: Examining the Elusive. 1987 Yearbook of the Association for Supervision and Curriculum Development*, ASCA, Arlington, Va.
Dubin, R. (1968) *Human Relations in Administration* (2nd edn), Prentice Hall, Englewood Cliffs, NJ.
Duke, D.L. (1986) The aesthetics of leadership, *Educational Administration Quarterly*, Vol. 22, no. 1.
Fiedler, F.E. (1967) *A Theory of Leadership Effectiveness*, McGraw Hill, New York.
Fiedler, F.E., Chemers, M.M. and Mahar, L. (1977) *Improving Leadership Effectiveness: The Leader Match Concept*, John Wiley & Sons, New York.
Goodlad, J.I. (1984) *A Place Called School*, McGraw-Hill, New York.
Greenfield, T.B. (1986) Leaders and schools: willfulness and non-natural order in organizations, in T.J. Sergiovanni and J.E. Corbally (eds.) *Leadership and Organizational Culture: New Perspectives on Administrative Theory and Practice*, University of Chicago Press, Urbana and Chicago.
Hersey, P. and Blanchard, K. (1982) *Management of Organizational Behavior: Utilizing Human Resources* (4th edn), Prentice-Hall, Englewood Cliffs, NJ.
Hodgkinson, C. (1983) *The Philosophy of Leadership*, Blackwell, Oxford.
Hoy, W.K. and Miskel, C.G. (1987) *Educational Administration: Theory, Research, and Practice* (3rd edn), Random House, New York.
Kelley, B.E. and Bredeson, P.V. (1987) Principals as symbol managers: measures of meaning in schools. Paper presented at the annual meeting of the American Educational Research Association. Washington, DC, AERA, April.
Lightfoot, S.L. (1983) *The Good High School*, Basic Books, New York.
Lipham, J. (1964) Leadership and administration, in E.E. Griffiths (ed.) *Behavioral Science and Educational Administration*, University of Chicago Press.

Pondy, L.R. (1978) Leadership is a language game, in M.W. McCall Jr and M.M. Lombardo (eds.) *Leadership: Where Else Can We Go?* Duke University Press, Durham, NC.

Purkey, S.C. and Smith, M.S. (1985) School reform: the district policy implications of the effective schools literature, *The Elementary School Journal*, Vol. 85.

Roueche, J.E. and Baker, G.A. (1986) *Profiling Excellence in America's Schools*, American Association of School Administrators, Arlington, Va.

Sathe, V. (1985) *Culture and Related Corporate Realities*, Richard D. Irwin, Homewood, Il.

Sergiovanni, T.J. (1984) Leadership and excellence in schooling, *Educational Leadership*, February.

Sergiovanni, T.J. (1987) The theoretical basis for cultural leadership, in L.T. Sheive and M.B. Schoenheit (eds.) *1987 Yearbook of the Association for Supervision and Curriculum Development*, ASCA, Alexandria, Va.

Sergiovanni, T.J., Burlingame, M., Coombs, F.S. and Thurston, P.W. (1987) *Educational Governance and Administration* (2nd edn), Prentice-Hall, Englewood Cliffs, NJ.

Sergiovanni, T.J. and Starratt, R.J. (1983) *Supervision: Human Perspectives* (3rd edn), McGraw-Hill, New York.

Shakeshaft, C. and Nowell, I. (1984) Research on theories, concepts, and models of organizational behavior: the influence of gender, *Issues in Education*, no. 2.

Sheive, L.T. and Schoenheit, M.B. (eds.) (1987) Leadership: examining the elusive, in *1987 Yearbook of the Association for Supervision and Curriculum Development*, ASCD, Arlington, Va.

Sizer, T.R. (1986) Rebuilding: first steps by the coalition of essential schools, *Phi Delta Kappan*, September.

Sowell, T. (1987) *A Conflict of Visions*, William Morrow & Co, New York.

Starratt, R.J. (1986) Excellence in education and quality of leadership. Occasional Paper No. 1. Southern Tasmanian Council for Educational Administration.

Stogdill, R.M. (1948) Personal factors associated with leadership: a survey of the literature, *Journal of Psychology*, Vol. 25, pp. 35–71.

Stogdill, R.M. (1950) Leadership, membership and organization, *Psychological Bulletin*, no. 47.

Stogdill, R.M. (1974) *Handbook of Leadership*, The Free Press, New York.

Vaill, P.B. (1986) The purposing of high performing systems, in T.J. Sergiovanni and J.E. Corbally (eds.) *Leadership and Organizational Culture: New Perspectives on Administrative Theory and Practice*, University of Chicago Press, Urbana and Chicago.

14

WOMEN DEPUTY HEADTEACHERS IN EDUCATIONAL MANAGEMENT

Colette Singleton

This material has been abridged

[*Editor's note*: Six women deputy heads in secondary schools were interviewed for this research study, and two male deputies as a control factor. This chapter comprises the analysis of results and conclusions of the study.]

ANALYSIS OF THE RESULTS

Having conducted all eight semi-structured interviews and accumulated a quantity of data the next step was to analyse this data and present it in some meaningful and useful form. [. . .]

The size and nature of the survey meant that inferential methods were seen as more suitable than descriptive methods. 'The purpose of such qualitative research is not to obtain a set of facts but to gain insight into a perspective' (Johnson, 1984). The perspective in this case was women's management styles, and whilst the research carried out attempts to be open, its declared intention is to illuminate, and it lays no claim to being representative.

A review of the literature on this topic [revealed] three distinct areas: leadership styles, roles and power. The questions which were developed for the interviews [and piloted] were designed to discover the extent to which the experiences of the women interviewed matched what had been revealed in the literature. Every attempt was made not to bias the results in any way by keeping the majority of the questions as open as possible. It was not until the final, unseen question that the objective behind the interview was revealed. [The list of questions sent out prior to the interview did not include the question: 'Have there ever been occasions in your present position when you have been aware that being a woman has been a help or a hindrance?'] Yet, despite the fact that the interview now had a much more obvious feminist slant, none of the respondents altered their answers in any way. They merely used the final question as an opportunity to develop a number of the areas. [. . .]

In analysing the data it seemed most profitable to retain the structure established on the basis of the literature review: leadership styles, roles and power. As few of the questions dealt solely with one area it was not possible to work through the questions and their answers in a sequential manner. Instead the questions were first of all analysed in order to identify which of the three areas they contributed to, as shown below.

Then a coding frame was drawn up and the interview responses were coded. [. . .] The answers to the unseen question are discussed in a separate section in order not to bias the original findings.

LEADERSHIP STYLES

Man with the head and woman with the heart:
Man to command and woman to obey;
All else confusion.

                                        (Tennyson, 'The Princess')

[. . .] The answers given suggest that women may work in a more co-operative, participative, people-centred [style] than their male counterparts. The first person to be interviewed talked at length about needing to know how to handle people and how to treat them. She stressed that it was important not to be too concerned about your own status or position but to give others the opportunity to lead so that they too could develop. Although commitment and enthusiasm were important it was a positive disadvantage to appear too competent as this inhibited others who were then reluctant to get involved. She touched on this again at the end of the interview. Women, she felt, had a tendency to strive for perfection, but this could prove counterproductive as things didn't always get finished because people got bored.

Every one of the respondents echoed the need to work in co-operation with the staff (five of them had responsibility for staff welfare as part of their job description) and to a woman they all saw patience as a vital attribute. Other desirable attributes were: 'a sense of humour' (mentioned in three interviews), 'intelligence' (again mentioned in three interviews), 'the ability to delegate in order to encourage ownership and professional development', as well as 'having vision' and 'being able to motivate'. A number of these attributes were echoed by the two male deputies interviewed, including in one case 'the need to get on with people'. But both also stressed the need to 'lead from the front' as one described it, which contrasted somewhat with the more 'people-oriented', less forceful approach of the women.

The two interviews carried out with male deputy heads were an attempt to introduce some sort of control factor. [. . .] *All* the women found administration the least satisfactory, whilst they got most enjoyment and pleasure out of working with people, for example seeing pupils or staff develop and succeed.

The two men, however, found dealing with incompetence in people (staff in particular) very stressful and the least satisfactory part of their job, whilst most satisfaction came from things like 'achieving positive change' or 'completing the timetable'. On such a limited sample it would be unwise to draw anything but the most tentative of conclusions but these findings do offer further support for the idea of women having a more people-oriented approach.

Although this was only a small-scale study the women deputies interviewed were remarkably consistent in describing a management style that built on qualities and advantages they felt were the result of being a woman. Two main themes underpinned this style:

(1) A belief that women have access to more varied, 'softer' techniques in personal relationships;
(2) Greater understanding and sympathy for the needs of others.

Their approach to management was built on principles of co-operation rather than competition, a more 'low-key' or 'subtle' style than the one which appeared to be favoured by the two male deputies. One of the most experienced female deputies used the word 'devious' when describing women. She went on to expand this, explaining that women were able to get things done by subtle means, they had more options open to them than men who were, she felt, more constrained by traditional methods which were tied up with the male image.

ROLE

'There is no function in society which is peculiar to women as women or man as man; natural attributes are similarly distributed in each sex and it is natural to share all occupations' said Plato in the 4th century BC. The reality unfortunately is often very different. Jobs whilst not legally labelled 'for men' or 'for women' are still viewed by many people as just that. Moreover the belief that men and women have different 'natural abilities' means that whilst sharing the same title women can find themselves playing out quite a different role from their male counterparts. This was certainly the case for the female deputy head. In his analysis of management roles in schools, John (1973) states that 'One should be wary of the view that women deputy heads are mother figures particularly equipped by nature to dispense hospitality, aspirins and sticking plaster, to arrange flowers in the school entrance hall and to return lost property.'

Little appears to have changed in the years since this was written and the Equal Opportunities Commission is still drawing attention to the dangers of adopting such a stereotyped view of women's role. It also clearly indicates that knowledge of a situation alone is insufficient to change it. Why do people follow the dictates of role expectation? [Perhaps] 'he conforms because he personally considers such behaviour as meritorious and proper through his exposure to pressure to conform with expectations' (Open University, 1976, DT 352 Unit 8).

Role performance can also be defined by the complex series of relationships in which organizational members are involved and on which they depend for assistance and to some extent approval.

The questions which sought to elicit information about relationships with other members of the management team as well as relationships with the rest of the staff illustrated quite clearly that a number of the respondents had felt under pressure to conform to an accepted image of the old senior mistress role. At the same time, however, most of the respondents (five of the six) indicated through their answers that their behaviour was not limited to this structural conception of role. It was closer to Burnham's definition (1969): 'While what one is expected to do is prescribed, how one actually plays the role will be distinguished by personal nuances.' This led, however, to the problem of conflicting role expectations.

Kanter (1977) observes that establishing a viable identity in the male-dominated context of management is for many women 'a protective process'. The woman manager's attempts to reach out and create her own image are continually pre-empted by other organization members' expectations of her.

The problem of dealing with differing expectations was an issue touched upon by all the respondents. When dealing with areas of responsibility four of the six felt that because they were the senior women, it was accepted that any problems related to girls were automatically their responsibility, no matter how trivial. One respondent in particular noted that form tutors were selective about which deputy head to refer problems to and the criteria appeared to be the nature of the problem. 'Problems that appear to need a woman's touch, that is social or emotional problems, always end up outside my door. The discipline problems are always sent to . . . [male deputy].'

As well as being both a limiting and a frustrating factor this also has an effect on pupils' perceptions of male and female staff. It supports research carried out by Stanworth (1984) that pupils hold a general preconception that male teachers are more effective disciplinarians, who tolerate less 'mucking about'.

The age, and to a certain degree sex, of other members of staff seemed to be an influencing factor regarding role expectation. All the respondents agreed that their greatest problem lay with the older members of staff who had a far more traditional view of the role of senior women. This was more in keeping with the descriptions given by two of the respondents of the old senior mistress role, 'the flower and sandwiches brigade' or 'the dispenser of sympathy and sanitary towels'.

Interestingly, it wasn't just older men who presented a problem. Two of the respondents found their greatest difficulty lay with older women, in particular ones who had a strong relationship with the previous incumbent and appeared to resent any attempt to refocus the role.

Although younger members of staff appeared to hold less rigidly stereotyped views of women several of the respondents [. . .] felt that in the words of one of them, 'given the choice most of them would prefer a man leading the team. It sounds a bit pathetic when you say it out loud but I sense that a lot of the staff still feel that men have more power.'

Table 14.1 Distribution of major areas of responsibility

Respond-ents	Only girls welfare/ discipline	Staff welfare	Proba-tionary teachers	Students	INSET	TVEI	Curriculum	LMS	Timetable	Exam secretary	Co-ordinator of PSE
Female											
A	/	/	/	/	/	/					
B	/	/	/	/							/
C	/	/	/				/		/		/
D	/	/	/					/			/
E	/	/		/		/	/		/		
F	/	/	/			/	/				/
Male											
G						/	/		/		
H					/					/	

One respondent described how annoyed, but at the same time inadequate, she felt when, as a result of an external review of a major initiative she was involved in, she learnt that a female member of the team had told the assessor that one of the biggest problems facing the initiative was that it was fronted by a woman, which meant it had less credibility in the eyes of many of the male heads of department.

On the more positive side, four of the respondents described their heads as being very supportive and open to their interpretation of their role – a situation which had come about partially through them proving their worth by assuming responsibilities other than the traditionally accepted female ones.

In a number of their answers respondents recognized the need to overcome stereotyped roles. When discussing their areas of responsibility five of the six acknowledged that they were responsible for girls' welfare and discipline. In only one case was responsibility for the welfare of boys and girls shared with the male deputy on a year basis and not sex basis. When asked if they felt it was necessary for a woman to be responsible for girls' welfare the two oldest respondents felt it was, whilst the others agreed it was a custom they had accepted and not questioned.

Table 14.1 illustrates the distribution of major areas of responsibility. A large percentage of these responsibilities appears to fall in the caring or supporting areas with only two of the respondents having responsibility for curriculum development or timetabling, areas which have traditionally been seen as part of the male preserve. One respondent had been appointed as curriculum deputy, but a new appointment and internal reorganization put her into a pastoral role. Crosher (1984) notes a disturbing shift in responsibilities given to women in senior positions from management and curriculum to more domestic areas such as girls' welfare and lost property, which appears a retrograde step. But it is to some degree supported by the findings of this study.

One factor that became increasingly obvious was the way in which the women interviewed were expected to combine a number of areas of responsibility, generally more than their male counterparts. This factor supports research carried out by Torrington and Weightman (1989): 'When women hold senior posts they are much more likely than men to combine two specific posts of responsibility in order to enjoy the same salary grade as a man with a single responsibility.'

Analysis of all the jobs the women deputies were involved in, including the ones illustrated in Table 14.1, compared with those of the two male deputies also substantiated Torrington and Weightman's findings that 'men's' jobs are high profile and part of the natural progression up the hierarchy making moves to other schools straightforward, and that the jobs men are involved in have discrete activities that they can get on with and which don't require a great deal of cross-school liaison. Four of the female deputies, for example, had responsibility for the co-ordination of personal and social programmes. Two of them commented on how time consuming it was because it involved liaising with a large number of staff across the traditional subject boundaries. This was an area of responsibility one of the respondents would like to get rid of, but she felt it was a position that needed, in her words, 'a certain amount of clout as you are involved with a lot of staff, some of them heads of department, and I doubt if the job would get done properly if someone else tried to do it'.

A multiplicity of roles and a lack of clear role definitions were seen by three of the respondents as the greatest impediment to their doing an efficient job. Handy (1976) sees role ambiguity as leading to role stress as well as creating a lack of confidence in the focal person amongst other members of the group. One respondent felt very strongly that 'if people on the staff aren't clear as to exactly what your function is then they simply bypass you and go straight to the head'.

The major problem, however, with unclear roles was the fact that tasks were duplicated and time was wasted. Lack of time was the other reason given as the greatest impediment to doing an efficient job. This factor was cited by both male and female respondents but whereas the male deputies saw lack of time as the reason they were sometimes unable to do as effective a job as they would wish, all the women who mentioned it regretted not having sufficient time to spend with people, pupils or staff. One respondent admitted that she helped create the problem by being too available. Her justification was that 'You can either be like a machine and be very efficient, or you can maintain the human touch.'

In one sense the very availability that several respondents mentioned was illustrative of what Schmuck (1986) refers to when she describes women as exhibiting 'social-emotive roles' when working in mixed-sex groups. By displaying their concerns for people women trap themselves into the stereotyped roles described earlier in the study. For although they are quite capable of task-initiating behaviour their concern for people fulfils the expectations of a society riddled by patriarchal attitudes.

POWER

In a popular version of the legend of King Arthur and his knights of the round table, King Arthur posed the riddle, 'What thing is that which women most desire in this world?' The answer was 'What most women desire is to rule over men – yea even the greatest' (Green, 1953).

Is this really what women most desire or does it reveal more about male fears and fantasies than the ambitions of women? It has already been established that power or perceived power is essential for a person to have credibility in a management role. When asked how much autonomy they felt they had in carrying out their jobs, all except one of the female respondents felt that they had 'as much as you might expect for a deputy head'. One of the male respondents felt that this had increased over the years as the management of schools became more complex, a view supported by several of the female deputies. The main problem in this area appeared to lie in staff not recognizing or acknowledging that the deputies had any real power and so they found themselves bypassed. Once again the worst offenders appeared to be the older members of staff or members of a department with a very chauvinistic head of department. The one dissident voice on this topic felt that her freedom to act autonomously was severely restricted by the very hierarchical and autocratic decision-making process in her school. It wasn't altogether clear, however, how much of the problem in actual fact lay in the personality of the deputy and how much lay in the organizational structure of the school.

As the earlier research indicated there are various sources of power (Bacharach and Lawler, 1980). Position is one such source. Handy (1976) writes that 'The occupancy of a role entitles one to all the rights of that role in that organization.' But position power, he goes on to say, depends ultimately on the value the organization places on the person in the position. The role of deputy head is in no way a guarantee of power as Torrington and Weightman (1989) discovered. When analysing the work of the three deputies in one school their investigation uncovered the fact that the staff were generally disparaging of the role holders, seeing them as overpaid administrators with no real management role or power.

Three of the respondents in particular were very aware that staff perceptions were all important. When discussing the qualities needed for their post all three mentioned the need to be professional. When asked to develop this the following points were made:

'It's important to act in a clear, decisive manner. Women can just "faff" about or let themselves become obsessed by trivia.'
'You must be confident and know what you are talking about.'
'People will only respect you if you are reliable. It's no good saying you'll do something and then claiming you were too busy to do it.'

Awareness that power can be increased by being involved in certain activities was also apparent in the answers. Three of the respondents felt that their involvement in major initiatives had helped to increase their credibility although following the external review of an initiative mentioned earlier one of the respondents was now beginning to question this. Another respondent described the reaction of people both inside and outside her school when they learnt she had been given responsibility for the financial management of the school under LMS. 'They seemed very surprised,' she commented, 'that a woman should have anything to do with finance, probably because women aren't supposed to be very good at maths.'

The respondents were in agreement with the findings of Cook and Mendleson (1984) that men and women were no different in their capacity to wield power. Perhaps what was different was the way in which they chose to wield it.

BEING A WOMAN IN A MANAGEMENT POSITION

The final, unseen question gave rise to a number of interesting answers and reactions, which explored and developed further, issues related to all three areas. One respondent who had been so far unsuccessful in her applications for headships felt that being a woman was a decided disadvantage at county level and that a number of the inspectorate still had very stereotyped views of women. Within her own management team she sensed that the head was more comfortable when talking to the male deputy. She talked about there being a 'barrier' between her and him. It was difficult, she explained, to give concrete examples of this. 'I suppose you'll just have to put it down to feminine intuition,' she said and then made the observation that that wouldn't really be acceptable evidence, in an academic research topic!

Another respondent had talked of her frustration when senior management meetings deteriorated into what she regarded as trivia. In particular she acknowledged her hostility towards one of the male deputies who 'sprawled out on his chair', insisted on smoking his pipe and talking about cricket. Her comments about the management team in general seemed to substantiate work on group behaviour carried out by Solomons and Cramer (1985) who observed that although a female may have satisfied all the necessary qualifying criteria, complete integration into a predominantly male management team, especially if it had previously been all male, often involved a more complex process than mere entry. 'Observations of the dynamics of groups and the processes involved with minority person membership help to increase understanding about the nature of the psycho-social barriers to a professional woman becoming integrated into a group of male colleagues' (Cartwright and Zander, 1968).

It is important to be aware that this particular respondent spoke quite openly about her 'intolerance' and queried how much it had to do with her own temperament as well as her position as a woman. Moreover, three of the respondents described how they found both the head and other male members of the management team helpful and supportive, although this didn't really address the issue of whether or not they felt accepted by them.

What was interesting in this final section was that all the respondents felt that they had had, or were having, to work against stereotyped concepts of their role. Those who were still experiencing difficulties in this area were the two most recently appointed deputies. In both cases these had been internal appointments which may have a bearing on their present situation. [. . .]

Although recognizing the historical reasons behind it, it was still felt to be very unfair that men simply by virtue of being male had more status. This was very clearly summed up in one interview: 'Somehow people assume that men possess the necessary qualities to do the job and this only changes when they demonstrate otherwise, but with women, we have to prove over and over again that we can do the job before our abilities are recognized.'

The existence of double standards also proved to be an irritant: 'It's funny how when . . . makes a mistake everyone appears to be quite good-natured about it, but if I make a mistake I know for a fact they're far less charitable, not to my face of course, but behind my back.'

Women also had to be much more aware of the image they projected. Whilst it was acceptable for a man to act in a firm, directive fashion, or be bad-tempered and even sarcastic, in a similar situation women were considered to be either bossy or bitchy. In fact four of the interviewees identified either implicitly or explicitly the pressure on women to overperform, as compared to men, in order to achieve the same levels of professional recognition.

Another respondent felt that there were a lot of myths about women, myths that fell into the category of 'everybody knows that women . . .'. For example, it was a commonly held belief that women had a lot of time off, especially if they had children, yet the reality, revealed by her supply-cover record book, certainly didn't bear that out, at least in her own school.

Some of the issues raised at this stage of the interview dealt with the problems only women face and which would never confront a man. A major problem for some respondents was having two jobs, one at school and one at home. This, it was felt, placed a significant burden on women's shoulders no matter how helpful their partners were. The notion that children were the primary responsibility of the mother meant that women assumed the responsibility for organizing childminders and felt guilty whenever their own school functions clashed with those of their children.

Women's domestic function could also act as a potential source of discrimination and prejudice against them. One respondent described how during a discussion about her future the inspector asked her how old her children were. When he learnt they were in their teens he seemed relieved and more positive about her future career as her children would now be much more able to fend for themselves and not need her. Women's dual role, however, was seen by one respondent as the very reason why women make better managers than men. The fact that they had to cope with numerous tasks on different levels and work harder gave them an automatic grounding in many of the skills needed in management. It was interesting therefore that a few weeks later *The Sunday Times* (12 March, 1989) published an article which fully supported this deputy's claim. Dorothy Wade quoted the results of comparative studies of men and women in 65 different occupations carried out by Professor Cary Cooper of the Manchester School of Management. Apart from believing that women do their jobs better, Cooper also suggests that the necessity for women with families to be organized and juggle multiple commitments, makes them better potential managers (Wade, 1989).

Judi Marshall (1984) was surprised when she discovered that the way they dressed was an area of concern for a lot of the women managers she interviewed. It came therefore as no real surprise to this researcher that four of the respondents also talked about the problem of deciding what to wear. They felt that tailored suits were regarded as too masculine or even pretentious by some staff but at the same time clothes that were either too frilly or too casual were also not suitable in their own eyes. 'It's so much easier for a man!' explained one woman, 'they just wear a suit and no one comments one way or the other.'

It would be false to give the impression that all the respondents felt handicapped by being a woman or that even those who did express some reservations were entirely negative. What was apparent, however, was the way that women so often take on personal responsibility for the difficulties that can arise because they are women. A number were also keen to stress that they wanted to be thought of in their professional capacity rather than as a woman. Marshall (1984) develops this point at some length and concludes that such behaviour has a cost because 'central areas of the manager's being are partitioned off and are unable to contribute to her full capability and identity'.

One respondent felt that being a woman was a positive advantage because people were forced at times to adopt a different attitude. She gave as an example an occasion when a male member of staff was extremely aggressive with the male deputy, but when he came to speak to her about the same issue he adopted a far less aggressive stance. [. . .] Whilst accepting that being a woman did have some advantages this same respondent admitted that one of her greatest difficulties was earning the respect of those men who didn't believe women should be in a position of responsibility. They tended to be older male members of staff who had very traditional stereotyped views of women and their role in society.

Three of the respondents were firmly of the opinion that a woman should not use her sexuality in an underhand or unprofessional way. It was wrong for example to use your femininity in a 'fluffy way' according to one, whilst another described the difficulties she had in dealing with a female member of staff who had, on occasions, used her sexuality as a source of power to prejudice a decision in her favour. She had achieved this by deliberately bypassing the female deputy. 'She obviously recognized that hitching her skirt up as she crossed her legs wasn't going to work with me' was the rather caustic comment.

One final observation is based on a universal reaction of all the female deputies interviewed. Each one of them commented on the value of being able to exchange ideas with someone in the same position, an experience rarely open to them. This lends some support to the claims of writers like Marshall, (1983, 1984, 1985) Acker (1983) and others that women lack the informal networks open to men which offer *them* encouragement and support.

CONCLUSIONS

Much of the focus of this study has been on the extent to which the male-dominated nature of management, reflecting as it does wider social and historical patterns, affects the freedom women have to work within a management position and develop their own style of management. Shepard (1977) gives some clues as to how the value system within management arose. In the early 20th century, home, school and the church played an important part in preparing men for organizations. Conformity and obedience were rewarded and the need for loyalty and the acceptance of duty stressed. Within organizations, therefore, personal needs became irrelevant, communication was businesslike and depersonalized, all emotion was considered dysfunctional and asking for or giving help was a sign of weakness or a put-down.

More recently the growth in size and complexity of organizations has led to concepts such as teamwork, collaboration, problem solving, personal growth and trust being valued. Unfortunately these changes have not brought about a revolution in men's values or organizational life. Change is a slow process and, whilst accepting some of the new ways of managing, men are reluctant to let go of old ways.

A lot of the literature researched suggests that women, with their different upbringing and different role expectations find it difficult to participate in the male world of management. [. . .] The results of the interviews suggest that women may work in a more co-operative, participative, 'people-centred' way than do their male counterparts. But in order to achieve the freedom to manage in the style most appropriate to them women have to overcome a series of difficulties. These include:

(1) Stereotypes about women, for example that women's innate characteristics mean that they are 'emotional', 'unstable', 'not decisive enough';
(2) Stereotypes about the nature of management which adopts a 'male managerial model', taking as it does characteristics which are believed to be the male prerogatives as important;
(3) The belief that women have 'lower power orientation';
(4) The lack of female role models and women's isolation within organizations;
(5) The lip service paid to equal opportunities;
(6) The channelling of women into gender-appropriate kinds of work or areas within a job.

All of these have the effect of marginalizing women and preventing them from achieving their potential. This is a tragedy in any area but even more so in the field of educational management.

One of the axioms of good management practice is that it should relate to organizational needs. Good management is not a system imposed from without but is based on an understanding of the organization's aims. Yet the declared aims of many schools are often contradicted by actual management practice. In the past, schools were about moulding people and turning them into useful, productive citizens. Today schools are more about nurturing, encouraging pupils to find and develop their skills, stressing self-respect and respect for others. Yet whilst the aims of schools may have changed, often the way they are managed has not. A dominating, authoritarian, management regime cannot encourage warm, considerate, caring and intuitive behaviour in pupils. Yet this essentially masculine form of management is characteristic of many secondary schools (Leary, 1985) which require general conformity and are competitive, formal and punitive.

It was the fashion in the 1960s and 1970s to appoint populist, aggressive, ideological heads (Gray, 1987). They have now largely disappeared and the reason according to Gray is that they were unsuccessful. Their attempts to bring about quick, complete and fundamental structural change in schools in an aggressive, detached, authoritarian way may have fulfilled the common expectations of masculinity, but proved dysfunctional in organizations whose culture can be described in gender terms as a mixture of masculine and feminine. Interestingly, the heads who replaced them were chosen to 'nurse' the schools back to health, a far more 'feminine' concept.

Using a gender perspective allows a more creative view of the management role. If management is to be effective it requires a balance of feminine and masculine skills. One reason why a more 'feminine' style of management may be appropriate for schools could be that feminine styles are more accepting of differences than male. Male styles are strongly conformist while female styles are much more tolerant of deviance (Gray, 1987). Also the very nature of management, dealing as it does with areas of uncertainty, negotiation and policy-making, draws on feminine qualities of intuition, aesthetic consider-ations, dependence on colleagues and so on.

If good management depends then on such a balance, exhortations to women to gain acceptance in a male-dominated world by becoming like men threatens to cut off an essential side to management. If women are encouraged to accept male norms as the price of organizational membership they are cut off from looking inward to their own female resources. Keller (1980) de-scribes, for example, a female cognitive style which avoids the negative, dismis-sive labels usually associated with women's perspectives. Its main elements are: 'artistic, sensitive, integrated, deep, intersubjective, empathic, open, aesthetic, receptive'. If this profile were socially valued women would have a very distinc-tive contribution to make to organizational life.

More and more writers are considering the positive attributes women can bring to the management role. Farrell (1986) talks about 'an integrative perspective' which considers not only changes in power and structure to bring about changes in organizations but focuses on the relationships between men and women in organizations, in the hope that this more holistic approach might help to remove sexism from the warp and weft of organizations. Mar-shall (1984) concludes that the major task for both men and women is the uniting of masculine and feminine opposites. Following their large-scale study into management, Cooper and Davidson (1984) proposed that both male and female styles of management be enhanced, male managers being trained to adopt more efficient, sensitive, sympathetic and co-operative management styles whilst women managers were given training in assertion and confidence skills. Some recent work on the subject of women's management styles (De Lyon and Migniuolo, 1989) highlights research in the USA that indicates that it is women's rather different approach to educational management that suc-ceeds. US schools with women in senior positions produce higher achievements in subjects like maths and there is less violence and higher morale.

What organizations may need in future is what Sargent (1983) identifies as the androgynous manager. She defines androgyny as an integration of masculine and feminine qualities and androgynous management as a style that blends be-haviours previously thought to belong exclusively to men or to women.

In so far as this study illuminates women's management styles as a distinc-tive and discrete phenomenon it may help achieve the kind of creative synthesis which Sargent sees as crucial for the continued health and survival of any organization.

More particularly if pupils are to be taught in an environment that encourages them to grow up and develop as they truly are – in that common psychological androgyny that all adults share, then Gray (1987) contends that 'the styles of management must show that there is no single "masculinity" or "femininity" in being an adult and no single gender model for management behaviour'.

REFERENCES

Acker, S. (1983) Women and teaching: a semi-detached sociology of a semi-profession, in S. Walker and L. Baron (eds.) *Gender, Class and Education*, pp. 123–39, Falmer Press, Barcombe.

Bacharach, S.B. and Lawler, E.J. (1980) *Power and Politics in Organisations*, Jossey Bass, San Francisco.

Burnham, P.S. (1964) The role of the Deputy Head in secondary schools. Unpublished MEd thesis, University of Leicester.

Burnham, P.S. (1969) Role theory and educational administration, in G. Baron and W. Taylor (eds.) *Educational Administration and the Social Sciences*, Athlone Press, London, Ch. 5, pp. 72–94.

Cartwright, D. and Zander, A. (1968) *Group Dynamics: Research and Theory*, Harper & Row, New York.

Cook, S.H. and Mendleson, J.L. (1984) The power wielders: man and/or women managers? *Industrial Management*, Vol. 26, no. 2, pp. 22–27.

Cooper, C.L. and Davidson, M. (1984) *Women in Management*, Heinemann, London.

Crosher, J. (1984) The pattern of employment of women teachers: a perspective, *Secondary Educational Journal*, Vol. 14, no. 2, pp. 16–18.

De Lyon, H. and Migniuolo, F. (1989) *Women Teachers*, Open University Press, Milton Keynes.

Gray, H.L. (1987) Gender consideration in school management: masculine and feminine leadership styles, *School Organisation*, Vol. 7, no. 3, pp. 297–302.

Green, R.L. (1953) *King Arthur and his Knights of the Round Table*, Penguin, Harmondsworth.

Handy, C. (1976) *Understanding Organisations*, Penguin, Harmondsworth.

John, D. (1973) Senior staff roles in secondary schools, *Trends in Education*, no. 30.

Johnson, D. (1984) Planning small-scale research, in J. Bell, T. Bush, A. Fox, J. Goodey and S. Goulding (eds.) *Conducting Small-Scale Investigations in Educational Management*, Paul Chapman, London.

Kanter, R.M. (1977) *Men and Women of the Corporation*, Basic Books, New York.

Keller, E. (1980) Feminist critique of science: a forward or backward move? *Fundamenta Scientia*, Vol. 1, pp. 341–9.

Marshall, J. (1983) The identity dilemmas of being a woman manager, *Equal Opportunities International*, Vol. 2, no. 2, pp. 28–33.

Marshall, J. (1984) *Women Managers: Travellers in a Male World*, Wiley, Chichester.

Marshall, J. (1985) Being a woman: paths of personal and professional development for women managers, *Management, Education and Development*, Vol. 16, Part 2, pp. 169–79.

Schmuck, P.A. (1986) School management and administration: an analysis by gender, in E. Hoyle and A. McMahon (eds.), *World Yearbook of Education – The Management of Schools*, Kogan Page, London.

Solomons, H. and Cramer (1985) When the differences don't make a difference: women and men as colleagues, *Management Education and Development*, Vol. 16, Part 2, pp. 155–68.

Stanworth, M. (1984) *Gender and Schooling*, Hutchinson & Co., London.

Torrington, D. and Weightman, J. (1989) *The Reality of School Management*, Blackwell Educational, Oxford.

Wade, D. (1989) Feminine ways to get on with the job, *The Sunday Times*, 12 March, C4.

15

HEADTEACHER APPRAISAL

Cyril Poster and Doreen Poster

[. . .] To say that headteachers had in the past been given little indication by their LEAs of the criteria under which they might be appraised is an understatement of some magnitude. Morgan, Hall and Mackay (1983) had in their research into secondary headteacher selection, the POST project as it became known, found 'only one of 85 LEAs which . . . provided a written description of its view of the full range of secondary heads' duties'. They [. . .] differentiated between generic and specific elements in the job descriptions, but found no instance of selectors using these elements to identify the requirements for a particular post. Two years later the same team, now completing a follow-up study on the role of the secondary headteacher, concluded that 'a satisfactory definition of headship must include how heads approach the job as well as the tasks they perform' (Hall, Morgan and Mackay, 1985).

APPRAISING AGAINST WHAT CRITERIA?

If it is important for the appraisal of assistant teachers that they have a clear concept of goals agreed with their managers and consonant with whole-school policy, then surely it is no less important that headteachers have the same clarity about *their* goals. Indeed, since their goals are very much the determinants of that whole-school policy, unless there is that clarity how can the performance of other teachers within the school be properly appraised? This question in its turn raises another crucial issue: with whom will headteachers clarify their goals?

Increasingly the weight of administrative and managerial responsibility is leading many headteachers, particularly of secondary schools and large primary schools, towards corporate or collegial management. The senior management team is no longer, as it was once in many schools, a convenient shorthand form for the headteacher, the deputies and possibly one or two other senior members of staff, but without any clear definition of the team's function. It is now coming to mean a group of senior staff who not only share with the headteacher the decision-making but also severally assume responsibility for particular areas of management. Readers will not need to be reminded that the ultimate responsibility rests with the headteacher; but, the more the school is charged with complex and innovatory task networks, the more delegation *with authority to act* becomes the necessary mode. Implementing and monitoring the introduction of the National Curriculum, for example, may in a primary school become part of the job specification of the deputy head, working according to guidelines planned with the headteacher. Undertaking the budgetary control required by the introduction of local financial management may similarly become the province of a senior teacher in a secondary school.

In the mid-1970s, Meredydd Hughes contributed a chapter entitled 'The professional-as-administrator: the case of the secondary school head' to a symposium edited by Peters (1976). In it he sought, on the evidence of an extensive research project, first to differentiate between two models of headship, the head as chief executive and the head as leading professional, and secondly to reconcile and unify the two models. It is now patently obvious that 'the specialized work of maintaining the organization in operation' (Barnard, 1938) can no longer be reserved to the headteacher as chief executive, but must be shared if headteachers are to survive. Even more to the point, if one accepts the contention by Hughes that 'the chief executive is concerned both with what happens within the organization *and with the relation of the organization to the wider system of which it is part*' [our italics], the increasing contact between individual members of the senior staff of schools and officers and advisers of the LEA of itself leads to a corporate concept of the chief executive role.

In his attempt to reconcile the chief executive role with the leading professional role, Hughes draws a distinction between the traditional and innovative aspects of a headteacher's professionalism, and concludes 'an innovating emphasis is more easily reconciled with the head's managerial responsibilities'. Today few educationists would talk about the 'traditional', but rather would differentiate between the maintenance and innovative functions of leadership. The message here is surely that, if all the members of the collegial team are successfully to combine the chief executive and the leading professional roles, they must each have within their job specifications goals which are concerned with maintenance and with innovation. Needless to say, this applies also to the headteacher.

If it is accepted that headteachers' successful management of their schools will be heavily dependent on the achievements, at all levels, of their staff, it would seem to follow that their appraisal ought to focus largely on the processes of management rather than the quantifiable outcomes. Much energy is currently being expended on seeking to set up batteries of performance indicators whereby one school can be measured against another. Accountability is, of course, the vogue word for the new decade; but it may well be that the expenditure of energy and ingenuity in seeking measurements of 'throughputs' and 'outputs' will in the long run prove to be counterproductive to sound educational management. The appraisal of headteachers ought primarily to be concerned with the extent to which, on the one hand, they have facilitated, inspired, planned, evaluated and stabilized within the school; and, on the other hand, sought and achieved for the school a public image as a caring centre of learning. It is not easy to find measuring rods which will quantify achievements in these domains.

APPRAISING HEADTEACHERS

In one respect the role of headteachers is unique: however much they may have shared or devolved responsibility, they are the members of staff who are wholly accountable to their governing bodies and their LEAs for what goes on in their schools. Their appraisal must therefore look inward, to the success of their leadership of the school, and outward to the success of their relations with governors, LEAs and the public and their implementation of local and national policy. Not surprising, then, is the following recommendation (para 19) by the National Steering Group (DES, 1989): 'The pilot projects have demonstrated the advantages of arrangements in which headteachers are appraised by two appraisers. The additional appraiser adds a valuable further perspective on the complex job of the head and can assist in the task of collecting data for the appraisal.'

The draft National Framework (DES, 1990b) specifies that 'one of the two appraisers should be an officer of the LEA' and that 'where one appraiser is expected to play a larger role than the other' that person should have 'experience as a headteacher relevant to conditions in the phase in which the appraisee head works'.

There are two ways in which an LEA can nominate the peer group appraiser: it can identify from among its practising primary and secondary headteachers a number who will be offered secondment for a given period to act as headteacher appraisers; or it can identify a considerably larger number who will continue in post but be allowed extra staffing to compensate for the time that they will be engaged in appraisal activities. For this latter group, the NSG report recommends that a serving headteacher 'should not be involved in the appraisal programme of more than three other headteachers at any one time' (para 23).

The former proposal has the advantage that, as experience in this role grows, so will the expertise. This superintendent model, as it is generally described, was wholeheartedly commended by Graham in *Those Having Torches* (Suffolk LEA, 1985): 'We would . . . assert quite definitely that the "promotion" of experienced headteachers to fill this role [of area superintendents] is the only acceptable and logical way forward.' Later, in his contribution to the DES appraisal conference (DES, 1986), Graham waxed even more lyrical:

> I predict that we will find that a new breed of animal will emerge – from
> the ranks of heads, advisers, teachers, officers – those with a particular
> expertise in an exacting craft, and that they will conduct assessment of
> senior staff, and supervise the wider process within schools and in part-
> nership with heads.

This 'new breed of animal' has clearly not found favour with the NSG or with
the teaching profession at large. Even the phrase 'in partnership' does little to
ease the disquiet that 'conduct assessment' and 'supervise the . . . process' give
rise to.

Nevertheless, the rejection of the concept of superperson-appraiser does not
of itself rule out the concept of seconded headteachers. An obvious disadvantage lies in the fact that those selected for this role might well be seen by their
peers as increasingly losing touch with the day-to-day realities of running a
school, such is the rate of change in education today. There are problems too
for the LEA in selecting the secondees. The highly successful headteacher may
not be as enamoured as some might think with the prospect of being seconded
for, say, a three-year stint. Some headteachers well known to us who were
seconded to regional posts in the heyday of TVEI, for example, found re-entry
to their former posts not without attendant problems, some of which have
taken months, even years, to overcome. Furthermore, governing bodies have
now a far greater responsibility for decision-making in such situations. In
many parts of the country good applicants for headteacher posts are becoming
increasingly difficult to find; and why should we, some governors may think,
lose our good headteacher to an LEA secondment and have to face the daunting prospect of finding and working with a temporary substitute?

There is a strong possibility, then, that LEAs who wish to follow the path of
finding full-time appraisers for headteachers will make appointments rather
than seek agreement from governing bodies for secondments, looking particularly towards those who are within a few years of retirement. One issue
here is that many secondary headteachers so appointed would, if they were not
to be financially disadvantaged, have to be placed on salary scales that made
them senior to, for example, all advisers other than the chief adviser, a situation that would not be without repercussions for the good relations of CEOs
with their professional staff. Another issue is that the advent into the LEA
structure of a number of such postholders directly from long experience of
management 'from their side of the fence' may well lead to problems of assim-
ilation with existing LEA staff.

The alternative proposal is also not without its problems. At a time when
open enrolment under the conditions of the Education Reform Act 1988 is
forcing schools into the competitive mode, into 'marketing' as the profession is
reluctantly learning to call it, the selection of peer appraisers is a matter of
considerable delicacy. In circumstances other than those imposed on headteachers by the present climate, there would be much to be said for peer
appraisers being selected from within primary and secondary consortia of
schools. There would be an expectation of greater understanding of the issues
of the immediate neighbourhood; local colleagues would be better known and

their presence in the school would be less of a threat; corporate approaches to issues raised by appraisal would be likely to develop; the role of the appraiser as 'critical friend' would be easier to establish. Yet we have to face realities and accept that for many LEAs in today's climate this is a pipe dream.

The number of peer group headteacher appraisers that will be required, one-third of the total number of headteachers in the LEA, poses a further problem. Clearly, newly appointed headteachers are unlikely to be selected: from their point of view selection would be undesirable since they would regard themselves, even if they were already experienced headteachers, as having much to learn in their new LEA or new school or about their new colleagues; and from the LEA's point of view since they would lack credibility with their peers. If those on the verge of retirement and those whose own performance as headteachers renders them unlikely choices are removed from consideration, it seems very probable that the LEA will find their field of choice restricted to at best one in two of those eligible. Among these will be a number who will be too heavily committed with other LEA responsibilities to take on this additional role, and others who will prefer not to engage, in the current climate of rapid change and stress, in any commitments beyond those for which they are statutorily responsible.

It is therefore not too far-fetched to suggest that there will be some LEAs with too few headteachers willing and able to take on this role to make peer appraisal viable; and these LEAs will perforce have to opt for the superintendent model. Alternatively, LEAs and the DFE may find unworkable the recommendation of para 23 that a serving headteacher 'should not be involved in the appraisal programme of more than three other headteachers at any one time'. Indeed, it has already been observed that, on a biennial appraisal cycle, the time cost for the peer appraiser is not evenly balanced between the two years and that an increase to four appraisals which 'Box and Cox' would not be unduly burdensome.

We would not wish to make too much of these difficulties, though it would be poor management of the innovation if they were not given full consideration before decisions were taken which all parties might regret. If the introduction of appraisal is phased in over a number of years, as we are led to believe will be the case, there will come on line a succession of headteachers who, having themselves been through a biennial cycle and having gained experience of appraising within their own schools, will have the confidence and experience to take on the appraiser role for their own peer colleagues. At the same time it must be recognized that experience as appraiser within one's own school and as peer appraisee contributes to but does not equate with understanding of the role of peer appraiser. There would be a grave danger of the dilution of the necessary skills if this kind of cascade model were of itself considered all that was required.

The total time commitment for peer appraisers for their role in each headteacher appraisal is, we calculate, four to five days, possibly diminishing to three to four in the second and subsequent cycles. Details of how that estimate is arrived at are included in the sections which follow.

COMPONENTS OF HEADTEACHER APPRAISAL

Whether the appraisers are superintendent or peer, they will need to familiarize themselves with the circumstances of each school. This is not to be confused with data collection, much of which will be the responsibility of the CEO's officer or adviser. Rather it is because it is necessary for the appraiser to view the school in the light of its own management style, structure and circumstances and not to apply to it extraneous criteria.

Some idea of the context and the manner in which the school operates will be gleaned from a reading of the school's development plan, which will include a statement of its aims and objectives; of the staff handbook; of information prepared for parents at various stages of a pupil's passage through the school; and possibly of newsletters and other similar public materials. We would expect this activity, certainly for a secondary school, to occupy the appraiser for at least half a day. Ideally it should be followed by a discussion with the appraisee in which there can be further elucidation. However, it is more likely that, with time a valuable commodity, such a discussion will be incorporated in the initial meeting, for which a further half day must be allocated.

Initial meeting

If there is not to be suspicion on the part of the appraisee that, in some covert way, judgements are being made, it is essential that there is open behaviour and agreement over the way information will be collected: 'The clarification of sources and methods of collecting information for the appraisal [is] a particularly important function of this meeting for heads, given the diversity of their work' (DES, 1989, para 51). Furthermore, because it is clear that an appraisal interview can be no more than a sampling procedure, it is important that particular areas of focus are established and agreed. There are two arguments against the selection of these areas of focus at the beginning of the biennial cycle that we would like to refute.

The first is that, if headteachers know what they are being appraised on, they will bend all their energies to these targets at the expense of others. This is both cynical and unrealistic. Headteachers are nowadays required to manage highly complex institutions and cannot afford to let their management priorities become subordinated to mere self-interest. Furthermore, all managerial tasks are interdependent and the weakening of effort in one direction would undoubtedly have repercussions in others.

The second, a more reasonable argument, is that priorities may change over the biennial cycle. Although the selection should in fact be made not on priorities but on aspects of the headteacher's role which will give a broad view of managerial competency, there is no reason why there should not be a modification of the appraisal goals if this is the wish and in the best interest of the appraisee.

The selection of more than three areas of focus is counterproductive. In an appraisal interview of a headteacher it is extremely unlikely that the discussion of any major topic will take less than half an hour. No item of the appraisal agenda should be dealt with cursorily because time presses. If the true purposes of appraisal are to be met then it should be borne in mind that 'There is . . . benefit to be gained from the examination in depth of a few specific areas, provided that the selection is balanced and that key aspects of the head's work are not neglected over a long period' (*ibid*, para 52).

Self-appraisal

This activity is as important for headteachers as for all other members of staff. In one sense it is more important, since managerial goals are often long term and achievement may be less easy to evaluate. Headteachers, occupied as they are with the introduction of major innovations alongside dealing with day-to-day crises, can easily lose sight of their successes.

Although its use is recommended by the NSG (para 53) we have serious doubts about the applicability to headteachers of the proforma set out in Appendix B of the ACAS report. It is possible that some headteachers will not need any kind of proforma or prompt list, but for those who do we have

---

For each of the headings below where *in the period under review* you believe you have had a significant role, list the goal(s) which you set yourself. Assess the extent to which you have *so far* succeeded in meeting those goals.

What circumstances have helped you?
What have hindered you?

The development of . . .
- the school as a centre of learning
- the school as a caring institution
- the quality and contribution of the staff through in-service training and other means
- the managerial structure and style of the school

relationships with . . .
- staff, both teaching and ancillary
- parents
- the governing body
- the LEA
- the neighbourhood or community

the management of . . .
- the school budget
- the school fabric

liaison with . . .
- other schools and educational institutions to which pupils go/from which pupils come
- local business and industry

and finally . . .
- your personal development in this post
- any other goals

Of these, which do you regard as the area which has given you the most satisfaction? Which the least satisfaction?

© Routledge 1991

Figure 15.1   Prompt list: headteacher self-appraisal

devised one which is shown in Figure 15.1. It is not intended to be worked through from beginning to end, but rather to act as a series of reminders of areas of focus on which the headteacher might like to comment in preparation for the appraisal interview. Indeed, there is some merit in its more frequent, personal use, since it acts as a reminder of things achieved and may therefore be very reassuring. Those who have trialled it confirm that it acts as a useful focus for their consideration of their own performance.

Collection of information

The NSG report cites (para 54) the following sources of information useful to appraisers:

- publicly available data relating to the work of the school;
- task and/or classroom observation;
- interviews with staff, governors and parents;
- consultation with LEA officers and advisers.

Publicly available data

Some of this will have been covered in the peer appraiser's preparatory work. Other information will be known to the liaison adviser, described variously as the 'patch' adviser, pastoral adviser, consortium adviser or such other title as the LEA has coined. How public is *public*? We would suggest that *professionally available* is a better term, since the data must of necessity include matters about staffing, for example, not known to the public, or matters the knowledge of which is restricted to governors. Many authorities have recently become aware, as a consequence of the Education Reform Act and, in particular, the introduction of appraisal, that there are serious shortcomings in the communications system between the liaison adviser and phase and subject specialist advisers and advisory teachers. Some LEAs have begun to use information technology to remedy this defect.

Task and/or classroom observation

Except for those primary headteachers of small schools who have a full or nearly full timetable commitment, we can see little merit in classroom observation, unless the headteacher should specifically request it. The only plausible ground for such a request, we believe, is where the headteacher wishes to demonstrate to staff credibility as a practitioner; and in such cases we suggest that the observer might well be the curriculum co-ordinator or head of department of the subject being taught.

Task observation is another matter. For this, *shadowing* is one possibility. This entails the peer appraiser or the adviser accompanying the headteacher for a full day, or, better still, several half days, recording – with agreement –

activities and their outcomes and at the end of the period sharing impressions. This is a strategy used by many researchers (Richardson, 1973; Lyons, 1974; Hall, Mackay and Morgan, 1986) which participants have found valuable as a learning experience and often very revealing of the way they manage time.

Another strategy is for the headteacher to nominate a particular activity to be observed over a number of occasions. This might well be the introduction of a new practice in management: the first stage being the presentation to staff, giving the appraiser an opportunity to observe the way in which the head-teacher conducts a meeting; continuing by means of a log maintained by the headteacher and made available to the appraiser of relevant discussions and decisions since the initial presentation; and concluding with the meeting at which decisions are reached or promulgated. This is, of course, a time-consuming activity; but given that the local adviser would expect to visit the school on a number of occasions in any case, this might not so much add to that number as give further purpose to the visits.

Interviews with staff, governors and parents

We have serious reservations as to the propriety or efficacy of this strategy for the collection of information. First, we are dubious that it will contribute significantly to the data being collected, since there will not be the time for interviews with a representative sample of any of these groups, in particular of parents. Secondly, while the Code of Practice [. . .] is excellent as guidance for interviewers, and its purpose well understood by professionals, it will be very difficult to impose upon lay interviewees. Thirdly, we do not think it accords with the principle of open behaviour, which we have advocated as essential to any appraisal system, if these interviews do not take place in the presence of the headteacher; but, for parents in particular and for some staff, that may in itself be inhibiting.

We do not doubt that it is important that the voices of these groups are heard. Indeed, we are surprised at the exclusion of the prime client group of the school, the pupils. We suggest, however, that there are other, more general ways of collecting information from these groups: through an open staff meeting about general issues facing the staff; through the governors' meetings which liaison advisers or other representatives of the CEO will attend as a normal part of their duties; through the annual meeting for the school parent body or, more advant-ageously since they will undoubtedly be better attended and more representative, open or report evenings; and through a visit to classes to glean the impressions of pupils. In all these situations control of the observation of the Code of Practice rests with the appraisers. Except for the governors' meeting, at which the pres-ence of peer appraisers would be *ultra vires*, the attendance of either appraiser will be readily accepted or will pass unnoticed.

Consultation with LEA officers and advisers

We have already indicated [. . .] that LEAs need to devise, if they are not already in existence, effective systems for the collation of the written – and, we

trust, open – comments by members of the CEO's advisory staff on visits to the
school. Some of these visits will be formal, as when performance indicators are
being used to evaluate a school's performance. Others will be less formal, as
advisers and advisory teachers act in a supportive way to aid the school in its
development: its introduction of new aspects of the National Curriculum, for
example, or of local financial management. There will, however, on occasions
be the need to ask a particular officer or adviser for a specific update of
information, especially where the key result area being appraised lies within a
specialist field. The way in which special educational needs are being coped
with in the school is one instance; its personal, social and health education
programme another. It is important that the local adviser acts as a filter so that
the peer appraiser is not overloaded with irrelevant information. Equally, he or
she must be well informed on those areas which are on the agenda for the
appraisal interview.

Length of data collection period

It is difficult to follow the reasoning of the NSG in the recommendation (para
59) that the length of the data collection period 'should not normally be longer
than one term'. Understandably, the data should not include matters about
which all concerned will have to delve into their memories, but many managerial activities of necessity spread over quite lengthy periods. If one of the
purposes of appraisal is to enable the appraisee to assess the appropriateness of
a sequence of activities, there is little point in restricting the data to the most
recent events. The management of innovation follows a well-established cycle:
planning – preparation – performance – evaluation – stabilization. It is unrealistic to appraise the headteacher's role in that process by looking only at that
part which took place in a restricted period of time.

Conclusion

It is accepted that most of the data collection will be the responsibility of the
local adviser. Nevertheless, the peer appraiser must have some direct observation to bring to the appraisal interview, occupying in aggregate at least a
day, and must also spend some time with the adviser, both to discuss the data
and to plan the agenda and strategy for the appraisal interview itself. Finally, it
is advisable for both appraisers to be present when the agenda is agreed with
the appraisee, even though this may prove to be a mere formality.

The appraisal interview

This is rightly regarded as 'the central feature of appraisal for headteachers, as
it has been for teachers' (para 57). It should be conducted by the peer appraiser. The local adviser is thus free to take notes from which the appraisal
statement will be prepared and is likely to intervene only in order to give

information, clarify a situation or correct a misapprehension. Over many years of experience in interviewing we have come to appreciate that, in a duologue, after a short time the presence of a third party goes unnoticed, particularly when that person is already well known to the other two. On the other hand, being questioned by two or more very rapidly takes the 'conversation with a purpose' into the realms of an inquisition, in which interviewees rapidly find themselves adjusting their responses to the questioner rather than the questions. The formal interview that is part of most staffing appointments, for example, is likened by many at the receiving end to a game or competition in which their task is to satisfy the expectations of the interviewers, sometimes even the differing expectations of different interviewers, rather than to set their educational philosophy and skills in the balance against the demands of the post. The climate and the purpose of the appraisal interview must therefore be firmly established in the minds of all the participants. It must be remembered too that headteachers have, as appraisers, established their personal styles for the appraisals they have conducted and will therefore have certain expectations of how their own appraisals will be conducted. It is therefore important that the process is clearly explained and understood.

We reiterate, even more strongly if that is possible, our view that 'professional targets for action' (para 49) should be agreed, not at the appraisal interview, but on a separate occasion. That there will be some identification at the appraisal interview of actions to be taken and goals set – by no means the same thing – we accept. However, we remain convinced, as do most of those with whom we have worked, that it is asking too much of appraisees to focus in the same interview both on the appraisal of the activities of the previous biennium and on the identification of goals for that to come.

The appraisal statement

It follows from what we have suggested as the key role for advisers in the appraisal interview that they are the ones best placed to draw up the appraisal statement. This should be done without delay while the interview is fresh in the minds of all three participants. The draft needs to be considered by the peer appraiser and then agreed by the appraisee in the presence of both. It is now that it becomes possible to begin to consider goal setting, since agreement on the statement may be no more than a formality; but we would still sound a note of caution, since the climate may well continue to be retrospective rather than prospective and possibly not yet right for establishing future targets.

Follow-up and formal review meeting

As with other members of staff, this is an important element of the appraisal process. Follow-up, however, is less easy to bring about informally, certainly for the peer appraiser. Ideally one would like to see the concept of the 'critical friend' take root, whereby appraisees develop a relationship with their peer appraisers that enables them to contact them on the phone and ask for a meeting to tease out some particular issue that is associated with their previous appraisal or their current goals. For many headteachers the role is a lonely one and it is undoubtedly of benefit to share difficulties and successes; but the long history of the concept of 'captain of the ship', solely responsible for all that happens therein, even to the extent of going down with it rather than sending out a Mayday signal, dies hard. The more exacting the demands of the teaching profession, the more we ought to be looking at ways of breaking down traditional isolationism.

The formal review is easier to establish as a procedure. Without in any way attempting to conduct a mini-appraisal, the appraisers need to explore with the appraisee the way in which progress to declared goals is going. The appraisee should regard this as an opportunity: to point out unanticipated constraints, to seek resources, to discuss further training needs that have arisen since the appraisal and to test out perceptions of the progress that is being made.

We have seen in the past decade many of the barriers between headteacher colleagues breaking down, so that the sharing of problems is becoming more commonplace. Regrettably we still see too many examples of the lack of mutual understanding and respect between headteachers and advisers, often caused by a lack of appreciation on the part of the former of the tremendous increase in the range of tasks required of advisers and, despite the excellent work of the Centre for Adviser and Inspector Development (CAID) at Woolley Hall, of inadequate in-service training for advisers. Headteacher appraisal conducted by advisers and headteachers may do much to improve this relationship, as the two arms of the education service are seen increasingly as interdependent.

THE SCHOOL DEVELOPMENT PLAN

While it is important to distinguish between the appraisal of the headteacher and the review or audit of the School Development Plan (DES, 1990a), there is nevertheless a symbiotic relationship between the two. The School Development Plan is the joint responsibility of the staff and in particular the headteacher, the governing body and the LEA. It has to conform to the conditions set by both local and central government, but at the same time must reflect the distinctive nature of the neighbourhood in which the school physically exists and the community with which it relates and which it must serve. It is incumbent on every school to have a development plan and on every governing body and LEA to review it periodically. The ability of the institution to deliver the development plan is conditioned by the material and human resources available to it.

It is within this context that the appraisal of all staff necessarily falls. Their successes as teachers and managers will lead to the successful implementation of the development plan. For the classroom teacher some immediate goals will be easily perceived as relating to specific areas of the development plan:

curriculum development leading to the [. . .] consolidation of the National Curriculum is an obvious example. There will, however, be other areas of the development plan which they will perceive as relevant to the school as an institution but not so readily identifiable in terms of personal goals: the implementation of local management of schools, for example.

Those with senior managerial responsibility, and particularly the headteacher, have a heightened perception of these long-term goals, since they relate more particularly to the areas of management for which they are responsible. Yet no individual, not even the headteacher, can be appraised on institutional goals. They are appraised on their agreed and contracted contribution to the realization of that whole-school policy, not on the success or failure of the implementation of that policy.

One important reason for making this plain is that no LEA is likely to have the manpower to conduct development plan reviews to coincide with the biennial appraisal cycle; indeed, even if there were the human resources, we would question whether the enterprise was worth undertaking, since taking the watch to pieces to see what makes it tick usually results in its failure as an accurate timepiece. What is needed, however, is a temporal relationship between the appraisal of the headteacher and the review of the School Development Plan.

One LEA is currently proposing a cycle on these lines:

Year 1: School development review;
Year 2: Headteacher appraisal;
Year 3: Review update;
Year 4: Headteacher appraisal.

The review update would be undertaken by the local or phase adviser and would utilize the feedback from curriculum area and other visitations over the previous biennium. This interweaving of the personal element, the appraisal of the headteacher, with the institutional element, the review of the School Development Plan, brings into correct focus the relationship between the two, while making clear that they have different objectives.

REFERENCES

Barnard, C.I. (1938) *The Functions of the Executive*, Harvard University Press, Cambridge, Mass.

DES (1986) *Better Schools: Evaluation and Appraisal Conference*, HMSO, London.

DES (1989) Circular letter 'Report of the National Steering Group and the Government's Response', 2 October 1989.

DES (1990a) *Planning for School Development*, DES, London.

DES (1990b) draft of *School Teacher Appraisal: The National Framework*, DES, London.

Hall, V., Morgan, C. and Mackay, H. (1985) Defining headship – an impossible task? Secondary Heads' Association Review, London.

Hall, V., Mackay, H. and Morgan, C. (1986) *Headteachers at Work*, Open University Press, Milton Keynes.

Lyons, G. (1974) *The Administrative Tasks of Head and Senior Teachers in Large Secondary Schools*, University of Bristol, Bristol.

Morgan, C., Hall, V. and Mackay, H. (1983) *The Selection of Secondary Headteachers*, Open University Press, Milton Keynes.

Peters, R.S. (ed.) (1976) *The Role of the Head*, Routledge & Kegan Paul, London.

Richardson, E. (1973) *The Teacher, the School and the Task of Management*, Heinemann, London.

Suffolk LEA (1985) *Those Having Torches*, Suffolk Education Department, Ipswich.

PART 5:

The School and its Environment

16

PARENT–TEACHER PARTNERSHIP:
A Minimum Programme and a Signed Understanding

Alastair Macbeth

This material has been abridged

There are some signs that, among teachers, proclamation of parent–teacher partnership exceeds implementation. The Plowden Report (CACE, 1967, para 104) noted this tendency: 'In the course of our visits to schools, we were almost invariably told by heads that "we have very good relations with parents", however rudimentary the arrangements made.'

Practice has improved since 1967. One sign is that the 'minimum programme' advocated by the Plowden Report itself (para 112) now seems somewhat rudimentary: welcome to the school when a child is first admitted, at least two private consultations a year, open days, information booklets, clear written reports and some home visiting. Worthy objectives, and I shall return to them, but advances since then in our understanding of the educational importance of parents, although far from complete, suggest that rather more, both in terms of detail and of range, should be included in any minimum programme. To be fair to the Plowden Committee, they did also urge parental choice between schools (now consolidated by the 1980 and 1988 Acts), the development of the community school concept, the need to interest parents early, and the involvement of parents in extracurricular activities; but these were not part of their minimum programme.

The history of education has been one of constantly revising objectives, standards and techniques. Now, many years after Plowden, could be the right time to consider an updated minimum programme related to current knowledge and based on techniques which have been shown to be practicable. I shall offer for consideration such a revised minimum programme, but also go beyond it with additional ideas. I am limiting myself to the compulsory education age, so that those concerned with preschool (where parents are immensely important) may be disappointed, and I do not cover the difficulties of those who teach children with special educational needs (where, again, parents are crucial), nor the post-16 level at which young people replace parents as the school's main clients. [. . .] The ultimate test is always: is this to the educational benefit of children?

A REVISED MINIMUM PROGRAMME OF PARENT–TEACHER LIAISON

I consider that no school can honestly argue that it is treating its parents professionally as both clients and educational partners unless it initiates something comparable to the following twelve-point programme. It will be seen that some points in the programme relate to parents individually as those responsible for their child's education, while others are concerned with the parents as a group.

(1) The school might have a **welcoming system** not only when the child is first admitted, but all the time: welcoming both in the sense of being courteous and friendly and in the sense of encouraging parents to feel that they are part of the school community rather than outsiders. In terms of organization, this might include arrangements by which parents coming to the school always receive rapid and considerate attention.

(2) There should be a **written report or profile** on each child presented to his/her parents at least twice a year with thorough comments by teachers about the child's attainment, effort and behaviour, with a tear-off section containing questions about the child's progress to which parents are expected to reply. An assessment, a record and a planning document, the report should be the agenda for:

(3) **a consultation,** at least twice a year, private between parent(s) and teacher(s) of the child, with the report as the starting point, to plan the next phase of the child's learning. The reports and the consultations should not be seen as exchangeable alternatives; they are distinct, but related, actions.

(4) At least termly there might be a **class meeting** to explain to those parents with children in the same class (or age-group at upper secondary level) the nature of the coming term's curriculum and how parents can reinforce it in the home.

(5) **A parents' association** for the school (with class units) should be open to all parents with children in the school. It should not be run by teachers, though teachers should assist when asked by parents, especially in providing information. Its main concerns should be educational provision and parent–teacher links, its main functions consultation and information. Duplicating facilities and use of school buildings should be available free to the association at times which suit parents. Fund-raising should not be part of its remit, except to finance improved home–school liaison.

(6) **A governing body** (in Scotland a school board) for each school should make accountability of parents and teachers in regard to their educational obligations its main task. It should be recognized that the structure and

purposes of the parents' association and the governing body are different but mutually reinforcing.

(7) **Publications** by the school, to keep parents informed, should be prepared in collaboration with the parents' association.

(8) Parents should have the right to see, at any reasonable time, all **official records on their child held either by the school or by the education authority** (with certain exceptions . . .); and should have a means to challenge and correct inaccuracies or misrepresentations. The child's school record/file should be available at private consultations and the attention of parents drawn to any new entries. Apart from certain confidential references, no fact, assessment or opinion about the child should be conveyed in writing or by word of mouth by any member of the education service to anyone outside the education service unless it appears on the official record. [. . .]

(9) **Education according to parental wishes** is a principle already established in statute law. That law is not limited to choice between schools, though that is important. A list of main determinant decisions (e.g. setting, streaming, subject options, remedial provision, public examinations to be taken and when, transfer to another school, etc.) might be drawn up by each school's governing body or school board. Not only should the parent(s) be consulted in regard to main determinant decisions affecting their child, but in the case of disagreement in regard to a child of school age, every effort might be made to accommodate parental wishes 'so far as is compatible with the provision of efficient instruction and training and the avoidance of unreasonable public expenditure' (Education Act, 1944, Sect. 76). After the age of 16 the young person's wishes should predominate on the same conditions.

(10) A system of **home-visiting** might operate for exceptional circumstances.

(11) Teachers might constantly stress that they provide **both a service and a partnership**. Service implies the dedication of teachers' specialist skills and expertise to assist parents in fulfilling their parental duty on behalf of children. That service may, on occasions, involve expressing views contrary to those of parents. Partnership recognizes that much education happens in the home and that parents and teachers have differing but complementary educational functions which must operate in harmony to be most effective. Thus schooling is provided by teachers in a way which is responsive to parental wishes and in conjunction with parents' co-educative actions, but within an administrative and curricular framework informed by professional judgement.

(12) Teachers should also make it clear in their dealings with parents that although they provide a professional service for parents and act as partners with them, they are also **employees of the education authority** and they must operate within the objectives, systems and constraints laid down by both national and regional democratic processes. On occasions this may involve denying parental wishes or even checking upon parents (e.g. in regard to school attendance) on behalf of the state, for the welfare

of children. It may also mean parents providing information to the school. In brief, parents should to some degree be accountable to teachers, as teachers are to them.

Several points may be noted about this minimum programme. First, it accepts the philosophy embedded in current British law and normal in Europe that parents, not schools, are primarily responsible for their child's education. The programme does not represent radical change so much as rationalization of the existing position. Secondly, all the concepts are already operating somewhere to some degree. They are all practicable, and most are familiar to British teachers. Thirdly, the programme is a basic minimum, not a professional optimum. Schools can build upon it and, hopefully, in a decade's time it will appear to be insufficient as a basic minimum.

Fourthly, although an education authority may wish to adopt such a programme, most of the actions can be introduced by an individual school without waiting for national or regional instructions. Some details may need to be negotiated with the education authority, such as in areas where guidelines already exist about access to school records, but generally schools can take the initiatives themselves. Indeed, an individual teacher can (and some do) adopt much of the programme as personal practice. Hopefully, however, a programme of this sort may become mandatory in due time.

It was deliberate that fund-raising, the use of parents to carry out menial chores in the school, social events, speech days, extracurricular activities involving parents, open days and a variety of other activities commonly included as home–school liaison were *not* part of the minimum programme. Such activities, in my view, should be treated as peripheral and subsidiary to the main educational purposes and actions involving parents.

IMPEDIMENTS

A note of caution, even of pessimism, may be appropriate, for although this chapter seeks to advance positive suggestions to assist the growth of collaboration between parents and teachers, it must be recognized that there are problems to be faced. As Cullingford (1985, p. 7) asserts, 'there has been a significant rise in the involvement of parents in schools, and many successful experiments. But even in the best examples it is clear that the mutual suspicion between parents and teachers continues. Beneath the surface of well-intended meetings lies misunderstanding and indifference.'

Clearly the introduction of a programme such as I have outlined above in a school which does not already do these things will give rise to anxieties and difficulties. [. . .] But there are broader, more pervasive impediments which warrant preliminary mention. I shall consider these under [three] headings:

(1) Parental inhibitions and the signed understanding;
[. . .]
(2) Resources;
(3) Teachers' attitudes.

Parental inhibitions and the signed understanding

It is easier for parents *not* to liaise with schools than it is to do so. There are quite practical deterrents. For instance, it is usually assumed that to have contact, parents must go to teachers, not vice versa. To get to the school often requires time and expense of travel, and may involve finding someone to care for younger children at home. If contact is during school hours, some parents, especially fathers, may be prevented by work commitments, and if it is in the evenings or at weekends it may cut across other activities. Cultural differences, including language problems, can also deter some. School events to which they are invited may be unattractively advertised or irrelevant to their own child's schooling. Further, schools are sometimes cold, unwelcoming places and parents may retain distressing memories of their own schooldays.

Some schools make great efforts to overcome these deterrents, but they may still find the parental response to be disappointing. Why? The answer must surely lie in the realm of attitudes. Attitudes are a preparedness to act or not to act; and they are learned. There can be little doubt that many parents harbour an assumption that they are irrelevant to the schooling process. There is a substantial literature on attitudes and on attitude change. To belabour it here would be unproductive. However, it is worth noting that the more firmly a pre-existing attitude is held and the more often it is reinforced by those whose views are respected, the more difficult it is to change it. That parents have been on the periphery of schooling for so long, that this position is generally accepted by most parents, and that teachers, whose views are respected, reinforce this assumption – all these make a change of attitude difficult to achieve. It is therefore not just a matter of *permitting* parental involvement; the idea requires a 'hard sell' by determined teachers, supported by well-informed publicity. Indeed, such a campaign could go beyond mere exhortation (which has produced only patchy effects in the past) and aim to generate a sense of obligation. It is my view that, rather than implying to parents that liaison is optional, emphasis should be upon the responsibilities of parenthood, the legal duty of parents to provide education and the knowledge that active interest and co-operation by parents is likely to help the child to benefit from schooling. While the sales pitch by the school can be friendly, it must also be tough.

The twelve-point minimum programme for liaison listed above is a set of obligations on the school. However, there might be a comparable set of obligations upon parents. Since public servants and bureaucrats are hired to provide a service, teachers can be required, as part of their conditions of employment, to fulfil obligations; but the position with parents is different. Parents fulfil obligations either because they are legally bound to do so or because they feel moral compulsion to do so, not because they are employed to do so.

Legal requirements on parents are relatively scant, apart from the one massive and fundamental duty to provide education for the child suitable to his/her age, ability and aptitude. That duty is vaguely worded and, apparently, easily satisfied by ensuring that the pupil attends school regularly. In such circumstances, how can a sense of obligation be brought home forcefully to all parents? What now follows is an attempt to answer that challenge. It is an idea which builds upon the common procedure by which parents with children in trouble, especially those who have been persistent truants or who are under threat of exclusion from school, are asked to sign documents of co-operation. I first proposed it in a report for the EEC (Macbeth *et al.*, 1984).

In outlining this procedure I am not suggesting that it is a necessary con-comitant of the twelve-point minimum programme of liaison which, I believe, can stand on its own. However, as a simple formality to give emphasis to parental obligations, it may have some appeal.

The proposal starts with the prime parental duty, established by law, for parents to provide education for their child. Schooling is not compulsory, education is. Although a small number of families do successfully educate their children themselves without the aid of a school, the vast majority depend on schools to enable them to fulfil their duty. The suggestion is that, in exchange for taking a child into a school (relieving parents of the technical burden of education minimally), parents would be asked to sign an understanding that they have obligations related to that schooling process. The document might have wording along the lines of the example [in Figure 16.1].

I suggest that a copy is signed by the father and another by the mother (to overcome awkward 'I/we' wording) and by the one parent in the case of a lone-parent family or guardian (or by whoever is legally responsible in the case of a divorced couple). While such a document would not be used as a legally binding contract (though some authorities might wish to develop it into that) it could be the basis of heightening awareness among all parents and of applying moral pressure on defaulting parents.

Two obvious questions arise: what would be done if parents refused to sign, and what would happen if parents who had signed then defaulted on their

---

I, being the parent/guardian of .... (name of child) acknowledge that **I understand**:

(1) that prime responsibility for my child's education rests with me by law;
(2) that the school will assist me to carry out that responsibility;
(3) that my active support for my child's schooling may increase his/her likelihood of gaining maximum benefit from it.

Further, **I undertake** to do the following to the best of my ability:
(a) to attend private consultations with my child's teacher(s) at mutually convenient times;
(b) to read written reports sent by the school and to respond to them;
(c) to attend class meetings or other meetings arranged to explain the curriculum and the ways in which it can be reinforced at home;
(d) to provide suitable conditions and support for my child's homework;
(e) to provide such information as the school shall require for educational purposes;
(f) to support school rules;
(g) to abide by decisions made by the headteacher and the governing body with regard to the school's management.

Signature of parent/guardian .... Date ....

[Figure 16.1 Possible wording for signed understanding of parents' obligations] undertaking? The answer to each would seem to be simple. In regard to refusal to sign, parents would be denied a place in the school for their child. The onus is on them to provide education for their individual child. The education authority's two duties are to make facilities available for children and to check that parents are carrying out their duty. Parents who refuse to sign the understanding would thus be declining a school place offered by the authority and would either have to pay for independent schooling or educate their child at home. The latter process can be inspected and, if it is found to be unsatisfactory, proceedings relating to non-attendance and culminating in prosecution can be initiated. It is normal for other state services – medical, dental and so on – to be subject to signed conditions, so why not schools? As with those services, the vast majority will see the reasonableness of the arrangement and will sign.

What, then, if parents default on the undertakings which they have given through signature? Suppose that a parent never comes to private consultations? It is my view that persuasive rather than legal proceedings should follow. Contact could be made with the parents (if necessary at the home) and the importance of parental support and involvement would be explained in terms of benefit to the child. Where the parent speaks a minority language, an interpreter should assist. It could be added that continued failure to provide the specific support could result in details being entered on the child's school record and the matter being reported to a subcommittee of the governing body/ school board before which the parents might be summoned. If contributory problems emerge they could be reported to other welfare agencies. It is not in the child's interest, in my view, to debar him/her from school in this circumstance. The parent who fails (perhaps for genuine reasons) to provide minimal educational support is different from the parent who refuses to sign the document as a matter of principle.

I am aware that the signed understanding is a leap into the unknown and may, for that reason, be unappealing at this stage. Whether or not it is employed, information and publicity of the importance of parental liaison with the school can still give emphasis to obligations. [. . .]

Resources

[. . .] Teachers' time is the most crucial resource, but we may consider others. [. . . An] advantage for any school is the presence of a senior, respected member of each school's staff who has the co-ordination of parent–teacher liaison as a specified duty. I use the words 'senior, respected' since the importance of the function in the eyes of colleagues will, to some extent, be influenced by who has the task. If a raw junior or an incompetent is charged with the responsibility for relations with parents, staff will tend to see the function as having low status.

Similarly, the quality of presentation of publications for parents – report forms, handbooks, brochures, advisory booklets, newspapers – can inadvertently convey a message about the importance, or otherwise, of the communication itself. Scrappy, duplicated documents suggest that collaboration does not matter. Professionally printed, imaginatively presented and well-illustrated publications are more likely to be read and respected. [. . .] The point here is that they cost money. Having analysed report forms and school handbooks from several parts of Europe, I am convinced that expenditure on good printing and presentation is money well spent.

Schooling is a labour-intensive industry. Almost three-quarters of its cost is on personnel, and much of the rest goes on buildings. Relatively, expenditure on liaison publications is trivial. But at a time of economic cutback, consumables always seem to be disproportionately hit. When stocks of textbooks are at a dangerously low level, it is difficult to argue for expenditure on high-quality printing. [. . .] The choice should not be between textbooks and parental liaison. Partnership should be funded by government, and funded generously because it is important. However, two practical suggestions for a time of scrimpiness are worth considering. The first is advertising. Some Continental school handbooks and the publications of most national parents' organizations offset costs by carrying advertisements. Schools can do the same. The second is delegation to the PTA/PA. [. . .] I argue passionately to remove the fund-raising function from parental organizations; it deters parents and diverts the PTA/PA from its educational objectives. I offer one grudging exception, and that is when a home–school liaison activity is delegated to it. If one of a PTA/PA's main reasons for existence is educational partnership, then governors or a head, while retaining a veto and insisting on high quality, can delegate to it authority to design and produce school report forms, handbooks, newspapers and so on, thereby ensuring that these documents contain not only what the school wants but also what parents want. That delegation can include the raising of necessary finance, though I would argue strongly against the PTA raising funds for anything else.

The cost of implementing the twelve points of my suggested minimum programme of liaison is not high. Lack of time and will rather than lack of money are the main barriers. [. . .] Funding of educational partnership ought ultimately to be a government responsibility.

Teachers' attitudes

If parents' attitudes are crucial to home–school partnership, those of teachers are no less so. [. . .]

[Their] discretion includes links with parents which is an educational and therefore to some extent a curricular issue. The extent of those links, ranging from disdain to genuine partnership, is determined by the philosophies and attitudes of headteachers and teachers. Those attitudes may have a blocking or an enabling effect, irrespective of parental attitudes.

Rutter and his team (1979) have valuably stamped the notion of school ethos on the consciousness of British education. Even though there may be variations from teacher to teacher, a school can have a character, an atmosphere, a predominant set of standards which distinguish it as a whole. Elsewhere (Macbeth *et al.*, 1984, pp. 195–9) four broad stages of progression in the growth of home–school partnership have been suggested. The following is an adaptation of that.

Stage 1: the self-contained school;
Stage 2: professional uncertainty;
Stage 3: growing commitment;
Stage 4: the school and family concordat.

The self-contained school stage is characterized by teachers assuming that the school is a closed institution neither affected by nor influencing families outside. It tends to be associated with teacher autonomy; limited and formalized contacts with parents; non-routine contacts being related to crises; little parental choice or consultation; parent associations discouraged or confined to trivia; parents denied access to school records about their child; teaching content and methods regarded defensively as the teachers' domain only.

The second stage, that of *professional uncertainty*, results from the spread of evidence about the value of home–school liaison, the growth of participatory trends and increased recognition of parents as clients. As some teachers come to acknowledge home factors, others remain entrenched, but may 'soften' to the extent of blaming home background for low pupil attainment. Administrative structures tend to remain as in stage 1, routine contacts with parents being formalized, but with some teachers tentatively experimenting with liaison techniques individually.

The third stage, that of *growing commitment*, witnesses the school leadership increasingly encouraging liaison with parents and adapting the system. Parents are more welcome in the school and they no longer have to report to an inquisitorial head on crossing its portal. Not only the governing body, but the PTA/PA is encouraged to discuss and deal with educational issues. Emphasis is put on the value of home–school liaison, and parents are encouraged to teach their children at home, dovetailing with the school curriculum which has been explained to them. Parental choice in the school and access to their child's records increase, two-way reports are introduced and consultations become private planning sessions.

The similarity of stage 3 to the minimum programme of liaison outlined earlier in this chapter will be obvious. What, then, is left for stage 4? The features which characterize the ultimate stage would be an emphasis on obligation, the attempt to involve all families and a recognition that home-learning is part of education, not merely background to education. Stage 3 exhorts and permits participation with the acceptance that not all families would be involved. The shift towards obligation in stage 4 anticipates the signed understanding which I have described in this chapter with the objective of committing all parents and teachers.

It is evident that each stage is determined by teachers, and by their attitudes – especially those of the headteacher. The leadership styles of headteachers have been the subject of research on both sides of the Atlantic [. . .]. The extent to which a head is autocratic or democratic, defends existing structures or encourages innovation, is prepared to reassess goals and is sensitive to staff and client needs, to research evidence and to changes in society – all these can have impact on a school's home–school ethos. It is not easy for enthusiastic junior staff to initiate a different approach when the head resists it, especially since some headteachers still believe that they have a duty to act as a barrier to 'protect' teachers from parents. There is limited evidence of headteachers' attitudes differing from those of staff. Lynch and Pimlott (1976), for instance, found that Southampton teachers were more supportive of home visiting than were heads. The importance of heads finding sufficient time to read about, think about and discuss both objectives and future action cannot be over-stressed; the danger is that busy-ness stifles business, a tendency noted in a recent study of headship (Hall, Mackay and Morgan, 1986).

I like the anecdote told against himself by one primary headteacher who had accepted the traditional Scottish schools' indifference towards parents. One evening, having worked late, he noticed a light still burning in a classroom. Investigating, he found a probationer teacher discussing education with a group of mothers who were helping to prepare materials. Next day, prepared to indicate displeasure at the parental invasion, he quizzed her about this departure from convention. It is to the credit of both head and probationer that this discussion led to a total change of school policy.

Yet it would be wrong to suggest that the headteacher holds the key to everything. Staff, too, must be convinced. Even when the leadership of a school introduces the structures of partnership with parents (e.g. class meetings, consultations, two-way reports, and the like) their effectiveness can be substantially neutralized by hostile colleagues. Most schools have a group of staff who resist change and we should not underestimate their influence. There is a need for pre-service, in-service and in-school training and developmental work.

To some teachers the twelve-point minimum programme of liaison which I outlined above will seem commonplace, tepid and lacking in originality, building as it does on the established and the conventional. To others it could seem daunting and a challenge to established routines or difficult to fit in with other demands on time. While most schools could tick off some of the twelve points as being part of their current practice, few would score twelve out of twelve. Time, effort and resources are needed in order to create new routines, but staff attitudes, based on professional understanding and confidence in their own performance, are perhaps the most crucial factors.

Why should some teachers be resistant to collaboration with parents? I would suggest the following are possible elements of that resistance.

(1) Some teachers may have become accustomed to functioning without parents being central to their work.
(2) They may feel that they have enough child-centred work and mounting professional strains without the additional pressures of entering a genuine educational partnership with parents.

(3) Some teachers may find parents threatening, especially teachers who are unaccustomed to working with parents.
(4) Teachers' contracts and hours of work are not drawn up to include educational partnership with parents.
(5) Few education authorities have paid much more than lip-service to the educational importance of parents. So teachers, reasonably, may tend to reflect the stance of their employers.
(6) Teachers are constantly under pressure to alter the content of teaching and their working methods. Changes in technology, economic and industrial expectations, public examination systems and political demands are current examples. At a time of change, priorities have to be established for the implementation of changes. Parents tend to get low priority.
(7) Some teachers may simply be unaware of all the reasons why parents are educationally central to their work.

There can be little doubt that it is easier for teachers *not* to enter into educational partnership with parents. Equally, it is easier for parents *not* to enter into educational partnership with teachers, but to 'leave it to the specialists'. The evidence suggests that such inaction is to the disadvantage of pupils and, in particular, would reinforce the inequalities of opportunity inherent in current practice. [. . .]

REFERENCES

Central Advisory Council For Education (England) (1967) *Children and their Primary Schools* (The Plowden Report), HMSO/DES, London.
Cullingford, C. (ed.) (1985) *Parents, Teachers and Schools*, Robert Royce.
Hall, V., Mackay, H. and Morgan, C. (1986) *Headteachers at Work*, Open University Press, Milton Keynes.
Lynch, J. and Pimlott, J. (1976) *Parents and Teachers*, Schools Council Research Studies/Macmillan, London.
Macbeth, A.M., Corner, T., Nisbet, S., Nisbet, A., Ryan, D. and Strachan, D. (1984) *The Child Between: a Report on School–Family Relations in the Countries of the European Community*, Commission of the European Communities, Studies Collection, Education Series, EEC.
Rutter, M., Maughan, B., Mortimore, P. and Ouston, J. (1979) *Fifteen Thousand Hours: Secondary Schools and their Effects on Children*, Open Books, Wells.

17

EDUCATIONAL REFORM AND SCHOOL GOVERNING BODIES IN ENGLAND 1986–92: Old Dogs, New Tricks or New Dogs, New Tricks?

Rosemary Deem

INTRODUCTION

'At the end of the day there's no area of the school I expect governors to run without me' (headteacher, Firdene Comprehensive School, 1991). This quote illustrates the view of one headteacher in England about the nature of his own relationship to his school's governing body during the 1990s, a perception which may well be shared by many other headteachers. But is such a perspective on lay school governors, whose responsibilities and powers have undergone dramatic transformation since the late 1980s, still an accurate one? In this chapter I am going to explore some ways in which we might come to a better understanding of the changes that have taken place in the roles and responsibilities of lay school governors in England and Wales since 1986, during a period of intense educational reform. This will include considering the consequences of these developments for educational managers. I shall draw upon a variety of evidence, including an Economic and Social Research Council-funded case-study of ten governing bodies in two different local education authorities, which I and Kevin Brehony conducted between 1988 and 1992. I suggest that educational reforms involving greater local and lay control over schools may have a considerable impact on the relationships between laypeople and education professionals. Furthermore, it may be necessary to rethink how we conceptualize and understand lay governing bodies. In countries other than England and Wales, comparable bodies are often called school councils or school boards; they may, as in Scotland, differ in their composition and powers. But their similarity to what is discussed here lies in their use of laypeople to oversee the organization and management of schools in conjunction with professional teachers and headteachers or principals. The analysis set out here has, therefore, a much wider applicability than England or Wales.

GOVERNING BODIES IN ENGLAND AND WALES, 1944–88

Between the 1944 Education Act, which made governing bodies in their contemporary form legally possible and the 1980 Education Act which introduced
a right of parental representation on such bodies, governing or managing
boards were often of little educational significance and their activities and
discussions were frequently dominated by the local education authority (LEA)
nominees of the main political parties. Some LEAs had only one or two governing bodies for all their schools; parents had no right of representation on
these, although by the mid-1970s many LEAs did permit parent governors. In
1977 the Taylor Report (DES/Welsh Office, 1977) suggested that whilst LEAs
should remain responsible for the overseeing of school government, much
more power than previously should be delegated to governing bodies. These
bodies should comprise equal numbers of LEA, staff, parent, pupil (where
appropriate) and community representatives, with each school having its own
governing body. Many of the Taylor Report's recommendations have subsequently been implemented, although this does not include pupil governors or
the idea of numerical balance between different groups.

In 1980 a new Education Act introduced elected parent governors, teacher
governors and headteachers (if the latter so wished) on to governing bodies in
all LEAs. LEAs were no longer permitted to group numbers of schools together
under one governing body. However, as Kogan *et al.* (1984) point out, the
1980 Act was not very radical in its effects. LEA governors continued to
dominate many governing bodies and in some areas parents could only vote
for parent governors at their children's schools if they attended a meeting.

In the mid-1980s a further attempt at reform was made. The 1986 Act
altered the composition of governing bodies in maintained schools and clarified and extended the powers of governors. Using a formula related to school
size, the numbers of elected parent and nominated co-opted governors were
increased, whilst the number of LEA-nominated governors was reduced. These
provisions took effect in the autumn term of 1988. The Act specified more
clearly than did the 1944 Act, the involvement of governors in curriculum; for
example they were, in conjunction with their headteacher and paying due
regard to LEA curriculum policies, to establish a secular curriculum policy for
their school, including sex education if considered appropriate. Governing
bodies were also to undertake the task of ensuring that the curriculum was free
from political bias. Governors were to have a clear role in headteacher appointments. Each year governing bodies were to prepare a written report for
parents, which would then be discussed at an annual meeting.

The 1988 Education Reform Act further extended the powers of governors.
Governing bodies were asked to oversee the implementation of the newly
introduced National Curriculum and required to establish a charging policy
for 'optional extras'. Governors became responsible for ensuring that religious
education and collective worship occurred and were empowered to deal with
parental complaints about these and National Curriculum matters. Governors
would also hear appeals against permanent exclusion of a child from school.

The use of school premises outside normal school hours was to be under the control of governing bodies. If, when operating under open enrolment, the school became oversubscribed, governors would decide whom to admit. In LEA schools the greatest increase in governor responsibilities occurred under the provisions for local management of schools (LMS), where governors would approve school budgets, appoint and dismiss staff whilst ensuring compliance with employment law, and establish disciplinary and grievance procedures. Governors were also given the power under the 1988 Act to initiate the process by which a school can opt out of local authority control and become directly funded by the Department for Education.

PERSPECTIVES ON GOVERNING BODIES

Governing bodies as participants in systems of educational governance

Governing bodies in England have frequently been seen by those concerned with educational management as an adjunct to educational organizations, standing at the boundary between school and the outside world, rather than separate organizations in their own right. Governors have thus been regarded as one dimension of the way in which a school relates to its external environment (Glatter, 1989). Following this approach, governing bodies have typically been described as one feature of an overall system of educational politics or management, studied from the standpoint of political science. In the 1970s and 1980s this proved a fruitful avenue.

Thus, Kogan *et al.* (1984) found, in a study of governing bodies completed in the early 1980s, that 'it is the local authority which effectively sets the framework for governing bodies' functions, powers and modes of behaviour' (p. 14). The researchers saw the key variables determining governing body modes of operation as 'the Articles, instructions and resources handed to them from above' (*ibid*, p. 14), although it was accepted that 'no form of authority fails to be modified by the actions of those to whom it is applied' (*ibid*, p. 14). The Kogan study also argued that the values of the school were internalized by governors to such an extent that 'it is difficult for patterns of decision-making to be modified by gubernatorial action' (*ibid*, p. 71). Indeed the institutional boundaries were often so strong that the layperson was perceived as 'an outsider, a guest, on the territory of the professional' (*ibid*, p. 71). The models of governing bodies set up by this research suggested four types – the *accountable*, where governors ensured that the school operated satisfactorily within agreed procedures, the *advisory*, where governors legitimated and tested professional activities, the *supportive*, where governors supported the head and the school, and the *mediating*, where the governing body brought together different interests and negotiated between them. This set of models has been widely cited and utilized in subsequent research on governors.

Democracy and accountability

Another perspective on governing bodies which has been prominent is the extent to which governor involvement in schools reflects ideals of democracy and accountability (Bacon, 1978). Both of these are assumed to be key aspects of endeavours to involve laypeople, especially parents, more fully in the affairs of schools. Bacon's work looked especially at early attempts by Sheffield LEA to bring parents into greater participation in governing bodies, although he concluded that this exercise only involved a fairly narrow social group. More recently a Leverhulme Trust-funded research project, carried out by Golby and Brigley (1989) in Devon during 1987, focused mainly on parent governors and found that the democratic aims of greater parental representation introduced by the legislation of the early 1980s were not being totally fulfilled. Parent governors wanted to work with schools in achieving agreed educational aims but were often confused about their role. Parents sometimes felt sidelined by party political LEA appointees on governing bodies, were often overwhelmed by regulations and jargon and felt a tension between their desire for consensus and their wish, on occasions, to challenge some of the assumptions of teachers. Parent governors did not always find it easy to represent other parents' views in the meetings of their governing body, but many felt that they were there to do so. However, some parents, probably a minority, did succeed in becoming very active in, and knowledgeable about, their schools. The Golby and Brigley study also suggested that as parent governors became more confident, so democratic involvement and accountability of schools to parents and the community might be expected to increase, enabling parents to challenge the assumptions and power of the professional teachers where necessary.

Democratic participation arguments have been used not just by social scientists in their analysis of governing body functions but also by politicians as a means of legitimating changes to the composition and responsibilities of governors. Historically, England's governing bodies have been regarded as a way of involving voluntary effort in schooling, ensuring that not too much control over education is given to the centre and providing a means of achieving participation and accountability on behalf of the community, particularly those local ratepayers who have helped to pay for the costs of education (Deem, Brehony and Hemmings, 1990). More recently, it has been suggested by politicians that 'active citizenship' is an important duty for the adult population. Originally conceived of in relation to things like neighbourhood watch schemes designed to fight crime, it is possible to conceive of the notion that being a governor also constitutes 'active citizenship' (Brehony, 1992).

Democracy, accountability and notions of active citizenship all imply that those involved in governing schools include a cross-section of the population. However, recent data from the National Foundation for Educational Research (Keys and Fernandes, 1990) suggests that in the late 1980s many governors in England were white, middle-class professionals. Twenty per cent of non-teacher governors were found to be working in education and 44 per cent of those in a national sample survey had a degree or professional qualification. Our own research has followed the workings and progress of ten primary and secondary school governing bodies in two LEAs, during the four years following the 1988 Education Reform Act. The schools in the project have a range of catchment areas and locations, as well as differing social class and ethnic composition of pupil numbers. This research, whilst not intended to be universally generalizable, suggests that the social groups which comprise a school's student intake are not necessarily fully represented in the governing of those schools (Deem, 1991). We have found that whilst middle-class schools tend to have middle-class governors, the same correspondence between pupil intake and governors is not found, with one exception, where there are substantial numbers of working-class and ethnic minority pupils. Nor do governing bodies in mixed secondary schools necessarily represent the gender composition of the school roll. Democratic participation, then, so far as it exists within school governing bodies, is mediated by class and ethnicity, and gender (Deem, 1989; Deem, Brehony and Hemmings, 1992). Of course this pattern of governing body membership also influences the range of groups to whom education is supposedly being made accountable.

The views of headteachers

Headteachers have, as we might expect, developed their own views about governors. Some have tended to see governors as a necessary evil, to be humoured and when necessary manipulated. Others regard them as a pleasant group of people who undertake symbolic duties such as attending school concerts and sports days but have little wider significance. In general, it seems, heads in England have not regarded governing bodies as terribly important in the life of their school, nor seen them as a power-wielding group (Jones, 1987; Hall, Morgan and Mackay, 1984). Changes giving governors more powers do not necessarily seem to have altered this much, if a set of recent intensive interviews with primary and secondary heads is in any way typical (Mortimore and Mortimore, 1991a, 1991b). Although almost all the primary and secondary heads interviewed by the Mortimores referred to governors, only in one or two cases did involving governors fully in the work of the school come to be seen either as a major aspect of the way in which heads organized their school or a salient feature of the heads' educational philosophies. However, one primary head did comment:

> Now the Education Acts of 1986 and 1988 make it imperative for headteachers to ensure they have the right kind of working relationship . . . particularly with the governing body, whereas prior to that the relationship . . . could be best described as having to be no better than that of a vicar hosting his own tea party.
>
> (Ron Morton, quoted in Mortimore and Mortimore, 1991a, p. 37)

It remains to be seen whether this kind of changed role and view will affect not only the relationship between heads and governors but also the content of what each is required to do.

The view from the governing body

If heads are only slowly changing their own views about governing bodies, governors themselves are starting to perceive some of the complexities of their newly acquired powers. From the late 1980s, since when LEA schools in England and Wales have gradually been given delegated budgets, governing bodies began to undertake financial responsibilities for their schools and gained hiring and firing duties in relation to staff. Governors in LMS schools also took on at the beginning of the 1990s the task of deciding headteacher pay and operating staff grievance and pupil exclusion procedures. At this point the nature of the governing task itself began to undergo a sea change.

Two pieces of recent research have explored this change. The first of these is our own small-scale, intensive, longitudinal, study of ten governing bodies in two LEAs over a four-year period from 1988 until 1992. This project began with a pilot study of fifteen governing bodies, for the four school terms from October 1988 until December 1989 (Deem, Brehony and Hemmings, 1991) and has subsequently involved detailed observation of ten of the fifteen governing bodies at their formal and working group meetings, questionnaires, interviews with heads and governors and analysis of relevant documentation. Our concerns have been to discover how governors are learning to cope with their much increased workload, to explore the power relations (including those based on race and gender) of, and the decision-making processes operating within, governing bodies and to examine the nature of the changing relationships between schools, headteachers, governors and LEAs. The second piece of research is a National Foundation for Educational Research (NFER) project on a much shorter timescale but using, for some aspects of data collection, a larger sample of governing bodies. This study, conducted in 1990, involved gathering information from a representative sample of LEAs, a questionnaire sent to forty-one governing bodies in eight LEAs, a short period of observation of a subset of nine governing bodies, and interviews with members of those nine bodies (Baginsky, Baker and Cleave, 1991).

The main focus of the NFER study was the effectiveness of governing bodies as partners with schools. Their findings suggested that the four models of the Kogan *et al.* (1984) study mentioned earlier, might in time be replaced by a view of schools as businesses, with heads as chief executives and governing bodies as boards of directors. Such views were expressed by many governors, although some questioned still saw their role as that of a supporter or consultant. Baginsky, Baker and Cleave (1991) argue that it is not yet appropriate for new models of governing bodies to be developed, until all the planned changes have settled down. But they do attempt to identify, in their conclusions and recommendations, a number of ways in which governing bodies can become more effective in decision-making and direction.

The NFER researchers take the view, as do many who write on governors (Sallis, 1991a; *Governors' Action*, the AGIT Newsletter), that the new legislation gives governors considerable power not just over their schools but principally, and significantly, over headteachers. Thus in Sallis's regular Agenda

slot in the weekly publication *The Times Educational Supplement*, governors
writing in with queries have often asked about the power of heads to make
decisions without consulting governors. One such letter (Sallis, 1991b, p. 15)
ran as follows:

> **Question:** I am not the only one on my governing body ready to work
> hard for the school, but many of us are frustrated. Our agendas come
> from the town hall. . . . We have a delegated budget but all we do is
> approve it when everything has been decided. The head writes the annual
> report to parents and runs the meeting . . . once or twice we have tried to
> establish our right to an opinion (such as on one exclusion case) but we
> were told by the head and local authority that teachers would strike if we
> intervened.

Sallis in her reply advises the governing body to

> Muster what support there is to allow the school to assume the role the
> law intended; it is your agenda, your meeting, your chair, your clerk. . . .
> 'You' includes the head who stands to benefit greatly from your making a
> stand, if only he could shake off habits based on fear.

Such a perspective views governors as central to schools as organizations
rather than as bit-part actors. It also makes some rather reified assumptions
about the relationship between legislation and change, assumptions which
seem not to be entirely justified by the degree of ambiguity in the legislation
itself and the uncertainties identified in the political debate about its purpose.

In parallel with the changes of the 1980s, there has been a huge increase in
training materials to support governors and the production of many how-to-
do-it manuals. On the heads' side, lengthy documents have appeared from
their professional associations about how to manage their governing bodies.
All of the headteachers in our study said that they set out to manage their
governors; as the head of Little Rivers said in interview, 'My appraisers in the
pilot scheme told me my governors feel I keep them on a tight rein.' No doubt
many heads have always contrived to 'manage' their governors; but in the
present conjuncture, with so many more powers granted to governors, there is
more to play for and more to lose than in the past.

THE IMPACT ON HEADS OF THE CHANGING ROLE OF GOVERNING BODIES

The shift of emphasis from the traditional political science and educational
management notions of governing bodies as one component in a much wider
system of educational government, to perspectives which recognize that governors now play a major role in the running of schools, is not surprising. The
changes encompassed in the 1986 (no. 2) and 1988 Education Acts have had
very significant effects on the context in which state-maintained schools in
England and Wales operate (Flude and Hammer, 1990). The importance of
LEAs has been much reduced, parents and members of the local community

and those from industry and commerce have been encouraged to become governors and as governor responsibilities have grown, the distinctions between the powers of heads and those of lay governors have become much more blurred than previously.

It has accordingly become more difficult for heads to police the boundaries between their own job and the responsibilities of governors. Although some heads still want to hold on to the distinction between governing or rather 'the establishment of policy and the monitoring and evaluation of that policy', and managing as 'translating broad policy into practice and maintaining appropriate structures and processes to ensure that policy objectives are achieved' (Wilkins, 1990), it is becoming clear that this distinction is at odds with some interpretations of the late 1980s legislation. There are certainly governors in our own study who wish to challenge the distinctions between governing and managing as defined by Wilkins. But it is also the case that a more old-fashioned view about service to the community, which is more consistent with the idea that governing and managing are separable entities, still prevails amongst some governors. As illustration of the latter view, the Chair of Ashdene Secondary told us in an interview, on being asked why he was a governor: 'We enjoy arranging things for other people.' It was clear from the context of this comment that 'other people' referred to children and parents, not the head or teaching staff. Indeed the picture which prevails amongst the chairs of governing bodies we have interviewed, the majority of whom are LEA representatives, is that of an urban gentry, with a long tradition of voluntary work in many fields, from local politics to charitable concerns (Brehony, 1992).

However, our data also suggest that a new breed of governor, typically a co-opted business person with financial skills, legal knowledge or managerial expertise, is emerging with the onset of LMS. Such governors have little patience with the view of governors as people who rubber stamp decisions made by heads or teachers; they are concerned with exam results and standards and they wish to see schools run as businesses (Brehony and Deem, 1991). They want to know what heads are up to, they like to inspect the accounts regularly and they like to challenge what they regard as old-fashioned notions about schools being there to produce well-rounded members of society rather than future workers. One such governor at Firdene Secondary went to the trouble of preparing his own model grievance procedure for the governors to approve and adopt; whilst reflecting his own experience in industry, the procedure paid little heed to the nationally agreed working conditions for teachers. The beliefs and values of governors who hold 'schools are businesses' views may bring them into conflict with the values of their school. This presents a very different picture from the governors studied by Kogan who appear to have largely internalized the value systems of their schools, although our data indicate that there are still a good many governors who adopt the Kogan position.

Where a value and culture clash does exist, it may be quite starkly presented. A business governor at Moatmeadow Secondary, talking about the school's GCSE and A-level exam results, produced cuttings from the local paper where local councillors had been asking why the town's results were so poor compared to the national average. He then addressed the head:

> Why are ....'s schools' results below average? There are good staff, good
> levels of commitment and . . . it isn't genetic. . . . I don't believe you can
> get better science results with the current system – we need to turn against
> the ethos of the school . . . we shouldn't be delivering the science curriculum to all, there could be some streaming.

Although the head tried to persuade the governor that there were other ways of improving science exam results, this particular governor has a personal philosophy of education which is antithetical to that held by the school and he has spent time in school with the science staff, winning them round to his point of view. He is beginning to build alliances with other governors who share similar philosophies. In the end he may not persuade the school to change but he certainly has the capacity to challenge the head and he is quite open about the fact that he will not send his own children to this school when they are old enough.

At Birchdene Primary governors often pursue a line based on questioning the appropriateness of what the school offers, in relation to what they feel is required in the workplace. Mother tongue teaching, for instance, is especially poorly regarded by ethnic minority governors, since it is perceived as lessening the future employment chances of the pupils for whom it is provided. However, Birchdene's head was quite candid, during her interview with us, in saying 'I do not see my school as being here to turn out little workers.' In making this statement, she is also emphasizing the distance between herself and her governors.

Business-oriented governors have also been able to stretch their wings over the vexed question of headteacher pay, a decision they were asked to make in LMS schools during 1991, after the salary scales for heads had been changed by the Interim Advisory Committee on Teacher Pay. This responsibility for fixing headteacher pay has led, in some of our case-study schools, to long discussions about how to relate the head's pay to performance. At Firdene the following dialogue occurred.

> Cllr X   Under LMS all we can do is to look at performance – we don't
>   want the headmaster applying for a better post elsewhere.
> Mr G   There has been under Mr ... a significant change to the character
>   of the school – a smooth introduction of LMS.
> Mrs H   Does it bring it into line with industry?
> Mr P   Industry doesn't get a cost of living increase!
> Mr G   One million turnover is small in industrial terms.
> Cllr X   One of the biggest employers in the area . . .
> Mr P   It sounds reasonable to me. I propose . . .

It is impossible to imagine such a dialogue taking place at the time of the Kogan (1984) study in the early 1980s. Similarly, those conceptualizations of governing bodies which see them as standing at the external boundary of schools or which suggest that their activities are shaped by their LEAs and the institutional concerns of the schools they govern, may no longer be as useful or as appropriate as previously. However, it is clear from our research that the changes to governor and headteacher responsibilities occur in an uneven manner and it is often a slow process. The question then arises: in what ways can we now usefully consider and reconceptualize the work done by governors and the ways in which they relate to headteachers and to schools?

GOVERNING BODIES AND SCHOOLS AS MICROPOLITICAL ORGANIZATIONS

The theoretical approach which I favour, and whose analytical purchase has been strengthened rather than weakened by the findings of our research, is one which, along with Stephen Ball (1987) sees schools (and governing bodies too) as organizations which are 'arenas of struggle . . . riven with actual or potential conflict between members . . . poorly co-ordinated . . . ideologically diverse'. However, like Ball, I do not take this perspective to mean that schools and governing bodies are therefore locked in perpetual strife and struggle, within and between themselves. Rather, underlying day-to-day concerns which are often paramount, there are many conflicts of interest and ideological differences between those involved and the existence of these cannot be ignored. Furthermore I see governing schools as a political activity, in so far as it involves decision-making (or sometimes the absence of decision-making), questions about the values and purposes of schooling and the exercise of power over educational resources and choices.

The range of responsibilities given to governors under the legislation of the late 1980s also means rethinking the organizational status of governing bodies; are they still an adjunct to the school (old dogs but taught new tricks) or do they now have an organizational existence of their own (new dogs, new tricks)? We have to be careful that in concentrating on what Ball calls the meso level or the organizational features of something, we do not forget the macro picture. Ball suggests that 'it is all too easy to overestimate the degree and misconstrue the nature of penetration and influence of structural factors on the social dynamics of organizations' (1987, p. 23). But our data suggest that amongst the members of the governing boards we have studied, many are very aware of the wider social, political and economic interests invoked by reforms. Furthermore most of our governors appear to be influenced by the political tenor of the times, as well as by the substantive issues arising from the working through of substantive changes to school organization, curriculum and financing.

ARE GOVERNING BODIES NOW BEST UNDERSTOOD AS ORGANIZATIONS?

My theoretical approach has so far eschewed the question about whether governing bodies, in their current form, can usefully be conceptualized as organizations. I have shown that many previous approaches to the study of governing bodies, as well as the attitudes of headteachers, have assumed that governing bodies do not constitute organizations in their own right. In the past this view seems to have been well founded as governors were very dependent on factors like the political complexion and policies of the LEA and also often met as a body only once a term. However, the new legislation has changed the situation quite dramatically, for some if not all schools. In our own study formal meetings of almost all our governing bodies take place at least twice a term. The wide introduction of subcommittees also means that some governors meet more frequently; similar findings emerge in other studies (Keys and Fernandes, 1990; Baginsky, Baker and Cleave, 1991). A governor interviewed in the Baginsky case-study powerfully expressed this change when he said: 'In the past you only brought these strong personalities together three times a year. It was like a medieval joust really with its own rules of engagement. This is happening less now because as governors work together on subcommittees they get to know one another' (Baginsky *et al.*, 1991, p. 33). Governors in schools operating with delegated budgets also have a range of personnel functions, including staff appointments, where they are now expected to play a key role.

Increasingly governing bodies are coming to develop a culture of their own. This culture may not always be discernible to those education professionals involved because of its taken-for-granted nature but to new heads or to those with a great deal of experience gained in different schools, such cultural characteristics are very noticeable. Thus, in our study, the new head of Ivydene Comprehensive said in an interview: 'My first impression of this governing body was a kind of strangeness – sitting back in fairly comfortable chairs, not a great deal of paper, not as much going on as I'd anticipated.' Another very experienced primary head at Birchdene, a school with a largely Asian pupil intake and a governing body which, unusually, has a considerable number of Asian governors, said that decisions (in 1991) now took a long time because governors wanted to be involved in everything. She explained this partly in terms of the new legislation but also in terms of the ethnic culture and composition of the governing body itself: 'Some of the Asian governors feel that decisions are made in a caucus they don't know about and they think we [the school] are trying to make decisions without them. . . . I do at times find it very difficult.'

In our account of our pilot study of fifteen governing bodies from 1988 until 1989, we have described how much each governing body differed from each other in conduct of meetings, ambience, arrangement of seating, participation rates and philosophical outlook (Deem, Brehony and Hemmings, 1991). Distinct cultures are certainly being created in governing bodies. However, to what extent do the discernible cultural characteristics of different governing bodies still reflect the values of their respective schools or are they externally derived? At Ivydene, as described above by the new head, the governing body appears to reflect the rather sleepy nature of a comfortable successful middle-class school. At Birchdene Primary, however, where despite the deprived inner-city location and the largely Asian pupil intake, most teaching staff are white, the culture of the school and the culture of the governing body, which has a number of Asian members, seem poles apart.

Each governing body has its own set of rules and regulations, largely those laid down nationally by statute and described in the instruments and articles of government, but there are variations in the way these are interpreted. The various networks of subcommittees which our research governing bodies have established is one indication of the source of variation. The number of sub-groups varies from nine to none, and whilst in a couple of schools these subcommittee structures mirror those of the school's own organization, in most they do not. This lends credence to the view that governing bodies are becoming more autonomous from, but are still related to, the schools they govern.

Certainly governing bodies do not always follow the wishes of their head-teacher. Although the head of Little Rivers Secondary School said in our interviews that 'The governing body enhances my ability to run the school. . . . I think they trust me to do it. . . . I've never felt any kind of restrictions . . . and I normally get my way', most of the ten heads we interviewed recognized that they had to argue their courses of action much more than before the 1986 and 1988 Education Acts. Thus decisions about, for example, the employment of temporary staffing, priority setting or the purchase of new equipment, could no longer be made quickly or by the head and teachers alone.

Organizations have goals, they have a membership and they have tech-nologies for achieving their aims (Westoby, 1988). All of these characteristics apply in some measure to governing bodies. Furthermore, under the auspices of LMS, governing bodies are gradually becoming more autonomous from their LEA, something which is much more acutely achieved by the governing bodies of grant-maintained schools (Deem and Wilkins, 1992). In our obser-vation, primary school governing bodies, even those operating under LMS, are still much more dependent on their LEA than are the secondary school bodies in the study. In all the ten schools, governors are also heavily dependent on another organization, the school, for their very existence, despite possessing their own culture and rules. So the paradox remains: are governing bodies a separate organization or are they still best regarded as part of the school, albeit playing a more central role than prior to the mid-1980s?

LOOSE COUPLING AND ANARCHIC ORGANIZATIONS

I think it is helpful, in considering both the governing body's mode of oper-ation itself and the nature of the relationship between governing body and school, to introduce Weick's (1988) notion of loosely coupled systems. Weick describes the effects and appearance of this in the following terms: 'coupled events are responsive but . . . each event also preserves its own identity and some evidence of its physical or logical separateness. . . . Loose coupling also carries connotations of impermanence, dissolvability and tacitness, all of which are potentially crucial properties of the glue which holds organizations together' (Weick, 1988, pp. 58–9). All these characteristics seem applicable to governors. They are impermanent, serving a four-year term, with some resigning much earlier (Keys and Fernandes, 1990). We know that governors often lack knowledge about schools (Brehony and Deem, 1991) and frequently meet and act in ways which are separate from, though related to the school. Furthermore, as volunteers, the glue which binds governors and their schools together may often only be of the temporary kind.

If governing bodies can be described as having some distinct organizational features of their own, whilst being loosely coupled to their schools, it may be worthwhile going further down the road of organizational analysis. Cohen, March and Olsen (1972) suggest that educational organizations are far from conforming to the rational model of organizations often put forward. Instead, schools may be inclined to anarchy rather than predictability. By this they mean that the goals are diffuse and problematic, that membership is fluid and that the technology by which education is carried out is unclear.

Cohen *et al.*'s analysis can equally well be applied to governors. First there is wide evidence that governors are unclear about their role (Baginsky, Baker and Cleave, 1991; Sallis, 1991a; Deem, Brehony and Hemmings, 1991). In part this lack of clarity may be because the law itself is unclear. Thus, an extract from Section 10 of the Education Reform Act on collective worship and religious education, says: 'it shall be the duty of the local education authority and the governing body to exercise their functions *with a view to securing*, and the duty of the headteacher *to secure*' (author's italics). Such legal ambiguity can only be definitively resolved by a court. Second, the membership of governing bodies is fluid, although not perhaps in the precise sense meant by Cohen *et al.* Over a period of three years since the changed composition came into effect in October 1988, there are indications that there has been a substantial turnover of members, especially amongst co-opted governors (Keys and Fernandes, 1990). Also, although the sample used by Keys and Fernandes only showed an average of one vacancy per school (in 1990), our own research, while not claiming the same degree of generalizability, indicates that at any given moment governing bodies are often unsure of their membership. There may be persistent non-attenders and the notification of resignation and reappointment of LEA representatives is a slow process. Some of those who do attend are silent in meetings, so that their actual desire to participate, as well as the likelihood of their continued membership, must remain in doubt.

Finally the technology governors use to undertake their governorship varies from formal meetings and subcommittees or working groups to appointment and appeal panels, delegation of powers to heads, and visits to school. But the efficacy of these means can be questioned (Baginsky, Baker and Cleave, 1991; Deem, Brehony and Hemmings, 1991), both on grounds of the manner in which decisions are made and in relation to poor attendance patterns. A large number of subgroups in a governing body, particularly where the form of these does not mirror the school's own management structure, can also significantly add to the amount of time governors spend at both subcommittee and main meetings. Sometimes this extra time is spent without any particular benefit to either the school or governors being evident. Furthermore some of the technology requires a good working knowledge of the school, the teachers, the pupils and the curriculum, in order to discharge governors' duties in the area of curriculum, budget priorities and school aims, and staff appointments. But such knowledge, in our case-study schools, is often lacking. By contrast though, in fields like finance, buildings, and site maintenance, governors often do have the requisite knowledge (Brehony and Deem, 1991).

CONCLUSION

A considerable amount of recent empirical evidence about school governing bodies in England suggests that it may be useful in future to develop a perspective on governing bodies which incorporates some of the points raised here. These include the micropolitical nature of their activities, which directly challenges the view that governors should be apolitical and an acceptance of the extent to which gubernatorial activities and discussions are riven by conflicts. There is also an indication that some governing bodies are beginning to display a distinct organizational culture of their own. I have also noted, on the one hand, signs of the loose coupling of governing bodies to their schools and, on the other, similarities between the anarchic tendencies of schools and those of governing bodies. Adopting these reconceptualizations of governing bodies has many implications both for educational researchers and for those heads and teachers who have to work with governing bodies. The latter group too may need to review their own perspectives on the functions and roles of governing bodies, if they are to continue to work successfully with their newly empowered governors.

During the early 1990s, some English Conservative politicians, including the Secretary of State for Education, in outlining how they would wish to see teacher training reformed, have suggested that educational theory has no place in teacher education and development (Clarke, 1992). What I have argued here, however, is that theory and practice can and do inform each other. Thus, the theoretical conceptualizations of governing bodies constructed by researchers and the perspectives about governors held by teachers have much in common. Not only do they draw on a shared empirical base; both views have something valuable to offer the educational manager and the governor in coming to terms with changes in the way state education in England and Wales is now organized and financed. The article has focused specifically on the involvement of laypeople in the organization, governance, and management, of schools in England. But the insights offered here are, I believe, capable of application to other societies both inside and outside Europe, where laypeople have a formal role in schools, especially where recent educational reforms have included increasing the power of such laypeople and giving more local autonomy to schools.

ACKNOWLEDGEMENTS

The research project referred to in the chapter was funded by an Economic and Social Research Council grant (R000 23 1799). The researchers are grateful to the governing bodies involved in the study for their help and co-operation. Thanks to Sue Hemmings for the considerable amount of interviewing which she did for the project and the observational data she collected, whilst a researcher on the project from April 1990 until August 1991. Also particular thanks to Kevin Brehony for his contribution to the research discussed here and his comments on an earlier version of this article.

REFERENCES

AGIT, *Governors' Action*, Action on Governors' Information and Training Newsletter, CEDC, Lyng Hall, Blackberry Lane, Coventry CV2 3JS.

Bacon, A.W. (1978) *Public Accountability and the Schooling System*, Harper & Row, London.

Baginsky, M., Baker, L. and Cleave, S. (1991) *Towards Effective Partnership in School Governance*, NFER, Slough.

Ball, S. (1987) *The Micro-Politics of the School*, Methuen, London.

Brehony, K.J. (1992) 'Active citizens'; the case of school governors. Unpublished paper given to Westhill Sociology of Education conference, Birmingham.

Brehony, K.J. and Deem, R. (1991) School governing bodies: reshaping education in their own image. Paper given to BERA annual conference, Nottingham Polytechnic, August.

Clarke, K. (1992) Secretary of State for Education, Great Britain, unpublished speech to the North of England Education Conference, Southport, January.

Cohen, M.D., March, J.G. and Olsen, J.P. (1972) A garbage can model of organisational choice, *Administrative Science Quarterly*, Vol. 17, no. 1, pp. 1–25.

Deem, R. (1989) The new school governing bodies – are race and gender on the agenda? *Gender and Education*, Vol. 1, no. 3, pp. 247–60.

Deem, R. (1991) Governing by gender – the new school governing bodies, in P. Abbott and C. Wallace (eds.) *Gender, Power and Sexuality*, Macmillan, London.

Deem, R., Brehony, K.J. and Hemmings, S. (1990) Governing bodies and LEAs – who shall inherit the earth? Paper given to Education Reform Research Network seminar, University of Reading, November.

Deem, R., Brehony, K.J. and Hemmings, S. (1991) *The Reform of School Governing Bodies Project: A Report on the Pilot Study, October 1988–March 1990*, Open University Education Reform Research Group, Occasional Paper No. 3, Milton Keynes.

Deem, R., Brehony, K.J. and Hemmings, S. (1992) Social justice, social divisions and the governing of schools, in D. Gill, B. Mayor and M. Blair (eds.) *Racism and Education: Structures and Strategies*, Sage, London, pp. 208–25.

Deem, R. and Wilkins, J.A. (1992) Governing and managing schools after the Reform Act: the LEA experience and the GMS alternative, in L. Ellison, V. Griffiths and T. Simkins (eds.) *Implementing Educational Reform: The Early Lessons*, Longman, for BEMAS.

DES/Welsh Office (1977) *A New Partnership for our Schools* (The Taylor Report), HMSO, London.

Flude, M. and Hammer, M. (1990) (eds.) *The Education Reform Act 1988; its Origins and Implications*, Falmer, London.

Glatter, R. (1989) (ed.) *Educational Institutions and Their Environments: Managing the Boundaries*, Open University Press, Milton Keynes.

Golby, S. and Brigley, S. (1989) *Parents as School Governors*, Fairway Publications, Tiverton.

Hall, V., Morgan, C. and Mackay, H. (1984) *Headteachers at Work*, Open University Press, Milton Keynes.

Jones, A. (1987) *Leadership for Tomorrow's Schools*, Blackwell, Oxford.

Keys, W. and Fernandes, C. (1990) *A Survey of School Governing Bodies*, NFER, Slough.

Kogan, M., Johnson, D., Packwood, T. and Whittaker, T. (1984) *School Governing Bodies*, Heinemann, London.

Mortimore, P. and Mortimore, J. (1991a) (eds.) *The Primary Head: Roles, Responsibilities and Reflections*, Paul Chapman, London.

Mortimore, P. and Mortimore, J. (1991b) (eds.) *The Secondary Head: Roles, Responsibilities and Reflections*, Paul Chapman, London.

Sallis, J. (1991a) *School Governors: Your Questions Answered*, Hodder & Stoughton, London.

Sallis, J. (1991b) Agenda; Joan Sallis answers governors' questions, *The Times Educational Supplement*, 27 December, p. 15.

Weick, K.E. (1988) Educational organisations as loosely coupled systems, in A. Westoby (ed.) *Culture and Power in Educational Organisations*, Open University Press, Milton Keynes.

Westoby, A. (1988) (ed.) *Culture and Power in Educational Organisations*, Open University Press, Milton Keynes.

Wilkins, J.A. (1990) Restructuring education after the Reform Act and the role of school governors; a headteacher perspective, Open University Education Reform Study Group, Occasional Paper No. 1, Milton Keynes.

18

PERFORMANCE INDICATORS AND CONSUMER CHOICE

Bill Dennison

FINANCIAL INCENTIVES

The Education Reform Act 1988 and in particular those sections relating to the local management of schools (LMS) and open enrolment reinforce a trend which started when pupil numbers began to decrease. As soon as there is space in schools some parents want to exercise a right to choose. These rights were confirmed by the Education Act 1980, while the capacity of LEAs to plan provision efficiently, relative to shrinking pupil numbers, was strengthened. Effectively, the Education Reform Act extends these parental rights still further while blighting the planning capacity of LEAs. Their responsibilities to continue to provide sufficient pupil places will continue, but governing bodies, should they choose (and if they are able to attract enough pupils), can fill their schools to physical capacity.

There are several reasons why governors and staff will wish to follow this route. It means belonging to a school perceived as successful. For teachers it increases the likelihood of promotion, and a better paid job in the school. It reduces the risk of redeployment or redundancy. It involves working with children (and parents) some of whom at least have made a positive commitment towards the school. It should result in a better physical fabric, and more books, equipment, etc.

Financial factors are clearly important but do not dominate in such reasoning. They will become much more significant with LMS and open enrolment because of two features which have been allowed to develop in the cost structures of schools. First, fixed costs have been remarkably high; second, the marginal cost to schools of educating a few additional children can be minimal. Without exception, spending on salaries and premises has absorbed well over 90 per cent of total expenditure on each school. With financial retrenchment and falling rolls, the main way that LEAs could lower fixed costs was to reduce staffing (redeployment, early retirements, etc.), but this did no more than shrink these costs in real terms. Indeed, they rose in most schools as a percentage of total expenditure, leaving even less to spend on non-staffing and non-premises items.

In earlier times, as the system grew, extra pupils attracted additional funds, yet many, particularly secondary schools, found they could increase the size of classes by one or two children, apparently without any educational costs. As a result, many schools raised the number of options in the upper school to offer pupils more choice. Of course, in doing so, they employed more staff and made their fixed costs as high (proportionately) as before. When cutbacks had to be made, and pupil numbers fell, they were badly placed because they had little control over the staff that left while having a commitment to an expensive curriculum.

Financially the main change prompted by LMS will be formula funding. Most schools have some experience of such arrangements, in that their funding by LEAs has been broadly in line with pupil numbers. However, what neither they, nor the schools, have had to confront is the mechanistic imposition of a rigid formula to determine each school's budget share and the inflexibilities such arrangements can induce. Above all, in such circumstances, the two features of school cost structures will be of crucial importance. If a school's fixed costs exceed budget share, governors will have to consider dismissing staff. Alternatively, extra pupils, because of the full additional funding they will attract, must prove very appealing, especially if they can be accommodated without the necessity of more spending.

CONSUMER SOVEREIGNTY

With one relatively simple piece of legislation, the consumer (parent or pupil) becomes sovereign. A school will want to attract as many pupils as possible both for positive reasons – the extra activities it can provide, the better quality of school life it can organize, and the enhanced status of all concerned – and the negative reason of avoiding the threats posed by even a small percentage reduction in funding. To maximize this attractiveness, however, a school has little alternative but to offer parents and older pupils what it perceives they most want from the school. An approach in which professional staff determine what is appropriate based upon their training and experience, with little concern for consumer preferences, has been severely inhibited by the Reform Act.

In the UK, professionals have been reluctant to market their services. Public providers (in social services, education and health) have avoided such activities almost completely. In the private sector, architects, lawyers and accountants have given them some attention (more so recently) but rather discreetly. From a professional perspective, the avoidance of marketing is understandable. Once a service is marketed it becomes subject to scrutiny. Potential consumers require guidance about the quality of the service, what they may gain from it, and (sometimes) at what cost. They need criteria on which to base judgements about whether to use a service, or which parts of a service they should choose. Such processes, by offering consumers some measure of determination, reduce the control and the autonomy of professional staff.

Moves towards a firmer consumer orientation should come as no surprise to professionals. They have seen considerable legislation to strengthen the position of consumers (including themselves) of goods and non-professional services. These new rights of consumers, and the obligations of providers, have received substantial publicity. There has been a proliferation of activities to raise consumer awareness. Clearly such developments had to extend to professional work.

Indeed, calls for their extension were strengthened by two main factors. First, such services can impinge dramatically on an individual's well-being – the law, education and health being the best examples. Second, there exists a strong perception among consumers of vested interest – professionals placing their own needs before their clients'. Therefore, governments of all persuasions having been seen to sponsor consumerism became committed to its furtherance. Rights and choices, once conferred, are difficult to deny in a democracy. More significantly, the transfer of some consumer power in itself increases demands for further transfers.

The prominent influence of parental choice in LMS and the resultant rise in inter-school competition for children must be placed, therefore, in the wider context of greater obligation to the consumer. Increasingly parents (and older pupils) will need to be conceived of as consumers of the service a school provides. If they do not like the quality of the education offered, they are free (and in a consumer-oriented society encouraged) to go elsewhere and take the funding they attract to another school.

Of course, the notion of consumer sovereignty has its limitations in this context. Not all parents wish to make a choice. As a result, their children will attend the most convenient school. In many rural areas geographic factors eliminate choice. Even those pupils and parents willing and able to choose normally make one decision only – when a child joins a new school. On most occasions it requires exceptional circumstances for parents to be so dissatisfied with the quality of service as to move their children to another school.

Yet such marginal decisions, relating only to a minority of children, can profoundly affect a school's development because of the influence of the two dominant features in its cost structure. High fixed costs, and the small sums that have to be spent educating additional pupils, mean that a school which grows from 1,000 to 1,100 children (say) will be highly advantaged; by comparison, a school whose roll declines from 1,000 to 900 will be greatly disadvantaged. The difference between the two circumstances will be large; so big in fact that the expanding school will stand to gain extra pupils as it uses additional funding to make itself still more attractive to potential consumers, while the other struggles to fulfil statutory obligations and find enough income to cover its fixed costs.

THE COMPETITIVE EDGE

Successful marketing involves discovering consumer expectations and then gaining the confidence of potential consumers that these expectations are likely to be fulfilled. As a public service, education has been reluctant to investigate the two issues that flow from this definition: what parents and children expect from a school before they register, and the extent to which such expectations are being changed both during and after school attendance (Stillman and Meychell, 1986). Such reluctance is easily explained. The systematic collection of relevant information would be a complex affair. Also there was little incentive to collect such material.

National surveys of parental opinion about education, or efforts to find overall levels of satisfaction with schooling, are of minimal value because of the uniqueness of each school. For governors and staff five key questions emerge for their school. The questions are written in the present tense. Transferred to the future (relating to the children likely to attend) they assume, if anything, still greater importance:

(1) How many of our children attend the school because it is convenient, i.e. no decision has been made?
(2) How many children attend the school following a positive choice, even though it is convenient, i.e. other schools were considered but rejected?
(3) How many children attend the school although other schools are more convenient, or would have represented a more natural choice?
(4) How many children, where a choice in favour of this school would have been convenient and natural, are being educated elsewhere?
(5) What are the factors which influence these choices, particularly the positive (and negative) decisions demonstrated by the answers to questions (2), (3) and (4)?

The number of children in each category, and the factors which influence the choices, will characterize a school. Any attempt to generalize, therefore, can mislead. However, staff and governors are searching for guidance, and an opportunity to gather some evidence arose while working with a wide range of audiences during LMS training. They were composed mainly of professional staff but included governors, and parents and some older pupils. In discussion a large number of factors were suggested which, according to the perceptions of participants, had been an influence in an attendance choice 'for' or 'against' a school known to them. Over a period of several months these factors have been consolidated (but not prioritized) into a list of 25 items, which seem to represent potential contributors to a decision. They are presented in outline (Dennison, 1989) in Table 18.1.

There are obvious deficiencies inherent in the construction of this list. Essentially it represents the views of one group (professional staff) about the perceptions of another (parents and children). However, in the absence of a rigorously conducted market survey of opinions there is little else available to guide schools about why they appear more (or less) popular than their

Table 18.1   Influential factors on school choice

Quality of the buildings
Physical location of the school
History and traditions of the school
Characteristics of the 'natural' catchment area
'Caring' attributes of the school
Organization of parents' evenings and other visits to school
Examination and test results
Quality of the teaching (including the implementation of homework policy)
Range and quality of extracurricular activities
HMI and LEA published reports on the school
Length and arrangement of the school day
Links with feeder schools, nurseries and playgroups
Links with receiving schools and (for secondary schools) with employers, further and higher
   education
Children's behaviour outside school
Children's behaviour in school
School uniform policy
Unofficial grapevine of comment about the school in homes, workplaces, pubs, etc.
Quality of information sent to parents
Quality of the school brochure
Number of feeder schools receiving the brochure
Adverse comments made about competitor schools
Attitude of the media towards the school
Volume of good publicity about pupil achievements, etc.
Level of school involvement in (and with) the local community
Profile achieved by the head, staff and governors of the school

---

neighbours. Such a survey, though, would need (unlike the list) to concentrate upon the consumers of one school, for the significance of factors must vary from school to school; not all groups of parents will have the same priorities, nor place the same emphasis upon them. Nevertheless, the 25 factors are a starting point from which a school can consider its competitive edge, and how it might go about attracting and retaining pupils.

PERFORMANCE INDICATORS

In most respects the factors constitute performance indicators as determined by consumers. They provide a very crude 'shopping list' that might be used by prospective parents. Of course it would be highly improbable for a parent to work systematically through all factors, comparing one school with others. It is far more likely that individual choices occur as a result of considering a few (or maybe one only) factor. Perhaps even a single event – seeing children misbehave on their way to school or reading a report on pupil achievement in the local press – is sufficient to trigger a decision. Such caveats, though, cannot disguise that the factors do represent a form of performance indicator according to what consumers expect of a school.

One immediate criticism of many staff as they reviewed the list was that it reinforced unfairness, particularly because it included influential factors over which their school had no control – most notably its physical location, its history and traditions, and the characteristics of its 'natural' catchment area. They were not prepared to accept that those factors over which their school has considerable autonomy – organizing parental visits, uniform policy, the school brochure, and their own profile as a staff – provide an effective counterweight.

Yet a common theme that links all factors is the mix of school and non-school determinants that they demonstrate. The quality of school buildings represents a good example. Structure, achitecture, when built, etc., are all features beyond the control or influence of a school staff. However, with LMS, day-to-day maintenance, cleanliness and the tidiness of the premises become a school responsibility. Quite possibly a potential parent will be more influenced by whether the buildings appear clean, tidy and cared for (with an absence of litter and graffiti) than their age or the style of the architecture.

Test scores and examination results provide another good example of dual determinants. The literature on school effectiveness (as measured by pupil performance) is vast and somewhat contradictory. However, in this context, two issues seem beyond dispute. Schools can influence the performance of children in tests and examinations but these influences are generally less than those that result from non-school variables, like the socio-economic status of pupils and the expectations of their parents. A school can achieve through its own efforts outstanding examination performance relative to the background of its children, while still producing lower overall results than a neighbouring school. The critical perception of a potential consumer ought to be the results achieved relative to those expected.

Even with a factor such as a policy towards uniforms, a school is not wholly autonomous. If such a factor influences a choice it is not so much whether a policy exists which matters, but rather how well it appears to be implemented; and here a school must rely to some extent on supportive parents and prevailing local attitudes. The existence of similar links between school-controlled and external variables in most competitive-edge factors is hardly surprising given the closeness and the complexities of the relationships between a school, its pupils, parents and the local community.

However valid the criticisms of unfairness, it is unlikely they will have much practical effect. Undoubtedly some schools will find it easier than others to attract additional pupils for demographic reasons. Clearly many more parents will be influenced by the actual examination results of a school than are likely to make allowances for achievement relative to pupil background. However, the twin effects of rising consumerism and the mechanics of LMS mean that many performance indicators which professional staff might have selected (and may still wish to use for their own educational and managerial purposes) will be displaced in actual significance by those which parents and pupils elect to rely upon.

Yet it would be a resourceless and unimaginative staff (and teaching profession) who accepted such a state of affairs without an alternative strategy. The real art in effective marketing, whatever the product, is to lead consumers towards situations where their expectations coalesce with those of the suppliers. On this basis, therefore, a school needs to organize an education whose content and quality both meet the requirements of what professionals think they ought to be doing, and gives them satisfaction, and satisfies the needs of pupils, parents and the local community.

However, this can only happen when the consumers are sure that the professionals appreciate their perceptions about performance indicators, and this appreciation is recognized in the characteristics of the education they organize. Perceptions are not fixed. They can be changed by the actions of the professionals. Teachers should be striving to assist their consumers to a more sophisticated interpretation of performance indicators more in line with those that they would use as professionals. If they do this they will have gone a long way in successfully marketing their school.

REFERENCES

Dennison, W.F. (1989) The competitive edge – attracting more pupils, *School Organisation*, Vol. 9, no. 2, pp. 179–86.
Stillman, A. and Meychell, K. (1986) *Choosing Schools: Parents, LEAs and the 1980 Education Act*, NFER-Nelson, Windsor, pp. 75–154.

PART 6:

Overview

19

SCHOOL EFFECTIVENESS, SCHOOL IMPROVEMENT AND DEVELOPMENT PLANNING

David Hargreaves and David Hopkins

[*Editor's note*: This chapter is taken from a book on the management and practice of school development planning. Here the authors examine the main themes of recent research on school effectiveness and improvement and their implications for development planning.]

SCHOOL EFFECTIVENESS

There is now a vast amount of evidence to support the common-sense notion that the characteristics of individual schools can make a difference to pupil progress. The research on 'effective schools', both in the UK (Mortimore *et al.*, 1988) and the USA (Purkey and Smith, 1983), has found that certain internal conditions are typical in schools that achieve higher levels of outcomes for their students. The first major study conducted in the UK was by Rutter and his colleagues (1979) who compared the 'effectiveness' of ten secondary schools in inner London on a range of student outcome measures. The 'effective schools', described in their book *Fifteen Thousand Hours*, were characterized by factors 'as varied as the degree of academic emphasis, teacher actions in lessons, the availability of incentives and rewards, good conditions for pupils, and the extent to which children are able to take responsibility' (Rutter *et al.*, 1979, p. 178). It was this constellation of factors that Rutter and his colleagues later referred to as the school's 'ethos'. The HMI survey reported in *Ten Good Schools* comes to similar conclusions. To HMI the 'good school' is one that can demonstrate 'quality in its aims, in oversight of pupils, in curriculum design, in standards of teaching and academic achievements and in its links with the local community. What they all have in common is effective leadership and a "climate" that is conducive to growth' (DES, 1977, p. 36).

The following eight factors are representative of the so-called 'organization factors' that are characteristic of effective schools (see Purkey and Smith, 1983):

(1) Curriculum-focused school leadership;
(2) Supportive climate within the school;
(3) Emphasis on curriculum and teaching (for example, maximizing academic learning);
(4) Clear goals and high expectations for students;
(5) A system for monitoring performance and achievement;
(6) Ongoing staff development and in-service training;
(7) Parental involvement and support;
(8) LEA and external support.

These factors do not, however, address the dynamics of schools as organizations. There appear to be four additional factors which infuse some meaning and life into the process of improvement within the school. These 'process factors' provide the means of achieving the organizational factors; they lubricate the system and 'fuel the dynamics of interaction'. They have been described by Fullan (1985, p. 400) as follows:

(1) A feel for the process of leadership; this is difficult to characterize because the complexity of factors involved tends to deny rational planning – a useful analogy would be that organizations are to be sailed rather than driven.
(2) A guiding value system; this refers to a consensus on high expectations, explicit goals, clear rules, a genuine caring about individuals, etc.
(3) Intense interaction and communication; this refers to simultaneous support and pressure at both horizontal and vertical levels within the school.
(4) Collaborative planning and implementation; this needs to occur both within the school and externally, particularly in the LEA.

Figure 19.1 Effective schools: organization and process factors

These descriptions of effective school cultures are similar to most others emerging from this line of research. The literature is also in agreement on three further issues. First, that these differences in outcome are systematically related to variations in the school's culture. Secondly, that the school's culture is amenable to alteration by concerted action on the part of the school staff. Although this is not an easy task, the evidence suggests that teachers and schools have more control than they may imagine over their ability to change their present situation. Thirdly, there is also broad agreement on the factors related to that difference.

In Figures 19.1 and 19.2 we have selected extracts from two studies of school effectiveness. The first is from a widely quoted American review of the research literature. In this paper Purkey and Smith distinguish, helpfully in our opinion, between organizational and process factors related to effectiveness. The second extract is taken from the ILEA junior school study conducted by Mortimore and his colleagues. This extract contains a great deal of reference to teaching methods, which is a point that we will come back to when discussing our third extract.

Although this research is extremely helpful in gaining a greater degree of understanding of what makes for school effectiveness, there are, however, a number of problems with its practical applications. The first is to do with the tendency of educational administrators, in their search for simple solutions to complex problems, naively to regard research evidence as a panacea for their pressing educational concerns. For as Cuban (1983) points out, too narrow an

(1) **Purposeful leadership of the staff by the head**
Key aspects: effective heads are sufficiently involved in and knowledgeable about what goes on in classrooms and about progress of individual pupils. Although they do not interfere constantly they are not afraid to assert their leadership.

(2) **The involvement of the deputy head**
Key aspects: a certain amount of delegation by the head and the sharing of responsibilities promote effectiveness.

(3) **The involvement of teachers**
Key aspects: active involvement in curriculum planning, developing curriculum guidelines, and participation in decision-making on school policy.

(4) **Consistency among teachers**
Key aspects: continuity in teaching staff and consistency of teacher approach are important.

(5) **Structured sessions**
Key aspects: teachers organize a framework within which pupils can work, encourage a degree of independence, and allow some freedom within this structure.

(6) **Intellectually challenging teaching**
Key aspects: use of higher-order questions and statements, pupils encouraged to use their creative imagination and powers of problem solving, teachers have an enthusiastic approach, and high expectations of pupils.

(7) **Work-centred environment**
Key aspects: much content-related work and feedback, relatively little time spent on routine matters, a low level of noise, and not an excessive amount of pupil movement.

(8) **Limited focus within lessons**
Key aspects: a focus upon only one curriculum area during a lesson.

(9) **Maximum communication between teachers and pupils**
Key aspects: a flexible approach, blending individual, class and group interaction as appropriate, including class discussion.

(10) **Record keeping**
Key aspects: record keeping linked to planning and assessment by both head and teachers.

(11) **Parental involvement**
Key aspects: help in classrooms, on educational visits, attendance at meetings to discuss children's progress, parents' reading to their children and access to books at home, informal open-door policy rather than parent–teacher associations.

(12) **Positive climate**
Key aspects: more emphasis on praise and reward than punishment and control, enthusiastic attitude of teachers, involvement of staff and children in a range of activities outside the classroom.

Figure 19.2   The twelve key factors of junior school effectiveness (adapted from Mortimore *et al.* (1988), pp. 250–6)

interpretation of the school effectiveness criteria leads to an increase in standardization, a narrowing of the educational agenda, and a removal of the obligation to improve from schools that have good examination results. Cuban argues that the question should really be: 'How can the broader more complex and less easily measured goals of schooling be achieved *as* we improve test scores?' In this respect, the effectiveness criteria have too narrow a focus for a practical strategy.

The second problem is raised by the increased sophistication of the recent school effectiveness studies. New analytical techniques have enabled more detailed investigation of the differential impact of school effectiveness on sub-groups. Mortimore and his colleagues (1988), for example, found that there was some variability in progress in reading between boys and girls in the same junior schools. Nuttall and his colleagues (1989), in their study of ILEA secondary schools, found that the effectiveness of a school varies along several dimensions, and that there are also variations over time. These findings suggest that the school effectiveness criteria lack the comprehensiveness required for a practical whole-school strategy.

We were [. . .] reminded of a third problem when reviewing a book of school effectiveness case-studies from the USA (Taylor, 1990). Although there was clarity and consensus in the cases about the effective school correlates, there was little discussion about the nature of the *process* that leads to effectiveness. Nowhere in the cases was the process of translating the correlates into a programme of action sufficiently articulated. And this of course is the third problem.

Even from this brief review, it is clear that [. . .] the effective schools criteria provide a necessary but not sufficient condition for school development. These characteristics can, however, be used in an audit or review [. . .]. For example: What can your school learn from them? How can aspects of them be incorporated into your development plan?

The research on school effectiveness is relatively recent and has been preceded by an extensive body of research on the effects of teaching on student performance. A summary of the research on teaching effects is given in Figure 19.3. This research, much of it from the USA, generally follows a 'process–product' design, where the amount and quality of teaching is assessed and correlated with student test scores. Within this framework the researchers attempt to identify those patterns of teaching that relate to enhanced achievement: the focus is on teaching as a means to an end. Although researchers in this area speak confidently to their conclusions, we must remember that at best their results are correlations, and do not prove 'cause and effect'. The health warnings that we gave to the research on school effects apply here also.

We discuss this research for two reasons. The first is that, as the Mortimore study on school effects shows, teaching is an important aspect of school effectiveness. Indeed some researchers claim that the major contributor to school effectiveness is teaching rather than school culture. Be that as it may, we do know that the more structured and reflective the approach to teaching, the more likely it is that students' academic performance will improve. These specifications can therefore be used by teachers as a basis for auditing and reviewing their own teaching.

The second and related reason is that teacher development and school development are inextricably linked. [. . .] Management is everyone's responsibility and the school's development plan provides a structure for integrating classroom and whole-school developments. On the one hand, classroom improvement is about enhancing teaching skills and strategies, curriculum

A summary of the substantive findings from studies of teaching effects falls into three broad categories:

(1) **Time and curriculum.** Student achievement is influenced by the way time is allocated by teachers and used by students in classrooms. It follows that interventions which affect instructional time are likely to affect achievement. But time alone is not the measure of quality in teaching. At the very least, our conception of time in classrooms must include a dimension of curriculum. Curriculum most often shows up in studies of teaching as content covered and/or opportunity to learn. The most sophisticated form of this measure is 'academic learning time', i.e. the time students spend working successfully with content measured on the criterion achievement test. In thinking about instructional time it is necessary to consider not only whether students are paying attention, but also what they are doing: solving work problems, answering comprehension questions, writing expository essays – and whether these 'pursuits' are related to the curriculum being tested. When alignment occurs, students achieve. In this sense opportunity to learn is a fundamental condition for student achievement.

(2) **Classroom management.** Whether students actually utilize their opportunities to learn depends in part upon how well teachers organize and manage classrooms. Central to this view of classroom order is a *work system* consisting of activities which organize students for working and rules and procedures which specify actions for routine events. The most important features of the work system for a class are the *programmes of action* that define the nature of order for particular segments of time and pull students along specified paths. The teachers' role in management has at least three dimensions. First, they prepare in advance for how students as a group will be organized to accomplish work and what rules and procedures will govern movement and routine events. Secondly, successful teachers communicate their work systems clearly to students through explanations, written materials, rehearsals and sanction. Thirdly, successful teachers monitor classroom events to make sure that the work system is operating within reasonable limits and to notice early signs of potential disruptions.

(3) **Dimensions of instructional quality.** Given equal emphases on content and equally orderly classrooms, differences in student achievement will result among classes from differences in the quality of instruction, that is, the design of assignments, the clarity of explanations, the chances students have to practise, and the availability and accuracy of feedback. A complete picture of effective teaching must include, therefore, dimensions of instructional quality.

Classroom studies of teaching effects have generally supported a direct and structured approach to instruction. That is, students usually achieve more when a teacher:

(a) emphasizes academic goals, makes them explicit and expects students to be able to master the curriculum;
(b) carefully organizes and sequences curriculum experiences;
(c) clearly explains and illustrates what students are to learn;
(d) frequently asks direct and specific questions to monitor students' progress and check their understanding;
(e) provides students with ample opportunity to practise, gives prompts and feedback to ensure success and correct mistakes, and allows students to practise a skill until it is overlearned or automatic;
(f) reviews regularly and holds students accountable for work.

From this perspective, a teacher promotes student learning by being active in planning and organizing instruction, explaining to students what they are to learn, arranging occasions for guided practice, monitoring progress, providing feedback, and otherwise helping students to understand and accomplish work.

Figure 19.3 The findings of the research on teaching effects (adapted from Doyle (1987), pp. 93–6)

development and classroom management. On the other hand, school development is about improving the school's management arrangements, the structures, roles and collaboration necessary for sustained improvement. In the
middle, linking the two, is the teacher. It is only he or she who can bring
together in a practical and meaningful way these two crucial elements for
enhancing quality in schools.

We believe that some of the research quoted and alluded to above may help
teachers become more precise in their search for increased effectiveness. But we
must remember that research in general has, as we have noted, many limitations. In terms of school development it becomes useful only when it is subjected to the discipline of practice, through the exercise of the teacher's
professional judgement. For as Stenhouse (1975, p. 142) said in a slightly
different context, such proposals are not to be regarded 'as an unqualified
recommendation but rather as a provisional specification claiming no more
than to be worth putting to the test of practice. Such proposals claim to be
intelligent rather than correct.'

The research discussed in this section is limited in one other respect: it has
been more concerned to describe the characteristics of school effectiveness,
rather than suggest ways in which effectiveness can be achieved. In the following section we examine some other research which is more concerned with the
process of improving schools.

SCHOOL IMPROVEMENT

School improvement studies tend to be more action oriented than the effective
schools research. They embody the long-term goal of moving towards the
vision of the 'problem solving' or 'thinking' school. This attitude was
exemplified in the work of the OECD-sponsored International School Improvement Project (ISIP) and the knowledge that emanated from it. School
improvement was defined in the ISIP as 'a systematic, sustained effort aimed at
change in learning conditions and other related internal conditions in one or
more schools, with the ultimate aim of accomplishing educational goals more
effectively' (Van Velzen *et al.*, 1985, p. 48).

School improvement is therefore about developing strategies for educational
change that strengthen the school's organization, as well as implementing
curriculum reforms. This obviously implies a very different way of thinking
about change than the ubiquitous 'top-down' approach so popular with
policy-makers. When the school is regarded as the 'centre' of change, then
strategies for change need to take this new perspective into account. The ISIP
served to popularize a school improvement approach to educational change,
and we have summarized so-called ISIP knowledge in Figure 19.4.

The ISIP approach to change is highly consistent with [our arguments]. We
too envisage the school at the centre of change, endorse the emphasis on
curriculum priorities being linked to managerial change within the plan, and
would like to see the school operating within a supportive environment.

The approach to school improvement taken by the ISIP rests on a number of assumptions:

(1) **The school as the centre of change**. This means that external reforms need to be sensitive to the situation in individual schools, rather than assuming that all schools are the same. It also implies that school improvement efforts need to adopt a 'classroom-exceeding' perspective, without ignoring the classroom.

(2) **A systematic approach to change**. School improvement is a carefully planned and managed process that takes place over a period of several years.

(3) **A key focus for change** is the 'internal conditions' of schools. These include not only the teaching–learning activities used in the school, but also the school's procedures, role allocation and resource use that support the teaching–learning process (in our words the school's management arrangements).

(4) **Accomplishing educational goals more effectively**. Generally speaking, educational goals are what a school is *supposed* to be doing for its students and society. This suggests a broader definition of outcome than student scores on achievement tests, even though for some schools these may be pre-eminent. Schools also serve the more general developmental needs of students, the professional development of teachers and the needs of its community.

(5) **A multi-level perspective**. Although the school is the centre of change it does not act alone. The school is embedded in an educational system that has to work collaboratively or symbiotically if the higest degrees of quality are to be achieved. This means that the roles of teachers, heads, governors, parents, support people (advisers, higher education, consultants, etc.), and local authorities should be defined, harnessed and committed to the process of school improvement.

(6) **Integrative implementation strategies**. This implies a linkage between 'top-down' and 'bottom-up' – remembering of course that both approaches can apply at a number of different levels in the system. Ideally 'top-down' provides policy aims, an overall strategy and operational plans; this is complemented by a 'bottom-up' response involving diagnosis, priority goal setting and implementation. The former provides the framework, resources and a menu of alternatives; the latter, energy and school-based implementation.

(7) **The drive towards institutionalization**. Change is only successful when it has become part of the natural behaviour of all those in the school. Implementation by itself is not enough.

Figure 19.4　A summary of ISIP knowledge (adapted from Van Velzen *et al.* (1985) and Hopkins (1987))

We also are concerned about the long-term impact of change. [. . .] All too often change efforts are short-lived; they either do not survive early enthusiasm or are replaced too quickly by another 'fad' or 'good idea'. The ISIP approach emphasized that effective change is a long-term process and a complex one at that. This complexity has been the subject of a number of investigations over the past ten years or so. Happily we now have a much better idea of what the change process looks like, and what are the factors making for success. We have summarized in Figure 19.5 the main stages of the school improvement process as it applies to school development planning.

We are pleased to report that other school improvement research is consistent with our general advice. This research is generally of two types. The first are the reviews of research that attempt to distil general guidelines from a synthesis of a number of studies. The second are the individual, usually in-depth, studies of school improvement.

In most schools development planning will initially be an innovation, a change from current practice. Even though development planning is supposed to help schools manage innovation and change, it may, particularly at the outset, represent a considerable challenge. For this reason it is helpful to regard the introduction of development planning as an innovation problem in itself, and to draw on the knowledge that we have of the change process.

The innovation process is generally considered to consist of three overlapping phases:

(1) **Initiation**. This phase is about deciding to embark on development planning, and about developing commitment towards the process. During this phase the purposes and process of development planning should be clearly spelled out, a key person in the school should be prepared to argue the case and encourage others to participate, and the focus of the whole process should be linked to issues that are important to a majority in the school. During this phase pressure to be involved is acceptable, as long as it is accompanied by support.

(2) **Implementation**. This phase normally includes the first cycle of development planning when the school is learning how to carry out the process. During this phase development planning needs to be well co-ordinated, have adequate and sustained INSET support, and 'rewards' (in the form of supply cover, positive reinforcement, etc.) should be provided. It is during this phase that skills and understanding are being acquired, some success is being achieved and responsibility is delegated to working groups of teachers.

(3) **Institutionalization**. This phase occurs when development planning becomes part of the school's usual pattern of doing things. Management arrangements [. . .] have evolved to support both development and maintenance, and are part of everyone's usual pattern of behaviour. There is widespread use of action plans by staff, the impact of development planning is being seen on classroom practice, and the whole process is not now regarded as being unusual.

The failure of many change efforts to progress beyond early implementation is partially explained by the lack of realization on the part of those involved that each of these phases has different characteristics and requires different strategies if success is to be achieved.

Figure 19.5 The process of school improvement and development planning (after Miles (1986))

An example of the first type is Fullan's (1991) *The New Meaning of Educational Change*. The book contains a comprehensive review of current research on educational change and practice. From this synthesis, Fullan identifies a number of assumptions about change which are important determinants of whether the realities of change get confronted or ignored. These assumptions about change are given in Figure 19.6.

An example of the second type of research is Louis and Miles' (1990) study, *Improving the Urban High School*. The book describes in depth school improvement efforts in five large American urban high schools. In contrast to studies of effective schools and effective teaching, they set themselves the task of answering the question, 'How do we get there?' They had five major findings on what it takes to really improve 'big-city' schools.

Their first is to do with *school–LEA relationships*. They found that this worked best when the LEA provided support and direction, and the school had a great deal of autonomy in choosing goals and strategies. Effective working relationships were the key.

(1) Do not assume that your version of what the change should be is the one that should or could be implemented. On the contrary, assume that one of the main purposes of the process of implementation is to *exchange your reality* of what should be through interaction with others.

(2) Assume that any significant innovation, if it is to result in change, requires individuals to work out their own meaning. Significant change involves a certain amount of ambiguity, ambivalence and uncertainty for the individual about the meaning of change.

(3) Assume that conflict and disagreement are not only inevitable but fundamental to successful change. Since any group of people possess multiple realities, any collective change attempt will necessarily involve conflict.

(4) Assume that people need pressure to change (even in directions which they desire), but it will only be effective under conditions which allow them to react, to form their own position, to interact with others and to obtain support.

(5) Assume that effective change takes time. It is a process of 'development in use'. Unrealistic or undefined time-lines fail to recognize that implementation occurs developmentally. Persistence is a critical attribute of successful change.

(6) Do not assume that the reason for lack of implementation is outright rejection of the values embodied in the change or hard-core resistance to all change. Assume that there are a number of possible reasons.

(7) Do not expect all or even most people or groups to change. The complexity of change is such that it is totally impossible to bring about widespread reform in any large social system. Progress occurs when we take steps which *increase* the number of people affected.

(8) Assume that you will need a *plan* which is based on the above assumptions and which addresses the factors known to affect implementation. Evolutionary planning and problem-coping models based on knowledge of the change process are essential.

(9) Assume that no amount of knowledge will ever make it totally clear what action should be taken. Better knowledge of the change process will improve the mix of resources on which we draw, but it will never and should never represent the sole basis for decision.

(10) Assume that changing the culture of institutions is the real agenda, not implementing single innovations. Putting it another way: when implementing particular innovations, always pay attention to how the institution is developing or not.

Figure 19.6   Assumptions about change (source: Fullan (1991), pp. 105–7)

A second factor [. . . is] that an *evolutionary approach to planning* 'works best, with plenty of early action (small-scale wins) to create energy and support learning' [Louis and Miles, 1990]. They also claim that 'planning is the first point where empowerment takes hold' (p. 292).

The third factor [. . .] is the importance of *shared images* 'of what the school should become' (p. 293). The importance of generating ownership towards the school's vision and aims and their reflection in the priorities of the plan is crucial.

Fourthly, Louis and Miles mention *resources* as a key variable. They call 'for a broad-based view of resources' in support of the school's vision. They emphasize the linking of developmental priorities to a cool appraisal of the resource implications.

Finally, Louis and Miles refer to *problem coping*. They found that 'problems during school improvement efforts are multiple, pervasive, and often nearly intractable. But dealing with them actively, promptly, and with some depth is the single biggest determinant of program success' (p. 295). 'Depth', they emphasize, is not about 'fire-fighting' but, to use our language, is about dealing directly with the school's management arrangements.

So there is a considerable body of research-based knowledge that can help with designing development planning initiatives, whether at the LEA, school or staff working group level. Once again we need to issue the familiar health warning. Not all of this advice need apply to every school, but much of it is by now well enough tested to warrant serious consideration.

So far the discussion has been on general strategic approaches to change. There is, however, one other area of school improvement research that needs mentioning briefly. This is the collection of specific individual approaches, that one commentator has recently referred to as being 'doors' which can open or unlock the process of school improvement (Joyce, 1991).

There are a number of familiar 'doors' that we have passed through during the recent history of educational change in the UK. A much-opened door in the early 1980s was the one named school self-evaluation. There were first the LEA-initiated schemes which tended to be accountability rather than development oriented (see Clift *et al.*, 1987). Later, the GRIDS approach sponsored by the Schools Council offered schools a more autonomous and developmental approach to whole-school evaluation which became very popular (see Abbott *et al.*, 1988). Other 'doors' have been the 'discovery' of management training in 1983, changes in INSET funding in the mid-1980s, and categorically funded curriculum projects such as TVEI.

The American research on these individual strategies has been more focused than that of their British counterparts. The tradition in the USA, as we have already seen, is to relate specific strategies to student test scores as a measure of effectiveness. Using this approach, in inevitably limited situations, some school improvement strategies have produced startling results. For example, the research on the application of different 'Models of Teaching', as described by Joyce and Weil (1986), has resulted in consistently higher test scores in some classrooms. Co-operative learning is currently achieving consistent improvements in many classrooms across the USA. The direct use of technology in classrooms, e.g. television programmes such as *Sesame Street*, and collaborative approaches to staff development, e.g. coaching, have well-documented positive effects on student learning (Joyce and Showers, 1988).

Unfortunately not all school improvement strategies work well all the time and in every setting. When they do not it is often because they do not affect the culture of the school. Many of these strategies implicitly assume that behind the 'door' are a series of interconnecting pathways that lead inexorably to school improvement. This is not so. Too often they focus on individual changes, on discrete projects and on individual teachers and classrooms, rather than on how these changes can fit in with and adapt the organization and culture of the school. As a consequence when the door opens it leads only into a cul-de-sac.

In addressing the same issue, Fullan (1988, p. 29) commented that

Without a direct and primary focus on changes in organizational factors it is unlikely that [single innovations or specific projects] will have much of a reform impact, and whatever impact there is will be short lived . . . school improvement efforts which ignore these deeper organizational conditions are 'doomed to tinkering'. . . . Strategies are needed that more directly address the culture of the organization.

To conclude this section, let us restate the main problem with most attempts at school improvement. They are successful only to the extent that they satisfactorily address the complexities of school culture. This is something that [. . .] development planning as a school improvement strategy is well able to do. We return to this crucial issue in the final section.

SCHOOL DEVELOPMENT

It is now [many] years since Ron Edmonds asked his felicitous question: 'How many effective schools would you have to see to be persuaded of the educability of all children?' He continued, 'We already know more than we need to do that. Whether or not we do it must depend on how we feel about the fact that we haven't so far.'

Although we now know a lot more about school effectiveness and improvement than when Edmonds wrote, student achievement still lags far behind society's expectations. It seems to us that one of the major difficulties is the way in which this knowledge is used. Knowledge of the type discussed in this chapter is not a panacea; at best it is informed advice that schools may wish to test out in their own settings. [. . .] The advantage of development planning, however, is that it provides a means whereby this knowledge can be put to the test of practice. The knowledge is there to inform, not control practice. To return to Edmonds' question, [we suggest] that when research-based knowledge is put to the test of practice, the result will be more schools which educate *all* of their pupils.

For this to be achieved requires not simply better research, however practitioner friendly, but a profound change in school culture. Although few schools have yet achieved this cultural change, many are working on it. Where a school lacks the appropriate culture, development planning is a means of achieving it. The recognition by schools of this fact is the real and important condition of development planning. This is the key insight. If the school does so recognize, it will understand that development planning is not just about implementing innovation and change, but about changing its culture – or in more concrete terms, its management arrangements – to improve its *capacity* to manage (other) changes. A school cannot fend off change until it has recreated its culture. But it can self-consciously make changes to its management arrangements through its development plan, so that the *process* of development planning is strengthened simultaneously with implementing other kinds of innovations.

The main purpose of our writing in this way has *not* been to contribute to the academic literature on school effectiveness, school improvement or management. Rather it has been to persuade heads and teachers that thinking about themselves, their work and their school in certain ways is empowering. It can help transform the culture of the school, and make it a better and more effective place for all pupils and teachers to learn.

REFERENCES

Abbott, R. *et al.* (1988) *GRIDS School Handbooks* (2nd edn), Primary and Secondary versions, Longman for the SCDC, York.

Clift, P. *et al.* (1987) *Studies in School Self-Evaluation*, Falmer Press, Lewes.

Cuban, L. (1983) Effective schools: a friendly but cautionary note, *Phi Delta Kappan*, Vol. 64, no. 10 (June), pp. 695–6.

DES (1977) *Ten Good Schools*, HMSO, London.

Doyle, W. (1987) Research on teaching effects as a resource for improving instruction, in M. Wideen and I. Andrews (eds.) *Staff Development for School Improvement*, Falmer Press, Lewes.

Fullan, M. (1985) Change processes and strategies at the local level, *The Elementary School Journal*, Vol. 85, no. 3, pp. 391–421.

Fullan, M. (1988) Change processes in secondary schools: towards a more fundamental agenda. University of Toronto (mimeo).

Fullan, M. (1991) *The New Meaning of Educational Change*, Cassell, London.

Hopkins, D. (ed.) (1987) *Improving the Quality of Schooling*, Falmer Press, Lewes.

Joyce, B. (1991) The doors to school improvement, *Educational Leadership* (May), pp. 59–62.

Joyce, B. and Showers, B. (1988) *Student Achievement through Staff Development*, Longman, New York.

Joyce, B. and Weil, M. (1986) *Models of Teaching* (3rd edn), Prentice Hall, Englewood Cliffs, NJ.

Louis, K. S. and Miles, M. (1990) *Improving the Urban High School*, Teachers College Press, New York.

Miles, M. (1986) Research findings on the stages of school improvement. Centre for Policy Research (mimeo), New York.

Mortimore, P. *et al.* (1988) *School Matters*, Open Books, London.

Nuttall, D. *et al.* (1989) Differential school effectiveness, *International Journal of Educational Research*, Vol. 13, no. 10, pp. 769–76.

Purkey, S. and Smith, M. (1983) Effective schools: a review, *The Elementary School Journal*, Vol. 83, no. 4, pp. 427–52.

Rutter, M. *et al.* (1979) *Fifteen Thousand Hours*, Open Books, London.

Stenhouse, L. (1975) *An Introduction to Curriculum Research and Development*, Heinemann Educational Books, London.

Taylor, B. (ed.) (1990) *Case Studies in Effective Schools Research*, Kendall/Hunt Publishing Company for the Center for Effective Schools, Dubuque, IA.

Van Velzen, W. *et al.* (1985) *Making School Improvement Work*, ACCO, Leuven, Belgium.

SUBJECT INDEX

AUTHOR INDEX